Welcome to Your Dream Home

Garlinghouse and Dream Homes of America are pleased to present this collection of Timber Crafted Homes. For nearly 100 years, Garlinghouse has helped build the American Dream. For over 35 years, Dream Homes of America has provided complete home construction packages for thousands of customers across the country and around the world. In this book, we team up to proudly offer you:

- A broad selection of popular designs with highly desirable features, created by the top designers in the country.
- The opportunity to build a house with top quality building materials, not available at your local lumberyard.
- The ability to have these high quality building materials delivered right to your construction site.
- The option to have an experienced construction crew build your home at reasonable prices.

Experience you can trust:

Almost one million customers have purchased Garlinghouse blueprints. Our success is based upon our reputation to provide the right designs for the right time. Garlinghouse markets home designs from 50 of the top designers in the country—more than half of whom have received awards in recognition of their excellence. As a result, Garlinghouse is one of the nation's top home plan providers. Dream Homes of America packages are customized to suit each client's specific needs and the materials are all supported by a full warranty. Dream Homes of

America has a high commitment to quality and service. Their outstanding reputation is the reason why Garlinghouse has teamed up with Dream Homes of America to provide you with this unique designer series of home packages.

A partnership that makes sense for you:

Garlinghouse has the designs to meet your needs. Dream Homes of America has the sales staff, design team, technical knowledge, and experience to help you use these designs to plan and then build your custom home, large or small, using quality building materials.

Please take the time to enjoy this book:

There are well over 100 spectacular photos in full color, with multiple plan illustrations, to help you select your home. Also, our editors have provided several pages of planning information to help you feel more comfortable with making such an important decision in your life.

We look forward to helping you Live Your Dream.

COVER HOME (WESTMINSTER) DESIGNED BY DAVID GILLETT DESIGN, ORILLIA, ONTARIO

From our family to yours...

About Dream Homes of America

Since 1968, we have been making new home dreams come true. We are dedicated to bringing you the very best, and affordably priced, selection of timber crafted home packages available. Our commitment to unsurpassed selection, quality, and service has brought many of our customers back when they were ready to build a second and third home. No wonder we are one of the fastest growing home suppliers in North America today.

With Dream Homes, you not only choose your house design—you can customize it, order all the quality materials to create it, and have all those components shipped anywhere in the world. You can even locate the closest recommended builder to construct it for you. Plus, you'll have one of the strongest warranty programs in the industry backing you up, every step of the way.

The individual members of our group of companies specialize in different styles of homes. These businesses include Linwood Homes, the Hampton Timber Frame Company, Mill Bay Log Homes, and Country Heritage Homes. Under one owner, these companies are committed to giving you the best possible value in building your new home.

In this outstanding new book, we are proud to showcase over 90 distinctive designer home plans to inspire you. These designs feature a variety of popular types of construction with broad appeal to anyone interested in fine timber crafted homes.

Why buy just a plan when Dream Homes can give you the whole package?

www.dreamhomesofamerica.com

Custom Designed for You

Linwood has over 35 years of experience in designing and building custom cedar and other types of post and beam homes.

Spectacular homes don't just happen by accident. They happen when all the key elements needed to build are brought together in a carefully controlled process. In creating a complete custom home package, Linwood does this all for you.

High Quality Cedar

All Linwood cedar siding and interior cedar components are made with Western Red Cedar —one of the finest building materials in the world. It's naturally durable, dimensionally stable, and exceptionally versatile to work with. *Above all— it's beautiful!*

We even operate our own sawmill, allowing us to control and maintain the quality of all our cedar components, from the log all the way to the finished product.

All Linwood framing lumber is certified by the North American Lumber Grading Association, and acknowledged as the best available.

Custom Design

You can customize any of our large number of plans to accommodate your own unique lifestyle needs. If you already have a home plan fully designed or even a sketch or a conceptual idea, our experienced design and building experts can work with you to make that plan a reality.

We'll incorporate your ideas into a set of preliminary drawings that show exterior elevations of the house from all four sides, detailed floor plans, and product specifications. Any changes that you request will be incorporated into these plans by our drafting and design team with no additional design costs. When you are satisfied with these drawings, detailed blueprints will be produced.

Our plans ensure full compliance with all Uniform/National Building Code specifications and are modified as required to meet local building department guidelines.

Our Sales & Design Consultants can provide you with assistance in selecting contractors, receiving and evaluating quotes, obtaining planning permits, and monitoring on-site job performance by the selected sub-trades.

Linwood Home ships worldwide from New York to Frankfurt to Osaka. Our home packages are delivered to building sites by truck, container, barge and helicopter. From the remotest island to the busiest metropolis, we'll deliver your dream home.

Visit our website at **www.linwoodhomes.com**

LINWOOD
custom cedar homes

Exceptional Homes
at Great Low Prices

Country Heritage Homes is proud to bring you an exciting new home collection, using a revolutionary approach to home design.

Our innovative **Opti-Bild**® computer modeling and rendering system allows us to design appealing homes with outstanding features, and then optimize the use of the materials required to build them.

The **Performax**® process selects the materials needed to construct each home based on the quality, price, and performance specifications of each individual component of the design. This process has been specifically developed to maximize effectiveness.

Country Heritage Homes is your reliable one-stop source for everything you will need to build your dream home. We offer superior pre-engineered designs, full construction blueprints, and all the quality materials required to build your home to the lock-up stage.

Low maintenance products with high structural strength and aesthetic appeal are supplied at the lowest possible price. Materials are pre-cut, and

pre-assembled where possible, to ensure rapid and accurate construction, as well as to minimize on-site construction waste.

Our long established industry relationships combined with our own production facilities enable us to offer you the benefits of volume buying, shipping coordination, and detailed construction information. As a result, your overall cost is reduced and the whole construction process is made as simple as possible.

The result is a beautiful home at a very affordable price. You can even see how your home will look before it is built. Check out our website for more designs and images.

Visit our website at
www.countryheritagehomes.com

Traditional Craftsmanship

The Hampton Timber Frame Company offers everything you need to construct your new timber frame home.

We can take your ideas and work with you to produce a unique timber frame design. Alternatively, we can adapt one of our stock plans to fit your needs. Once you have settled on a design that you like, we will provide you with a high-detail preliminary plan, showing floor plans and elevations from all sides, as well as the layout of the actual timber frame structure.

We want to provide you with all the resources you'll need to turn your timber frame dream home into a reality. If you wish, our affiliates can even provide decorating advice, finishing materials, and construction management.

Traditional Craftsmanship

Traditional timber frame uses the centuries old craft of interlocking timbers using mortise and tenon joints fastened with wood pegs.

These timbers are joined in a complete cross-section called a bent, or erected sequentially one at a time to form the complete frame structure. This assembly is strengthened by the addition of knee braces on the external walls.

Design Flexibility

Using the latest computer technology, we will take any revisions or changes to your preliminary plan and incorporate them into the production of the final professional construction blueprints.

These blueprints will meet National/Uniform Building Code requirements as well as the detailed needs of your builder.

Open House

If you wish, we can eliminate interior load bearing walls, which will open space and allow much more freedom in the interior design. We may also incorporate stylish walls of windows, a popular way to maximize light.

Whatever you choose to do, the result will be a warm and pleasing harmony of exposed wood and a variety of dramatic interior finishing options.

Visit our website at
www.hamptontimber.com

Log Homes Designed for You

In order to create a special log home, you need to bring together expertise in design, log selection, quality materials, and construction capability.

The award-winning Mill Bay design team offers full custom design in addition to an ability to modify the broad selection of popular designs showcased in our log home collection.

We have the widest selection of log profiles available in the industry today. Whether you want a simple 4"x 6" square shaped log, a massive 14" round log, or anything in between, we have it. We also offer a choice of Pine, Fir, and Spruce logs, and Western Red Cedar as a specialty log. Choose any log and any profile.

Our production facilities are situated in British Columbia, Canada, which allows us to offer you the finest timber in the world at a very competitive price.

We start the production process by selecting high quality logs, which are then machined to our exacting specifications. This procedure ensures a tight fit for maximum stability and the highest possible insulation values. For additional strength, the logs are thru-bolted for a sturdy, long lasting, and beautiful home.

Undertaking any construction project is a major investment both in time and money. When you build your log home with Mill Bay, we help you every step of the way, using our experience and knowledge to ensure your home project goes as smoothly and enjoyably as possible.

Visit our website at
www.millbaylog.com

MILL BAY
log homes

The DREAM HOMES *Advantage*
OF AMERICA

Custom Design

You can customize any of the 200 stock plans featured in our four full-color Plan Books to accommodate your own unique lifestyle needs.

Or, if you already have a home plan fully designed, or even a daydream sketch in your head, our experienced drafting and design experts can take your ideas and turn them into a beautiful home. Our team uses the latest computer technology to efficiently and professionally create detailed blueprints that your builder can depend on. Build on our decades of home design expertise at no extra cost!

Whether your heart's desire is a cedar contemporary, a traditional post and beam timber frame home, a log home, or a country heritage home—the Dream Homes team can deliver.

Complete Package

Every home package is complete and includes drafting and design, construction blueprints and all the high quality building materials required to finish and weatherproof the exterior of your home.

These materials include the framing lumber and sheathing to build floors and walls, windows and skylights, and exterior doors, as well as house wrap, nails, and roofing material.

High Quality Construction Materials

We operate our own sawmill in order to control and maintain the quality of all our cedar components, from the log all the way to the finished product. All framing lumber is certified by the North American Lumber Grading Association, and acknowledged as the best available.

All our other construction materials are supplied by major brand-name manufacturers and certified to national home building standard specifications. These include architectural laminated beams, plywood, windows, doors, and roofing material. Plus, we've searched North America to bring you a wide selection of specialty items. We put our buying power to work for you to obtain superior products at an advantageous price.

Last but not least, all cedar siding and interior cedar components are made with Western Red Cedar—one of the finest building materials in the world. It's naturally durable, dimensionally stable, and exceptionally versatile to work with. Above all—it's beautiful!

Full Warranty Program

There is a full structural warranty on all home packages good for 10 years. Our warranty is in turn supported by the individual warranties of all our suppliers. This powerful combination provides our customers with one of the strongest warranty programs available in the industry today.

World Wide Shipping Expertise

We have built homes all over the world from the U.S. to Germany to Japan. We specialize in hard to reach destinations where it is imperative that everything needed for construction is included in the package. Our home packages have been delivered to building sites by truck, container, barge, and even helicopter. You can depend on us to deliver! *(see page 12)*

Construction Support

We offer a variety of construction support— everything from detailed construction blueprints and manuals, to a recommended network of experienced builders. As an additional option, we even panelize wall units for rapid and easy assembly.

We have a toll-free hotline to answer construction questions, plus construction experts who can provide detailed instruction on the fastest and most efficient method of assembling one of our homes.

"It is a landmark."

~ Dr. Susan and Dr. Bob Carlson

Located at the top of a hill on a remote island near Sitka, Alaska, the Carlson's new relaxation retreat is already well known to Pacific coast fishermen.

"They use it as a landmark," laughs Dr. Susan Carlson of the getaway home she and her husband, Dr. Bob Carlson, recently finished building.

The isolated location posed a number of challenges, something the Carlsons were well aware of when they decided to look for a company that could help them build the home. With no roads, no outside communication, and no electricity, it was certainly not a conventional type of arrangement—nor was the design of the home they wanted.

"We were looking for something that would fit in with the environment," she explains.

The interest and cooperation they got from their Linwood sales representative impressed them enough to trust him and the rest of his crew to take on the challenge. And, as Dr. Carlson says, they're glad they did.

"It could have been a disaster if everything that was supposed to be sent up wasn't included," says Dr. Carlson, recalling how the materials were sent from British Columbia to Sitka, then transported by helicopter. "But it was all there."

They were also impressed with the company's dedication to the project after the delivery. "It wasn't just a drop-it-off and forget about the Carlsons," she says. "We could call them any time we wanted to, and they were very helpful to us throughout the whole process." Their contractor was appreciative of the follow-up as well.

see page 36

The Timber Crafted Homes Collection

The following pages showcase over 90 distinctive designer homes. There is a wide variety of styles and sizes, and many can be customized by our design experts to meet your individual needs.

This specially selected collection of homes share some characteristics that we feel make them particularly delightful:

- Outstanding interior design
- Open floor plans
- Use of distinctive windows and natural light
- Cathedral ceilings
- Luxurious master suites
- Gourmet kitchens
- Striking exteriors
- Porches & decks
- Architectural details
- The richness of natural wood

We are pleased to bring this unique collection to you for the first time. Contact us to start turning your new dream home into a reality.

DREAM HOMES
OF AMERICA

2,241 sq. ft.

• This new design has rapidly become a Linwood best seller. It's easy to see why with its classic lines and contemporary comfort.

• The magnificent open-plan living area allows for formal or family entertaining. Any chef would be delighted to work in the large gourmet kitchen. The cedar lined vaulted ceiling adds warmth to this very spacious area.

• The generous master suite has its own private deck and is located on the main floor. With two large bedrooms upstairs, the additional main-floor bedroom can easily be a cozy entertainment room or home office.

~ MAJESTIC ~

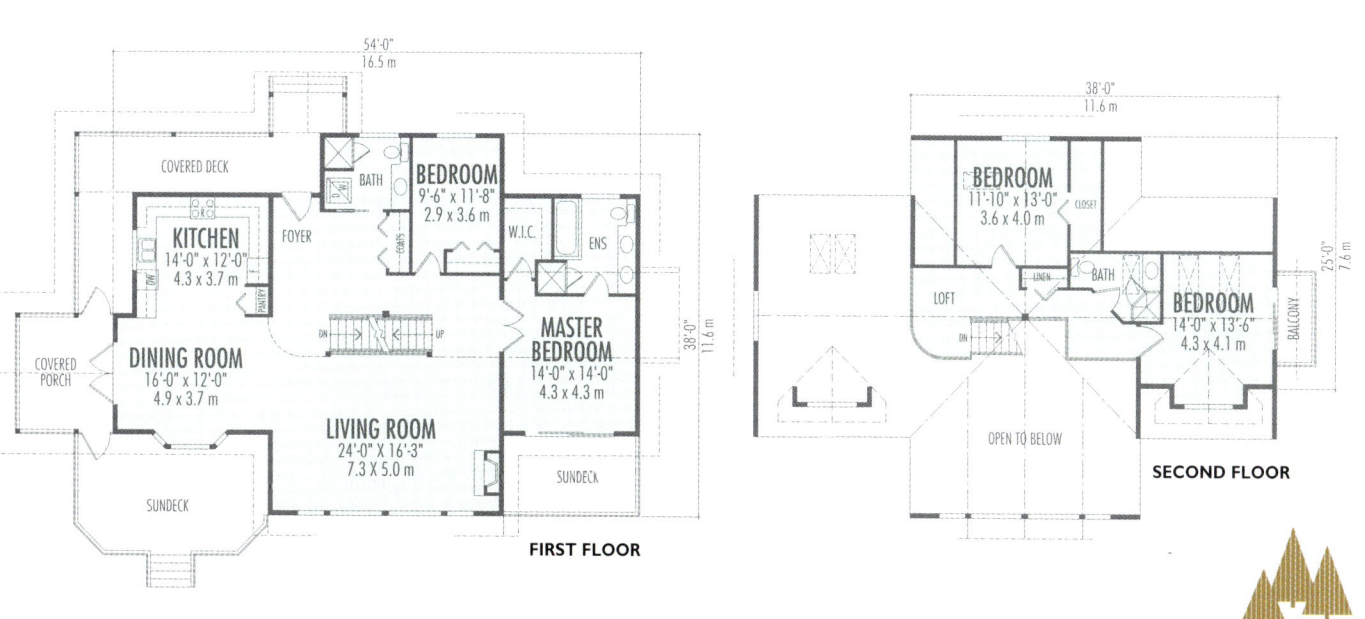

FIRST FLOOR

- COVERED DECK
- KITCHEN 14'-0" x 12'-0" 4.3 x 3.7 m
- FOYER
- BATH
- BEDROOM 9'-6" x 11'-8" 2.9 x 3.6 m
- W.I.C.
- ENS
- DINING ROOM 16'-0" x 12'-0" 4.9 x 3.7 m
- COVERED PORCH
- MASTER BEDROOM 14'-0" x 14'-0" 4.3 x 4.3 m
- LIVING ROOM 24'-0" X 16'-3" 7.3 X 5.0 m
- SUNDECK
- PANTRY
- DN
- UP
- 54'-0" 16.5 m
- 38'-0" 11.6 m

SECOND FLOOR

- BEDROOM 11'-10" x 13'-0" 3.6 x 4.0 m
- CLOSET
- LOFT
- LINEN
- BATH
- BEDROOM 14'-0" x 13'-6" 4.3 x 4.1 m
- BALCONY
- OPEN TO BELOW
- DN
- 38'-0" 11.6 m
- 25'-0" 7.6 m

PHOTOGRAPHY: JAMES YOCHUM PHOTOGRAPHY

2,038 sq. ft.

- A deck wraps around much of this home and, combined with a screen porch, enhances the outdoor living space of this gorgeous three-bedroom house.

- The master bedroom is located on the main floor with two additional bedrooms upstairs.

- The octagonal-shape living room has a soaring expanse of glass and the enormous windows let the sunlight flood in to highlight the beautiful interior finishing.

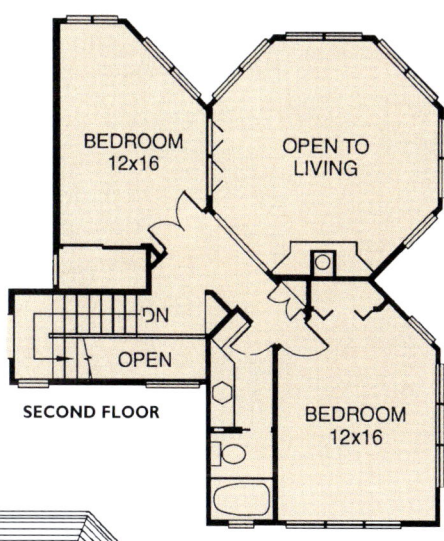

BEDROOM
12x16

OPEN TO
LIVING

DN

OPEN

BEDROOM
12x16

SECOND FLOOR

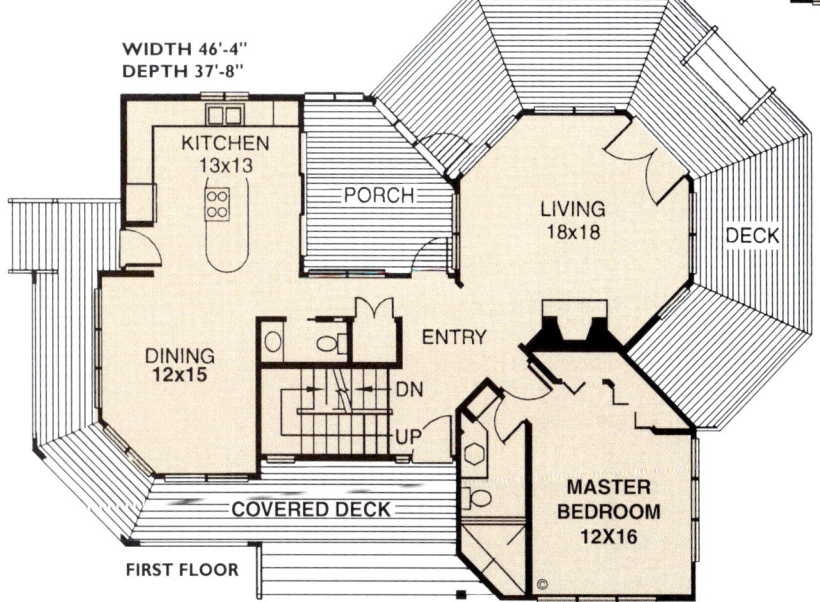

WIDTH 46'-4"
DEPTH 37'-8"

KITCHEN
13x13

PORCH

LIVING
18x18

DECK

DINING
12x15

ENTRY

DN

UP

MASTER
BEDROOM
12X16

COVERED DECK

FIRST FLOOR

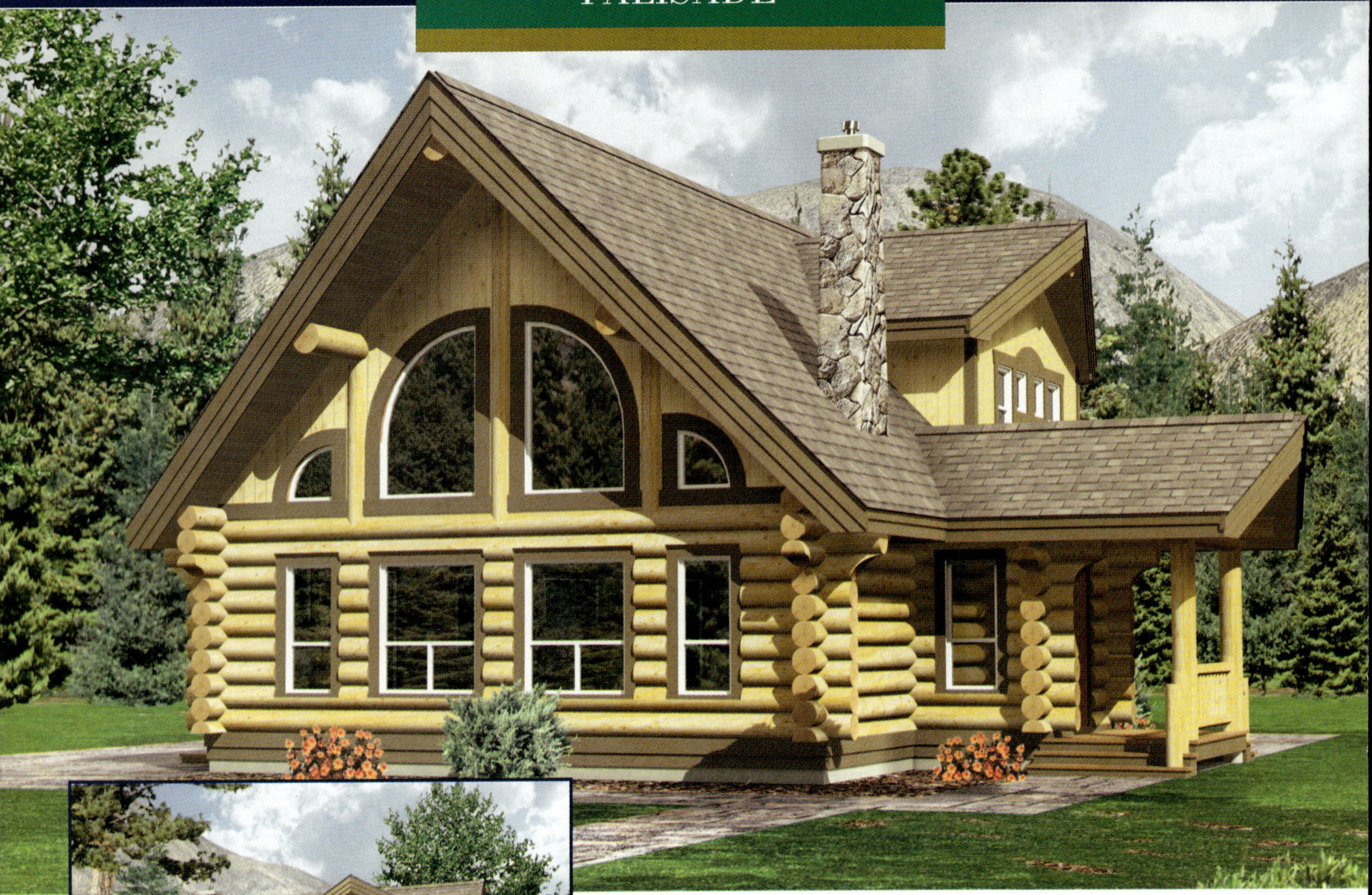

1,800 sq. ft.

- exterior dimensions 40' x 40'
- covered entry, vaulted master bedroom, living and dining rooms
- 3 bedrooms, 2 bathrooms
- huge master bedroom with 5-piece ensuite

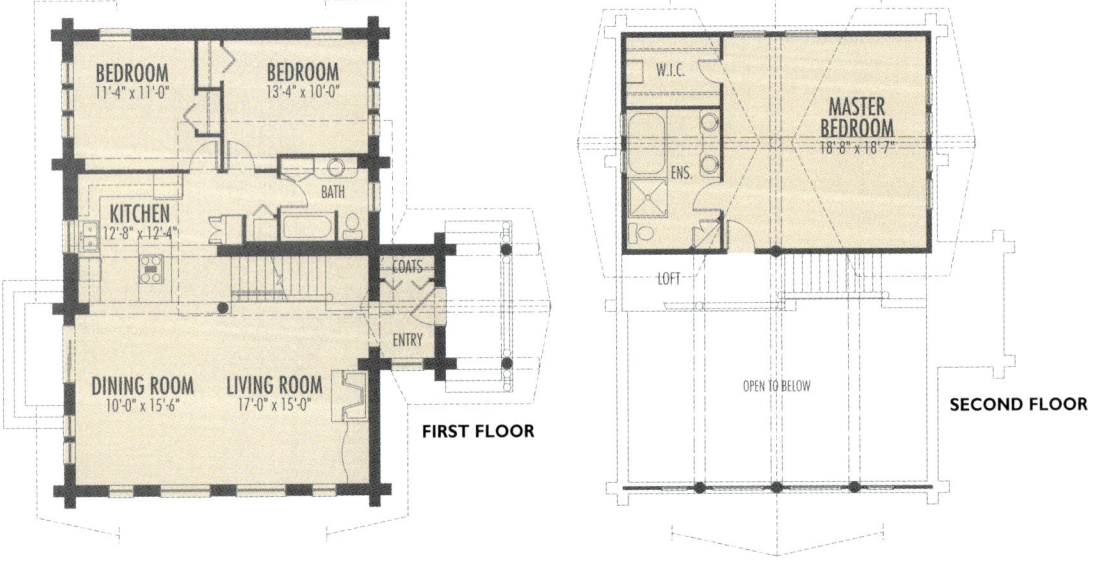

FIRST FLOOR

BEDROOM
11'-4" x 11'-0"

BEDROOM
13'-4" x 10'-0"

KITCHEN
12'-8" x 12'-4"

BATH

COATS

ENTRY

DINING ROOM
10'-0" x 15'-6"

LIVING ROOM
17'-0" x 15'-0"

SECOND FLOOR

W.I.C.

MASTER BEDROOM
18'-8" x 18'-7"

ENS.

LOFT

OPEN TO BELOW

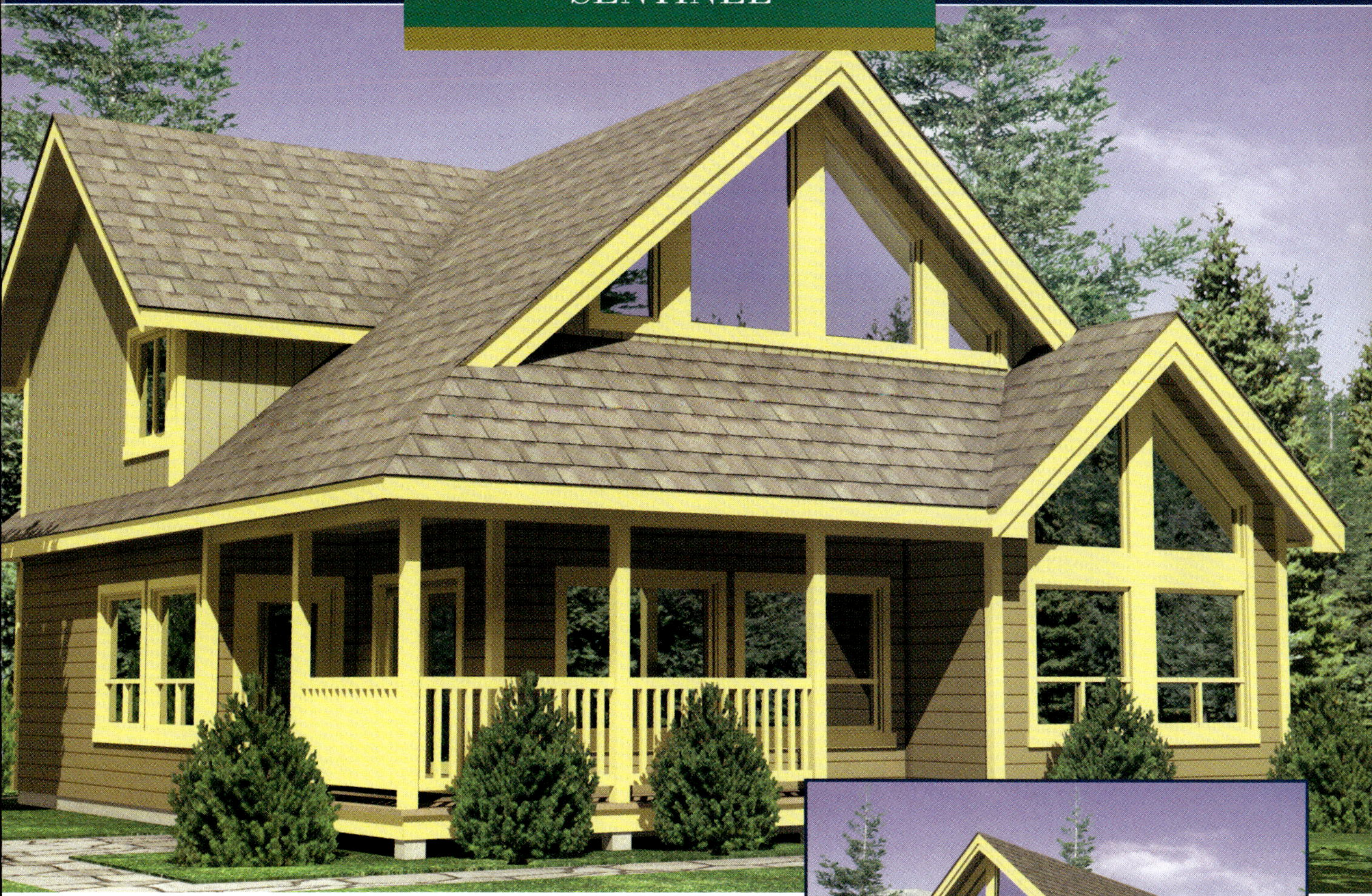

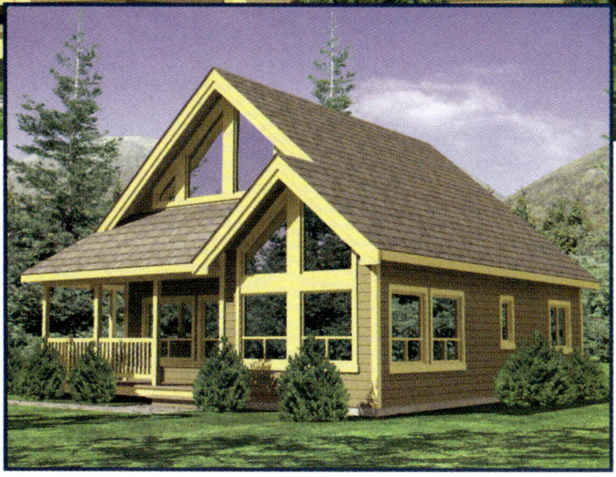

1,689 sq. ft.

- exterior dimensions 36' x 38'
- vaulted living room and family room
- 3 bedrooms, 3 bathrooms (upstairs vaulted)
- covered verandah

FIRST FLOOR

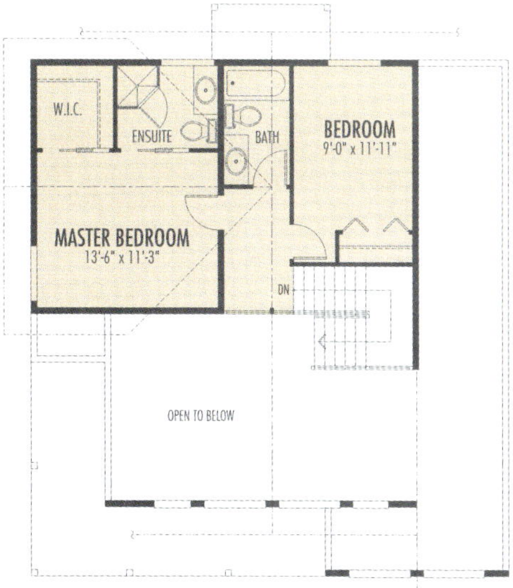

SECOND FLOOR

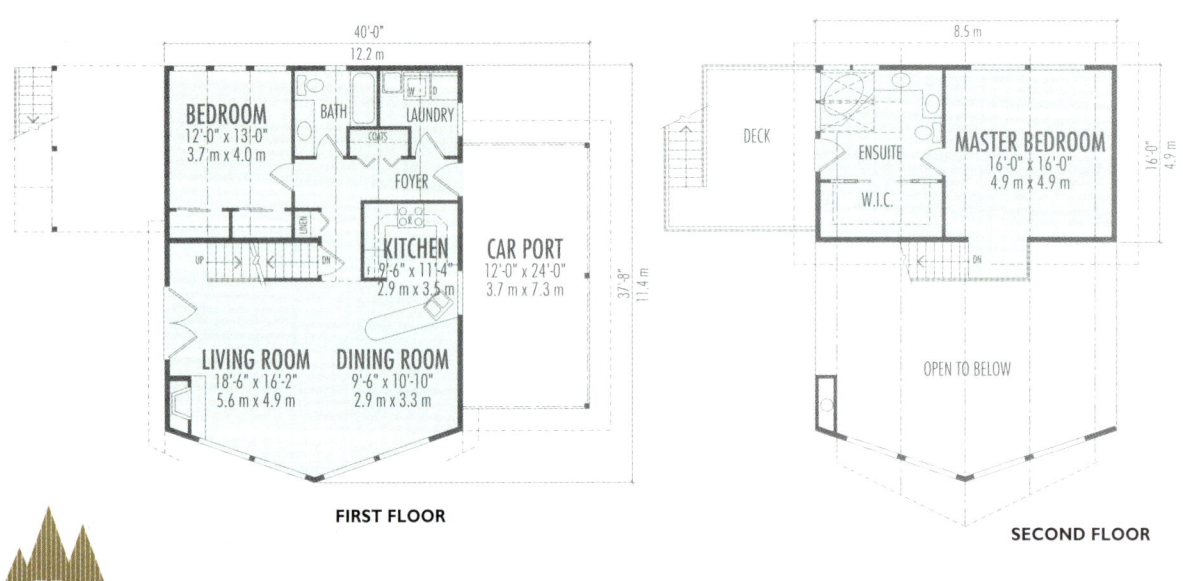

1,457 sq. ft.

- exterior dimensions 40' x 38'
- vaulted living and dining room
- 2 bedrooms, 2 bathrooms
- large private deck off master suite

FIRST FLOOR

40'-0"
12.2 m

BEDROOM
12'-0" x 13'-0"
3.7 m x 4.0 m

BATH

W. D
LAUNDRY

COATS

FOYER

LNEN

UP   DN

KITCHEN
9'-6" x 11'-4"
2.9 m x 3.5 m

CAR PORT
12'-0" x 24'-0"
3.7 m x 7.3 m

37'-8"
11.4 m

LIVING ROOM
18'-6" x 16'-2"
5.6 m x 4.9 m

DINING ROOM
9'-6" x 10'-10"
2.9 m x 3.3 m

SECOND FLOOR

8.5 m

DECK

ENSUITE

W.I.C.

MASTER BEDROOM
16'-0" x 16'-0"
4.9 m x 4.9 m

16'-0"
4.9 m

DN

OPEN TO BELOW

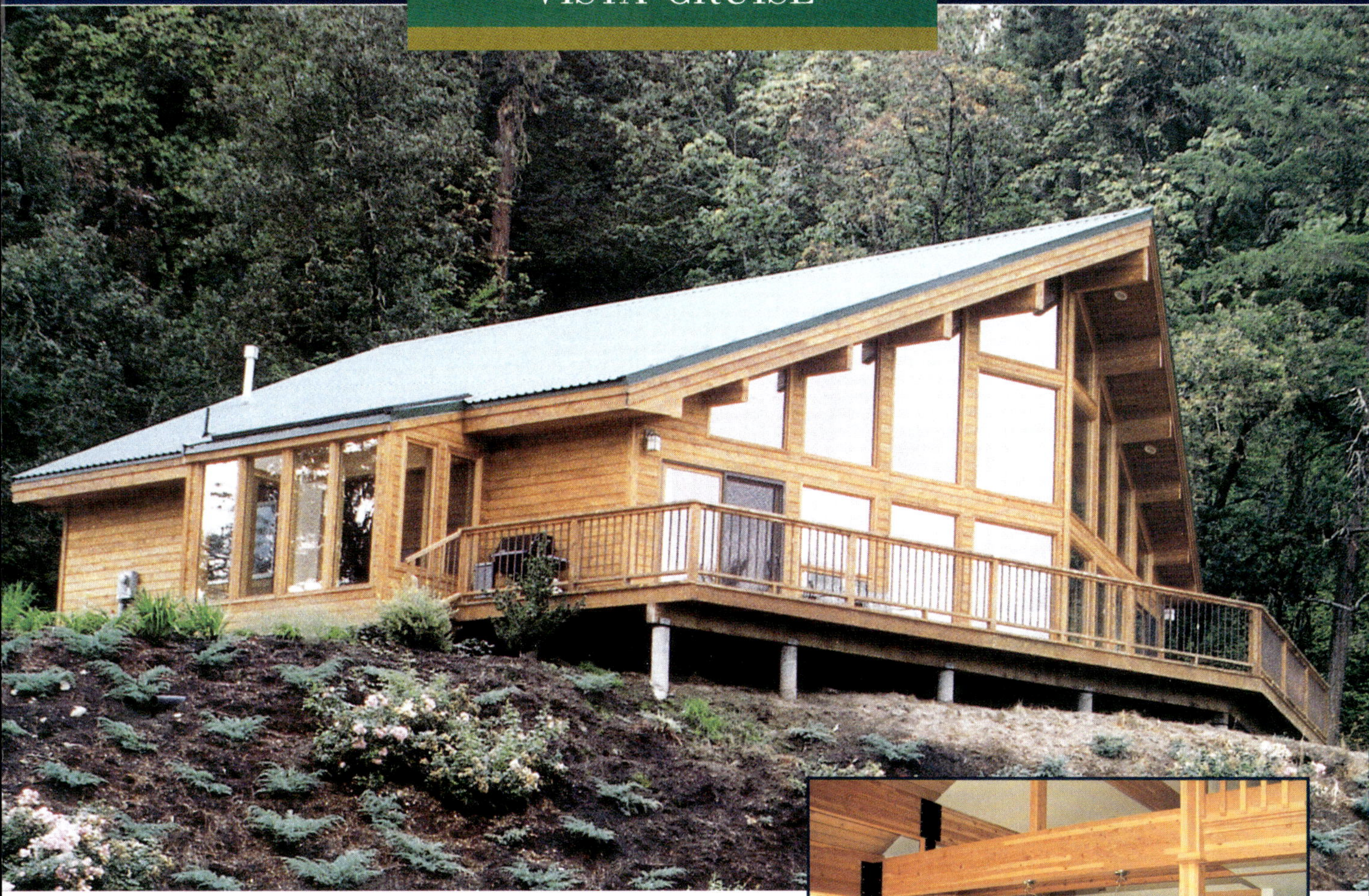

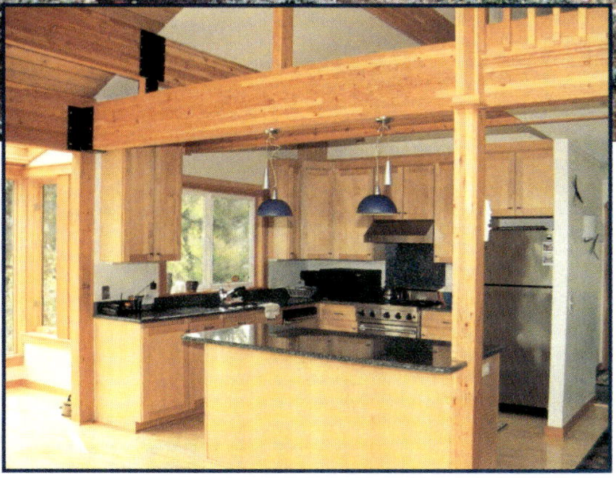

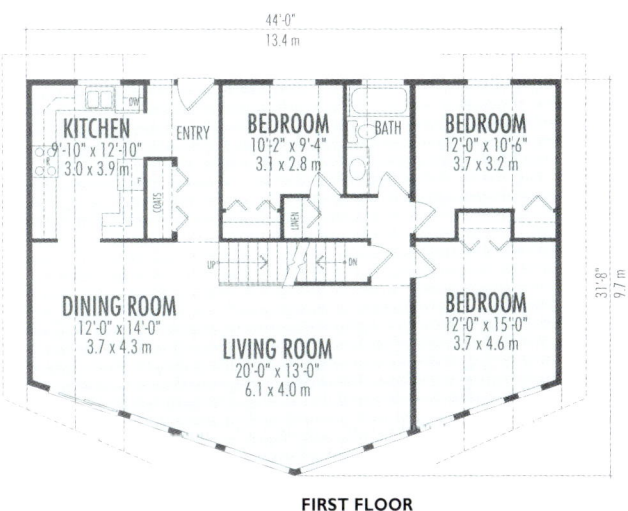

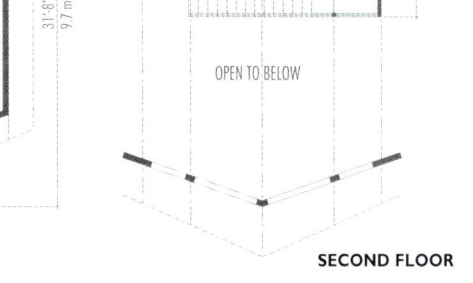

1,512 sq. ft.

- exterior dimensions 44' x 32'
- vaulted master bedroom, dining and living rooms
- 3 bedrooms, one bathroom, and a large open loft
- French doors access large front deck from living area and master bedroom.

FIRST FLOOR

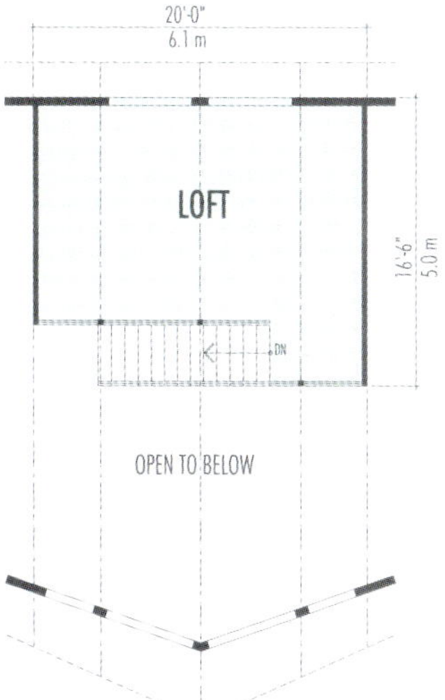

44'-0"
13.4 m

KITCHEN
9'-10" x 12'-10"
3.0 x 3.9 m

ENTRY

BEDROOM
10'-2" x 9'-4"
3.1 x 2.8 m

BATH

BEDROOM
12'-0" x 10'-6"
3.7 x 3.2 m

DINING ROOM
12'-0" x 14'-0"
3.7 x 4.3 m

UP

DN

LIVING ROOM
20'-0" x 13'-0"
6.1 x 4.0 m

BEDROOM
12'-0" x 15'-0"
3.7 x 4.6 m

31'-6"
9.7 m

SECOND FLOOR

20'-0"
6.1 m

LOFT

DN

OPEN TO BELOW

16'-6"
5.0 m

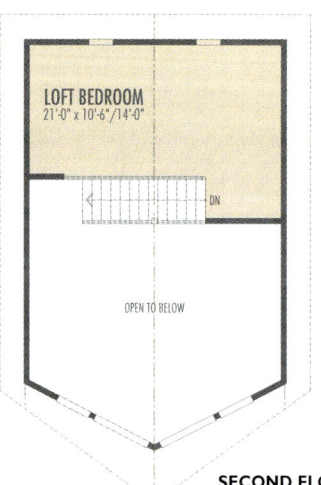

1,528 sq. ft.

- exterior dimensions 46' x 34'
- living room with prow front
- 3 bedrooms, 2 bathrooms
- all areas vaulted (except under loft)

COVERED ENTRY

KITCHEN
11'-6" x 12'-0"

ENTRY

W.I.C.

BEDROOM
10'-0" x 10'-8"

ENSUITE

BATH

W.I.C.

DINING ROOM
12'-0" x 11'-0"

UP

DN

MASTER
BEDROOM
11'-6" x 13'-1"

LIVING ROOM
21'-0" x 17'-11"

OPTIONAL SUNDECK

FIRST FLOOR

LOFT BEDROOM
21'-0" x 10'-6"/14'-0"

DN

OPEN TO BELOW

SECOND FLOOR

~ STANFORD ~

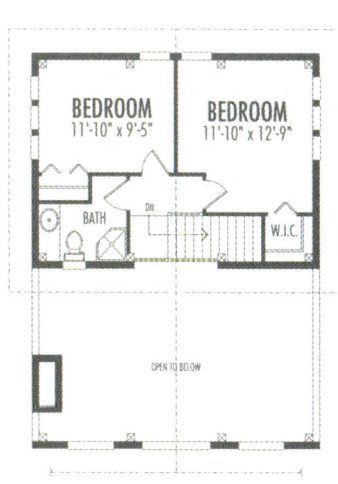

1,810 sq. ft.

- exterior dimensions: 51' x 39'
- large vaulted living room, dining room, and kitchen
- vaulted master suite with walk-in-closet and a 4-piece bath
- 3 bedrooms, 2½ bathrooms

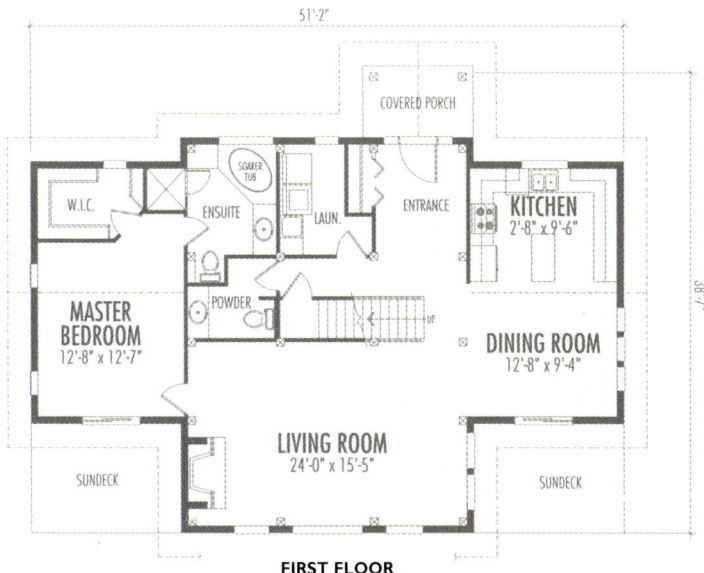

51'-2"

COVERED PORCH

W.I.C.

SOAKER TUB

ENSUITE

LAUN.

ENTRANCE

KITCHEN
2'-8" x 9'-6"

POWDER

38'-7"

MASTER BEDROOM
12'-8" x 12'-7"

DINING ROOM
12'-8" x 9'-4"

UP

LIVING ROOM
24'-0" x 15'-5"

SUNDECK

SUNDECK

FIRST FLOOR

BEDROOM
11'-10" x 9'-5"

BEDROOM
11'-10" x 12'-9"

BATH

DN

W.I.C.

OPEN TO BELOW

SECOND FLOOR

3,237 sq. ft.

- exterior dimensions: 51' x 62'
- elegant vaulted living areas, with large study on main floor
- vaulted bedrooms, one with its own loft
- large master suite with a 5-piece bath and walk-in-closet
- third-level loft
- 3 bedrooms, 2½ bathrooms

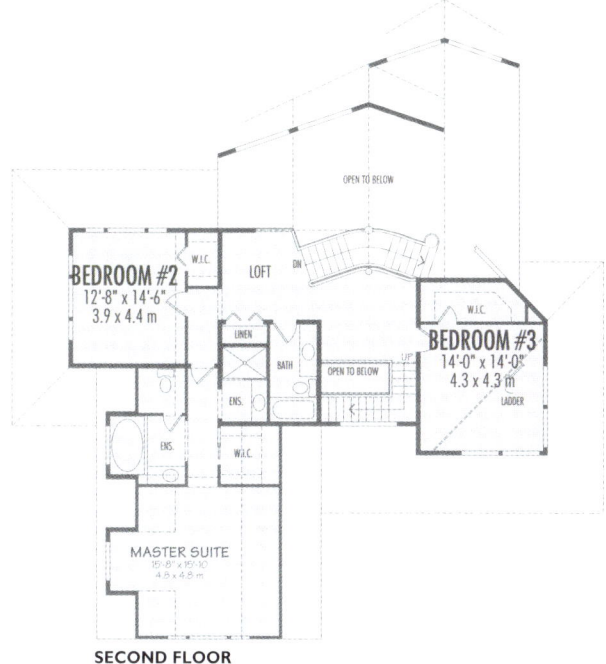

SECOND FLOOR

BEDROOM #2
12'-8" x 14'-6"
3.9 x 4.4 m

LOFT

W.I.C.

DN

OPEN TO BELOW

LINEN

BATH

ENS.

W.I.C.

BEDROOM #3
14'-0" x 14'-0"
4.3 x 4.3 m

OPEN TO BELOW

UP

LADDER

ENS.

W.I.C.

MASTER SUITE
15'-8" x 15'-10"
4.8 x 4.8 m

THIRD FLOOR

OPEN TO BELOW

STORAGE / PLANT SHELF

STUDIO/GAMES
21'-0" x 20'-6"
6.4 x 6.2 m

LINE OF 7'-0"
CEILING HT.

DN

OPEN TO BELOW

FIRST FLOOR

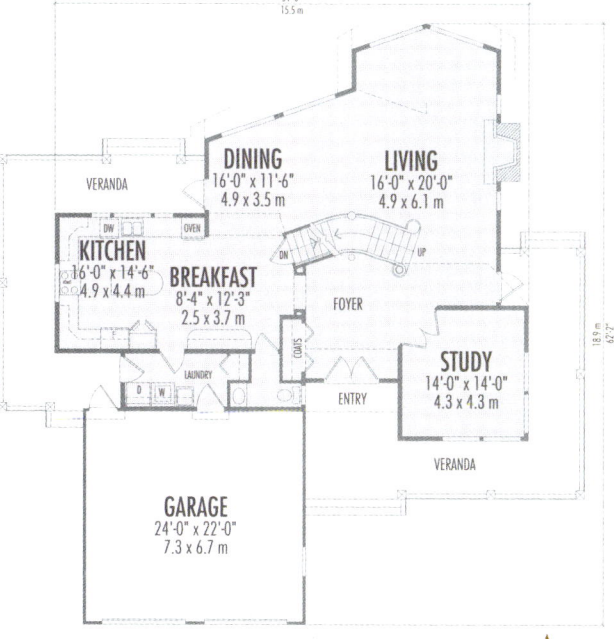

51'-0"
15.5 m

VERANDA

DINING
16'-0" x 11'-6"
4.9 x 3.5 m

LIVING
16'-0" x 20'-0"
4.9 x 6.1 m

KITCHEN
16'-0" x 14'-6"
4.9 x 4.4 m

DW
OVEN

BREAKFAST
8'-4" x 12'-3"
2.5 x 3.7 m

DN

UP

FOYER

COATS

STUDY
14'-0" x 14'-0"
4.3 x 4.3 m

LAUNDRY

D W

ENTRY

VERANDA

GARAGE
24'-0" x 22'-0"
7.3 x 6.7 m

18.9 m
62'-0"

1,584 sq. ft.

- Sunlight streams through the impressive windows of the living room in this stunning home. The open floor plan and the warmth of the magnificent log walls make this a special place for relaxing or entertaining.

- The master bedroom, with its own dressing room and bathroom, is upstairs, and separated from the other bedroom on the second floor to ensure privacy.

- A third bedroom on the main floor makes an excellent study or home office.

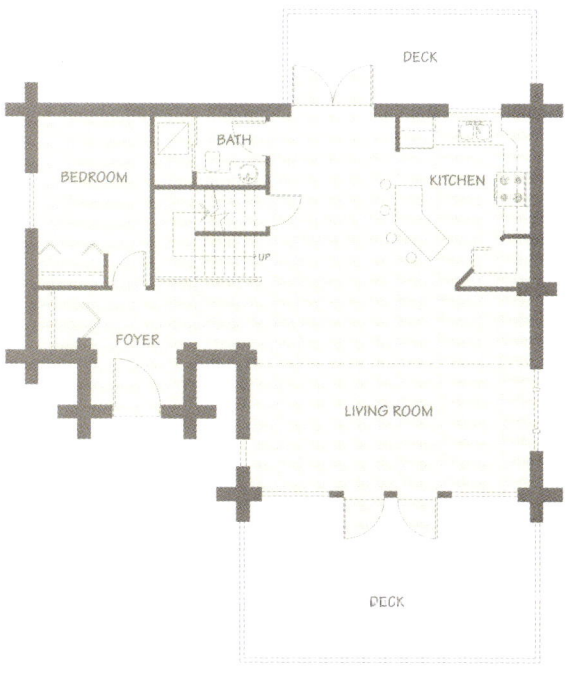

FIRST FLOOR

DECK

BATH

BEDROOM

KITCHEN

UP

FOYER

LIVING ROOM

DECK

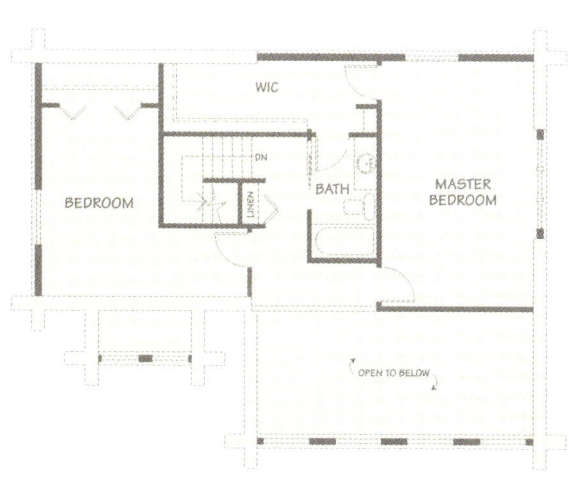

SECOND FLOOR

WIC

DN

BEDROOM

LINEN

BATH

MASTER
BEDROOM

OPEN TO BELOW

~ DORCHESTER ~

PHOTOGRAPHY: JAMES YOCHUM PHOTOGRAPHY

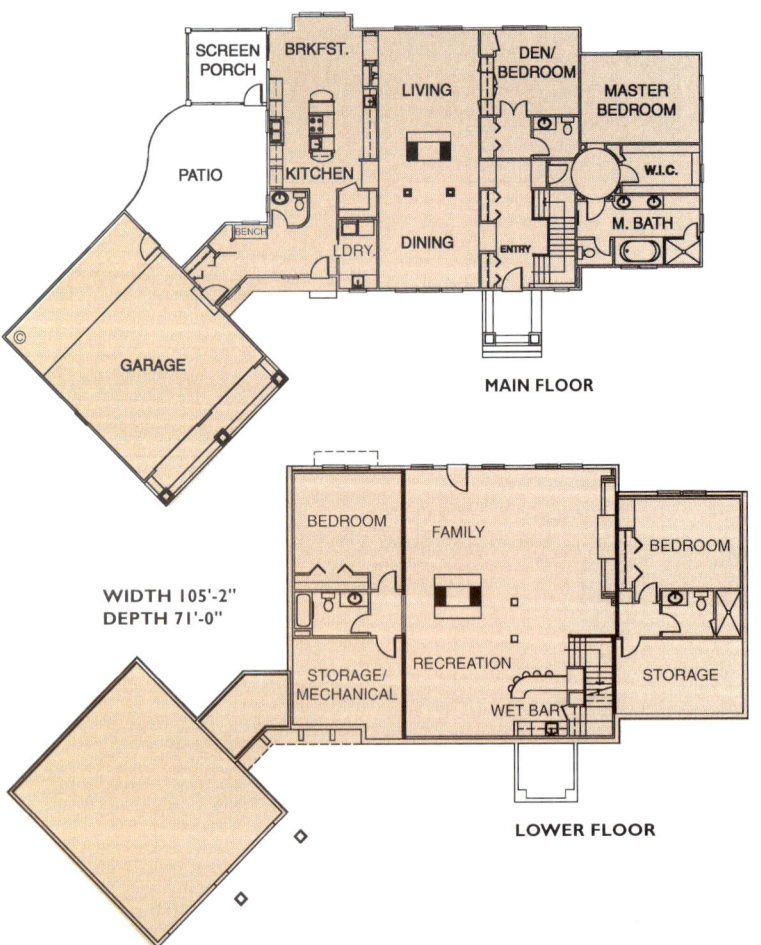

SCREEN PORCH
BRKFST.
LIVING
DEN/ BEDROOM
MASTER BEDROOM
PATIO
KITCHEN
W.I.C.
BENCH
LDRY.
DINING
ENTRY
M. BATH
GARAGE

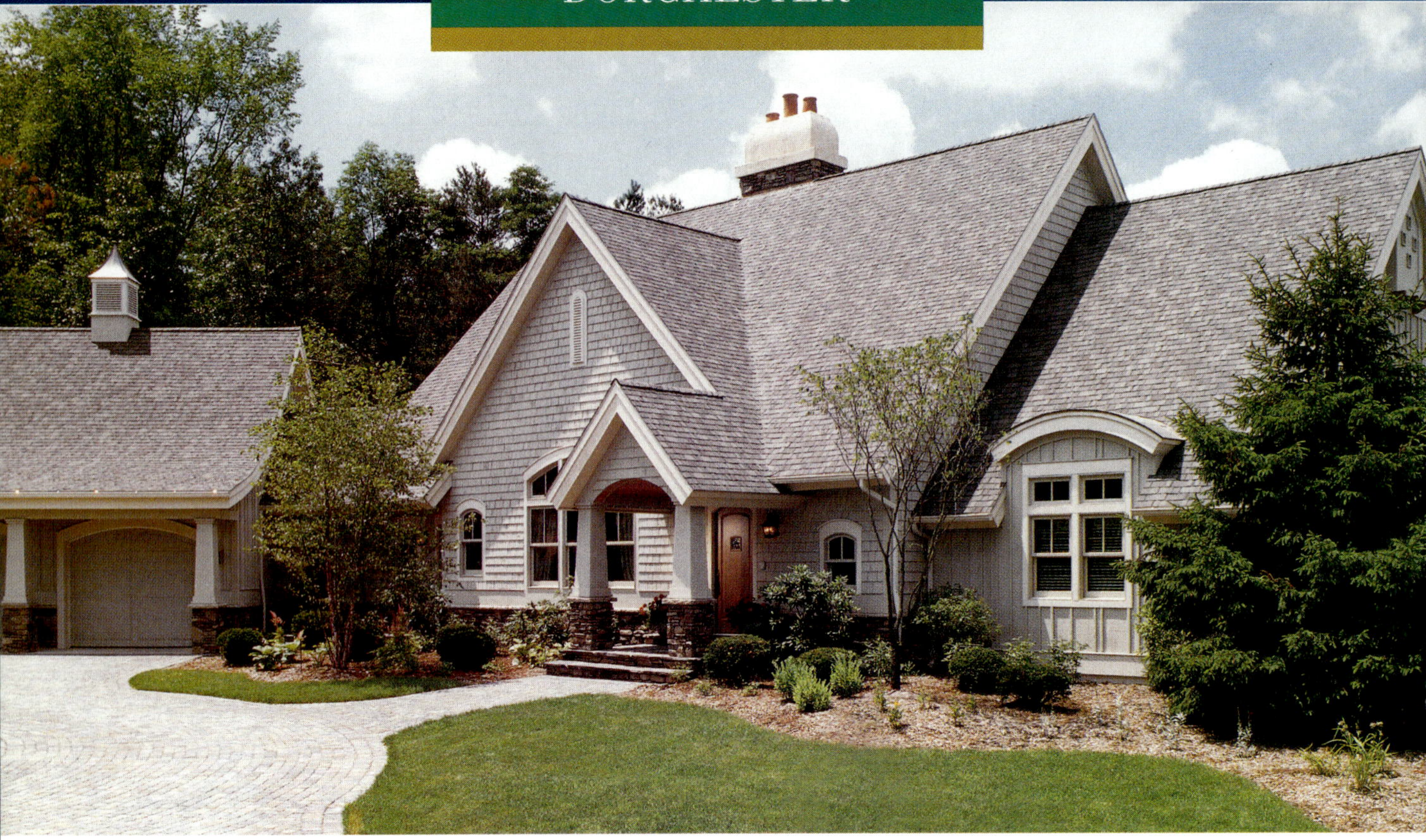

MAIN FLOOR

WIDTH 105'-2"
DEPTH 71'-0"

BEDROOM
FAMILY
BEDROOM
RECREATION
STORAGE/ MECHANICAL
WET BAR
STORAGE

LOWER FLOOR

4,292 sq. ft.

- The three-car garage set to the left of the home forms an inviting courtyard area rather than distracting attention from the home's facade.
- The well-appointed master suite features its own unique entry from the hallway.
- On the main level, a fireplace warms the living room, while elegant columns mark the dining room. Below, the family and recreation rooms share a fireplace.

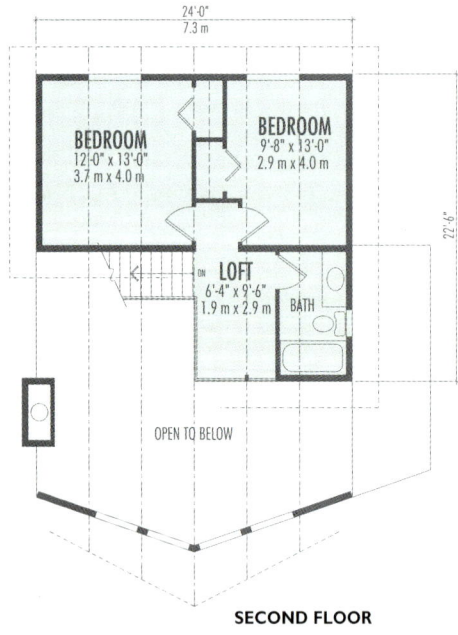

1,328 sq. ft.

- The splendid windows in the vaulted living areas seem to bring the outdoors into this elegant two-story chalet.

- In addition to the open-plan living and dining room, the main floor features one private bedroom, a 3-piece bath, laundry room, and a very functional kitchen with nook by the window.

- Two more bedrooms, a cozy loft open to the living areas, and a full bath are situated on the second level.

SECOND FLOOR

24'-0"
7.3 m

22'-6"
6.9 m

BEDROOM
12'-0" x 13'-0"
3.7 m x 4.0 m

BEDROOM
9'-8" x 13'-0"
2.9 m x 4.0 m

LOFT
6'-4" x 9'-6"
1.9 m x 2.9 m

BATH

OPEN TO BELOW

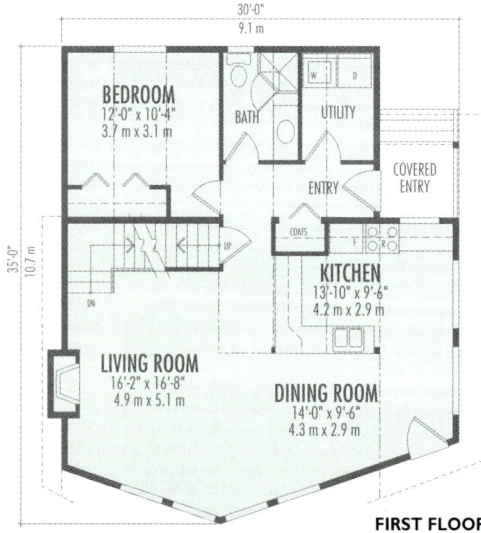

FIRST FLOOR

30'-0"
9.1 m

35'-0"
10.7 m

BEDROOM
12'-0" x 10'-4"
3.7 m x 3.1 m

BATH

UTILITY

W   D

COVERED ENTRY

ENTRY

COATS

KITCHEN
13'-10" x 9'-6"
4.2 m x 2.9 m

LIVING ROOM
16'-2" x 16'-8"
4.9 m x 5.1 m

DINING ROOM
14'-0" x 9'-6"
4.3 m x 2.9 m

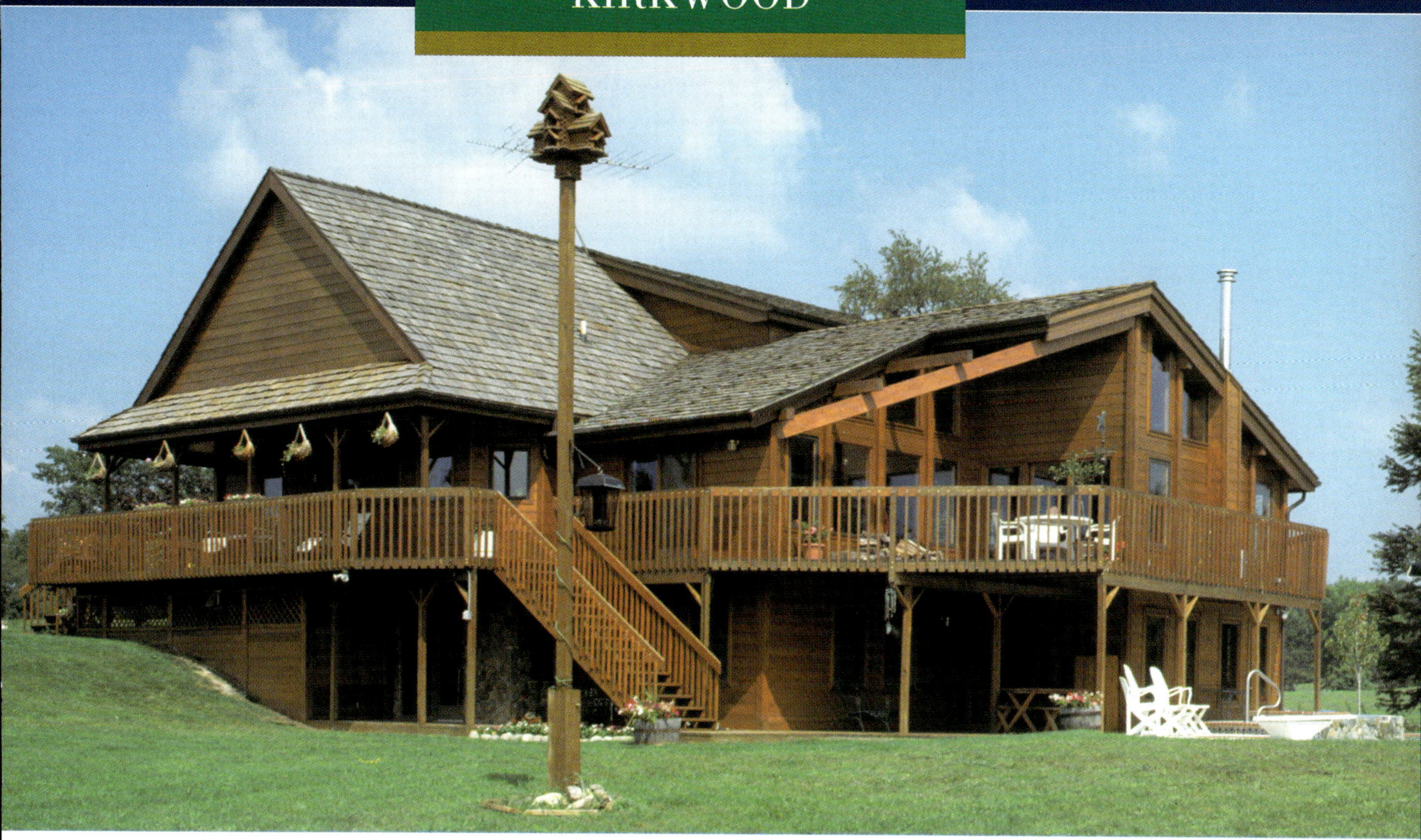

PHOTOGRAPHY: BETH SINGER

3,903 sq. ft.

- This impressive four-bedroom family home is anchored by the great-room, featuring a massive fireplace, built-in bookshelves, and access to the cozy loft study. The large country kitchen area, with its cooktop island and many other amenities, adjoins both the dining room and a spacious laundry/utility room.

- Also on the main floor is the master suite with private deck, built-in bookcases, two walk-in closets, and an ensuite bathroom with separate shower stall and skylit bathtub. A second bedroom on this floor has easy access to the full bathroom across the hall.

- The lower floor provides two additional bedrooms that share a full bathroom. A spacious recreation room with cozy fireplace and bar area opens to the downstairs patio.

MAIN FLOOR

LOWER FLOOR

LOFT

~ CHESTNUT ~

1,454 sq. ft.

- exterior dimensions 38' x 36'
- large living room with full oratory windows
- 2 bedrooms, 2 bathrooms
- vaulted living areas and master suite

FIRST FLOOR

COVERED ENTRY

KITCHEN
13'-6" x 9'-1"

LAUNDRY

BATH

FOYER

UP

DINING ROOM
14'-0" x 8'-0"

BEDROOM
8'-9" x 11'-8"

COVERED PORCH

LIVING ROOM
23'-1" x 14'-0"

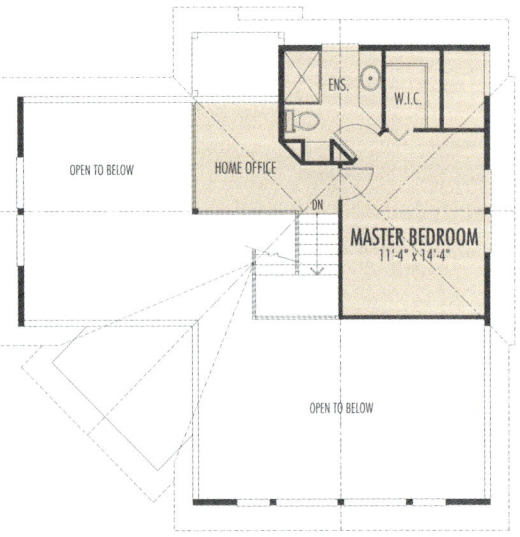

SECOND FLOOR

ENS.

W.I.C.

OPEN TO BELOW

HOME OFFICE

DN

MASTER BEDROOM
11'-4" x 14'-4"

OPEN TO BELOW

1,836 sq. ft.

- exterior dimensions 66' x 38'
- family room with vaulted ceiling
- clerestory windows in kitchen and family room
- 3 bedrooms, 2 bathrooms
- bathroom with corner soaking tub and shower

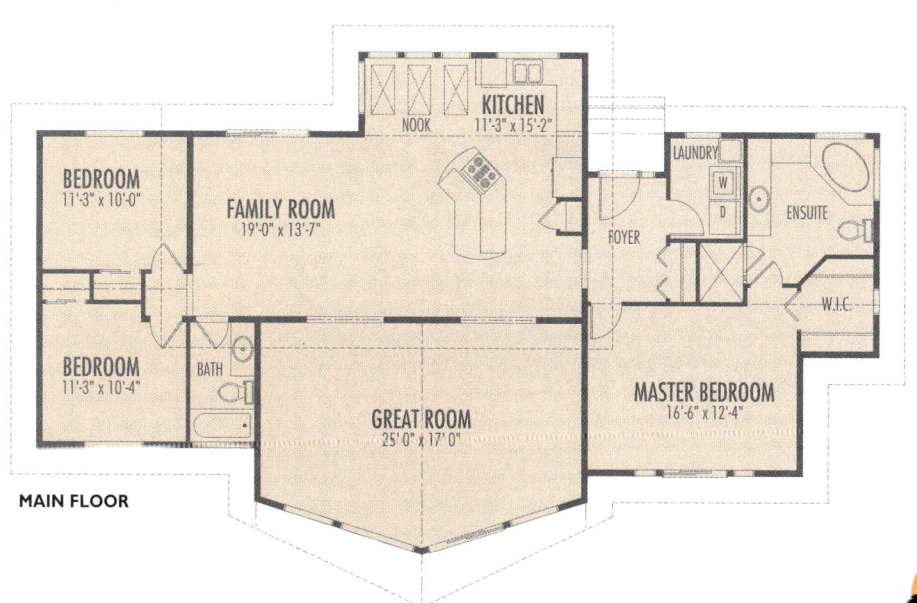

MAIN FLOOR

BEDROOM
11'-3" x 10'-0"

FAMILY ROOM
19'-0" x 13'-7"

NOOK

KITCHEN
11'-3" x 15'-2"

LAUNDRY

W
D

ENSUITE

FOYER

BEDROOM
11'-3" x 10'-4"

BATH

W.I.C.

GREAT ROOM
25' 0" x 17' 0"

MASTER BEDROOM
16'-6" x 12'-4"

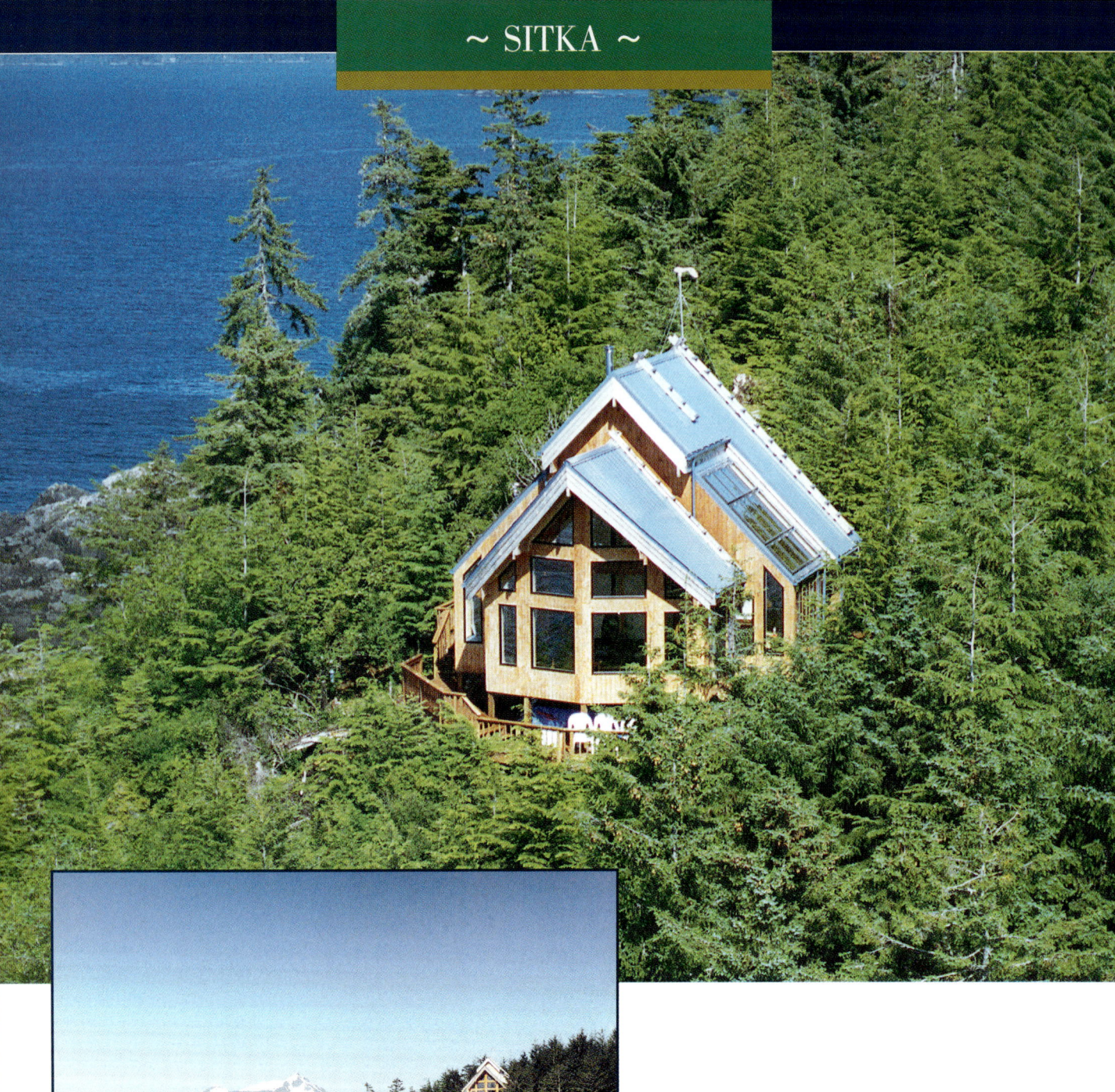

1,187 sq. ft.

- This unique getaway features two very private bedrooms.

- Many picture windows and skylights facilitate the flow of natural light from all directions.

- The stunning spiral staircase adds architectural interest to this truly one-of-a-kind home design.

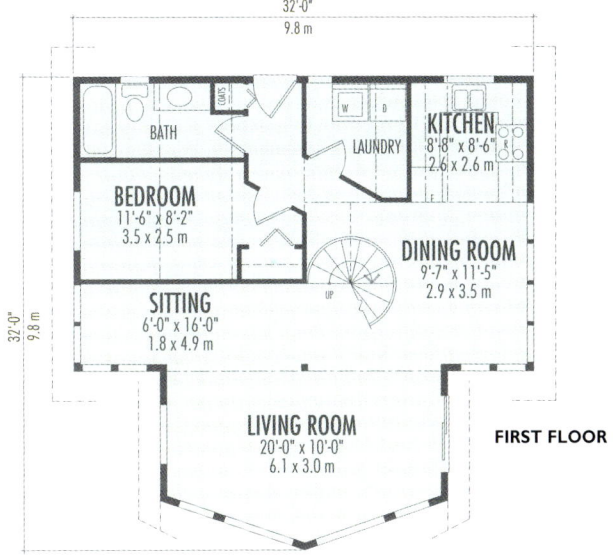

FIRST FLOOR

- 32'-0" / 9.8 m
- 32'-0" / 9.8 m
- BATH
- COATS
- W / D
- LAUNDRY
- KITCHEN 8'-8" x 8'-6" 2.6 x 2.6 m
- BEDROOM 11'-6" x 8'-2" 3.5 x 2.5 m
- DINING ROOM 9'-7" x 11'-5" 2.9 x 3.5 m
- SITTING 6'-0" x 16'-0" 1.8 x 4.9 m
- UP
- LIVING ROOM 20'-0" x 10'-0" 6.1 x 3.0 m

SECOND FLOOR

- 32'-0" / 9.8 m
- 20'-0" / 6.1 m
- BALCONY
- BEDROOM / LOFT
- DN
- OPEN TO BELOW

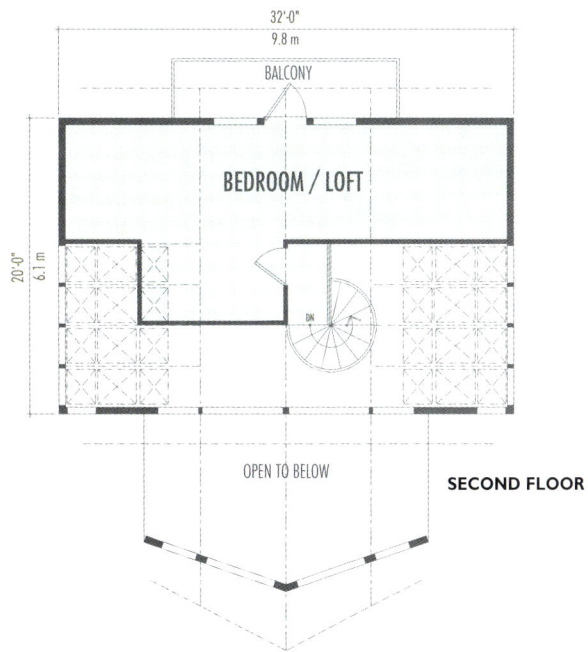

please see testimonial on page 12

~ CASTLEWOOD ~

PHOTOGRAPHY: GLENN GRAVES

2,563 sq. ft.

- large 4 bedroom, 3½ bathroom Country classic
- living room features a 17' ceiling
- hearth room, which opens onto deck, has a high sloped ceiling
- cozy two-way fireplace between the living and hearth rooms

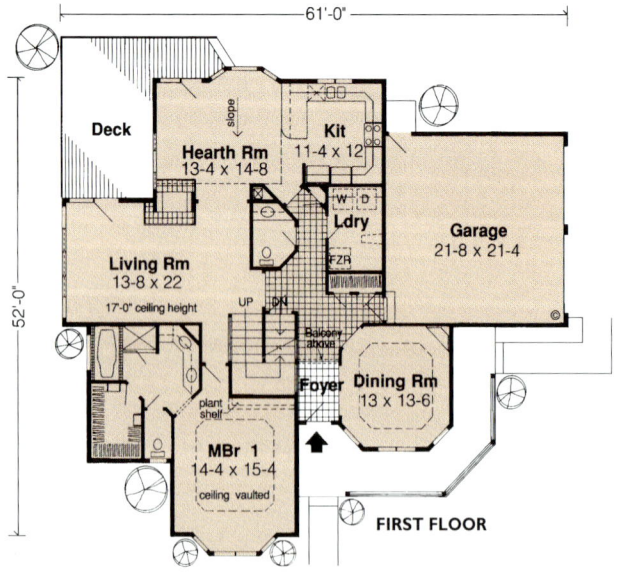

FIRST FLOOR

61'-0"

52'-0"

Deck

Hearth Rm
13-4 x 14-8

Kit
11-4 x 12

Ldry

W D

FZR

Garage
21-8 x 21-4

Living Rm
13-8 x 22
17'-0" ceiling height

UP DN

Balcony above

plant shelf

Foyer

Dining Rm
13 x 13-6

MBr 1
14-4 x 15-4
ceiling vaulted

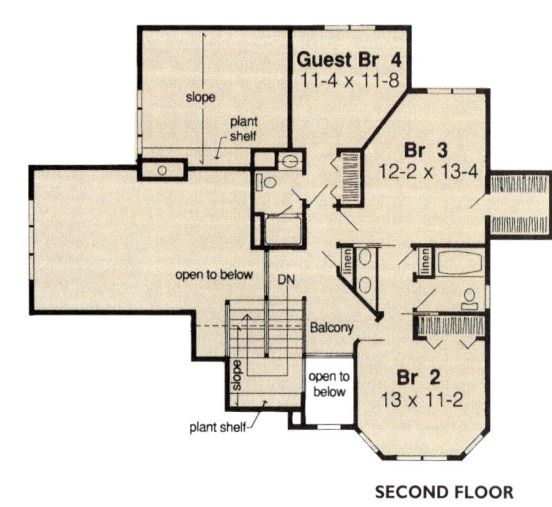

SECOND FLOOR

Guest Br 4
11-4 x 11-8

slope

plant shelf

Br 3
12-2 x 13-4

open to below

DN

Balcony

linen

linen

open to below

Br 2
13 x 11-2

slope

plant shelf

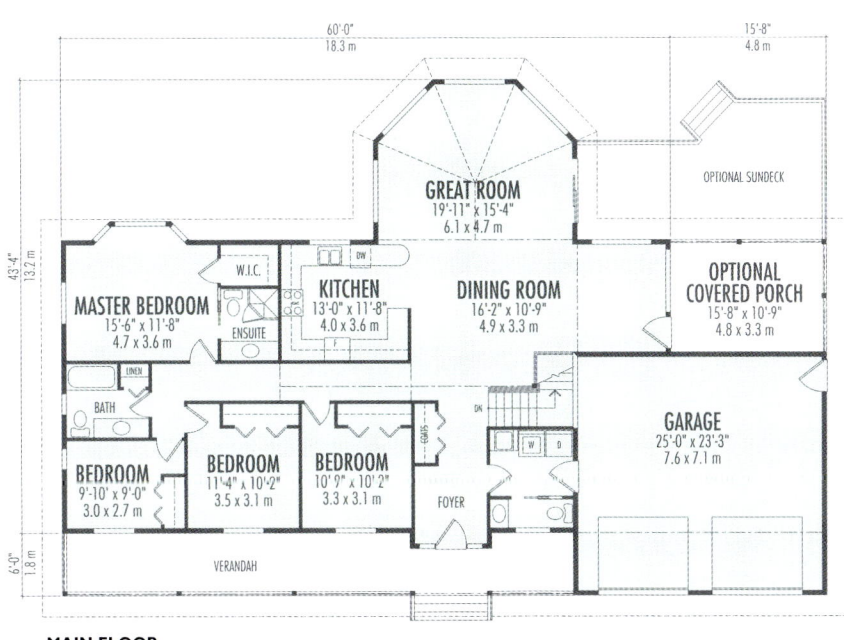

~ JACKSON ~

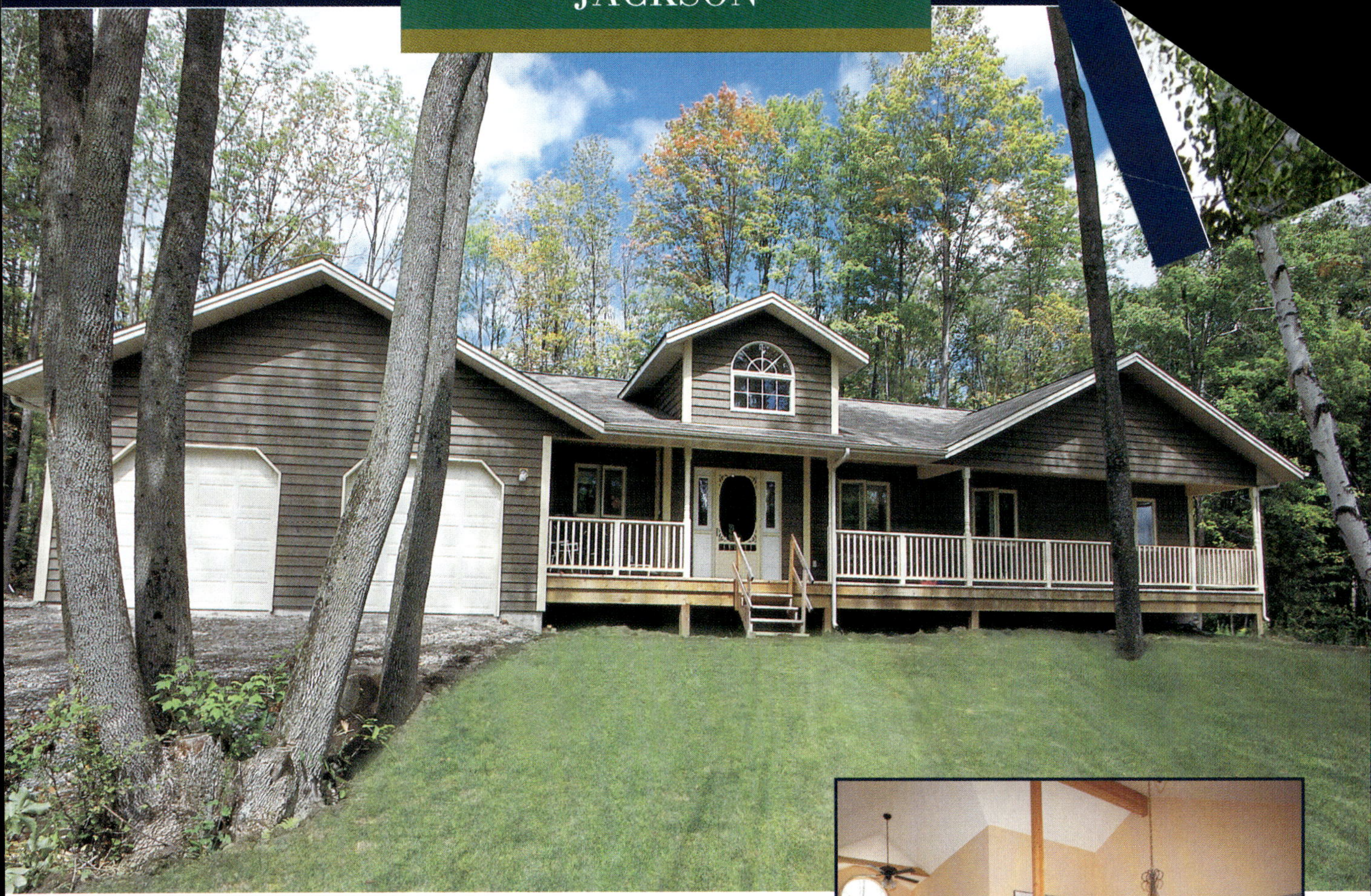

1,821 sq. ft.

- exterior dimensions 76' x 50'
- octagonal shaped great-room brings in light from all sides
- covered verandah in front
- 4 bedrooms, 2 bathrooms

MAIN FLOOR

60'-0"
18.3 m

15'-8"
4.8 m

43'-4"
13.2 m

6'-0"
1.8 m

GREAT ROOM
19'-11" x 15'-4"
6.1 x 4.7 m

OPTIONAL SUNDECK

W.I.C.

DW

KITCHEN
13'-0" x 11'-8"
4.0 x 3.6 m

DINING ROOM
16'-2" x 10'-9"
4.9 x 3.3 m

OPTIONAL COVERED PORCH
15'-8" x 10'-9"
4.8 x 3.3 m

MASTER BEDROOM
15'-6" x 11'-8"
4.7 x 3.6 m

ENSUITE

LINEN

BATH

BEDROOM
9'-10" x 9'-0"
3.0 x 2.7 m

BEDROOM
11'-4" x 10'-2"
3.5 x 3.1 m

BEDROOM
10'-9" x 10'-2"
3.3 x 3.1 m

W   D

DN

GARAGE
25'-0" x 23'-3"
7.6 x 7.1 m

FOYER

VERANDAH

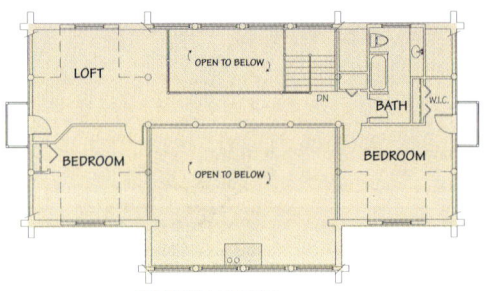

2,629 sq. ft.

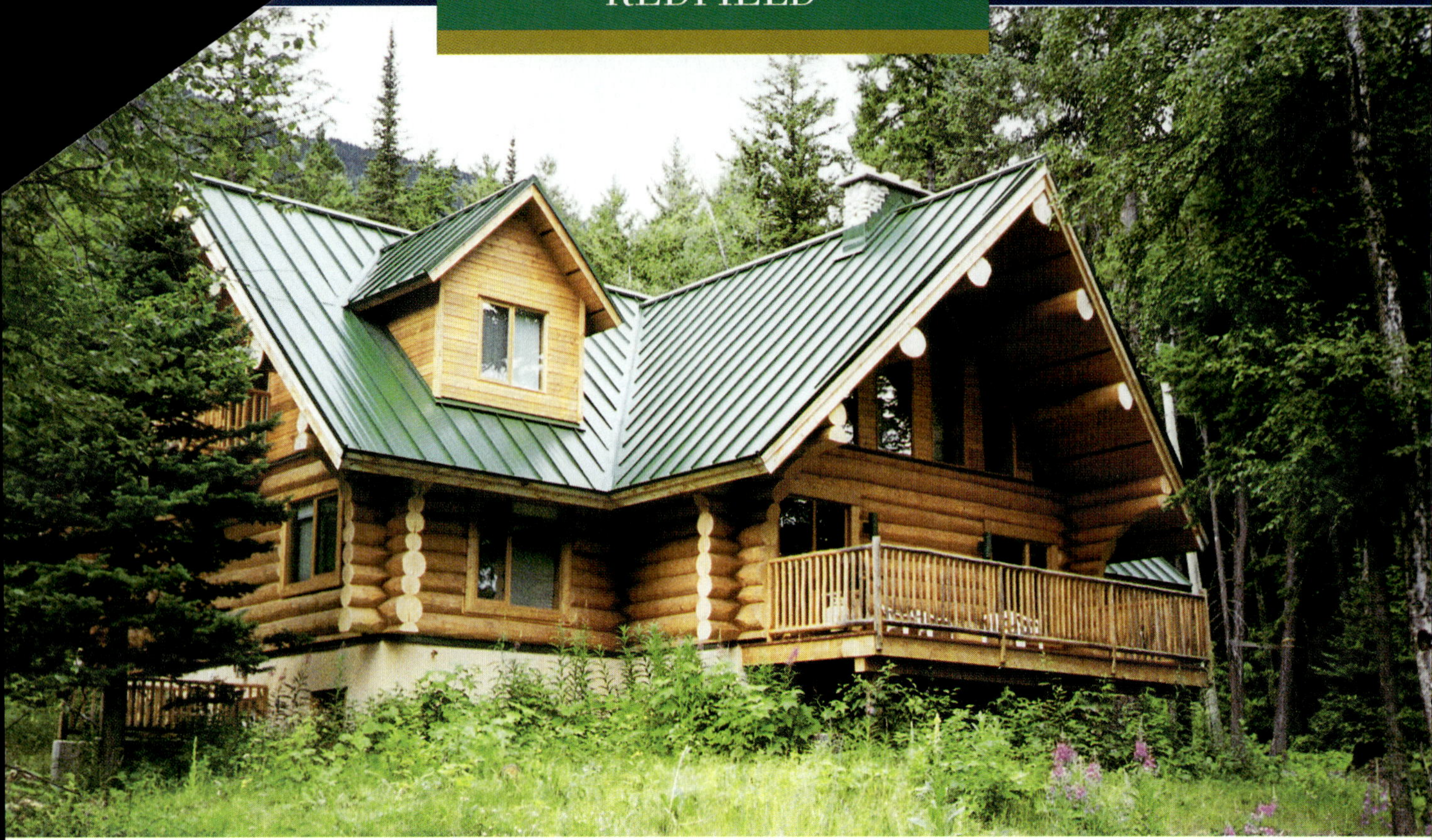

- The appeal of this delightful design begins with gabled dormers on the second level and finishes with a beautiful yet functional layout with remarkable comfort. An impressive and welcoming foyer opens up to the bright and airy cathedral-ceiling great room, which highlights a floor to ceiling fireplace. Tucked away by the dining room is a generous gourmet kitchen with ample counter space.

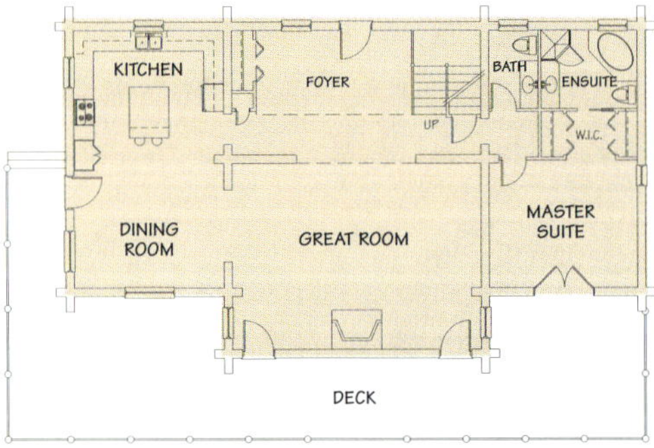

- Upstairs, many charming features await, including an open-sided walkway which looks down onto the great room and foyer, a large master suite with a full ensuite tucked into one of the dormers, and a cozy loft. Let your imagination soar when you personalize this adaptable design to fit your family's needs.

SECOND FLOOR

FIRST FLOOR

PHOTOGRAPHY: JAMES YOCHUM PHOTOGRAPHY

1,881 sq. ft.

- An inviting veranda and varied rooflines add to the appeal of this two bedroom with den, or three-bedroom New England cottage.

- The open-plan kitchen, dining, and living rooms flow together to create an open and airy atmosphere.

- The bay window in the kitchen fills the working space with ample natural light.

- The upper floor offers a large master bedroom and a good sized second bedroom, each with access to a full private bathroom.

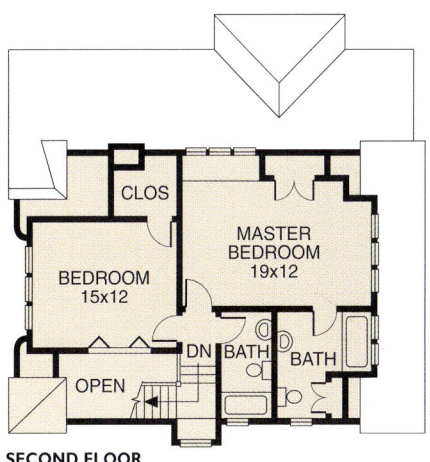

CLOS

MASTER BEDROOM
19x12

BEDROOM
15x12

DN   BATH   BATH

OPEN

SECOND FLOOR

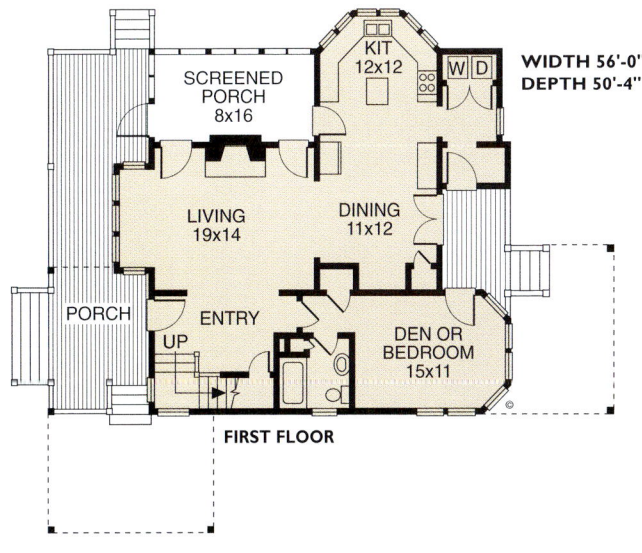

KIT
12x12

W D

WIDTH 56'-0"
DEPTH 50'-4"

SCREENED
PORCH
8x16

LIVING
19x14

DINING
11x12

PORCH

ENTRY

UP

DEN OR
BEDROOM
15x11

FIRST FLOOR

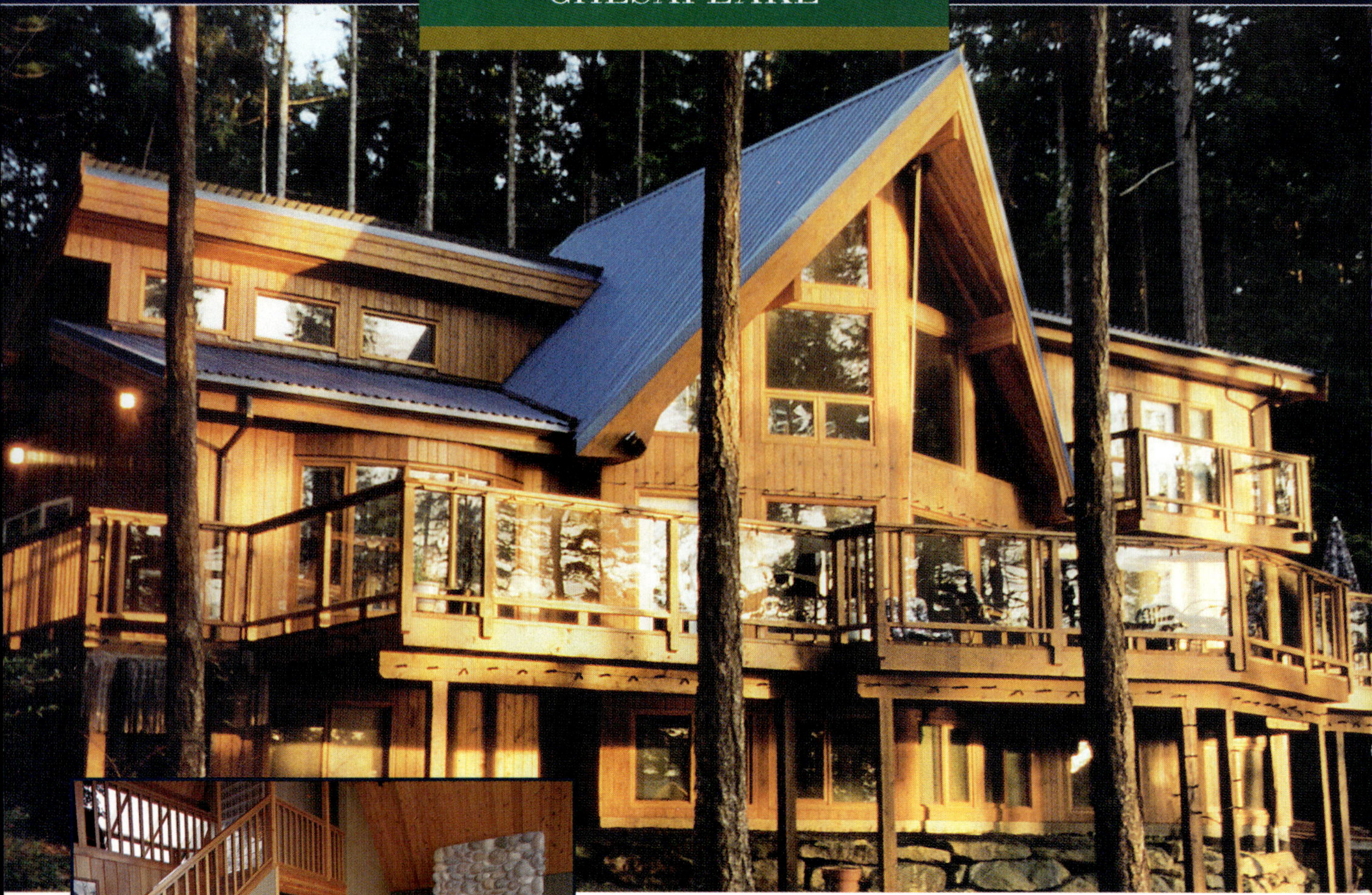

2,643 sq. ft.

- exterior dimensions 60' x 41'
- vaulted living room and family room, with lovely sunroom at the back
- 3 bedrooms and den
- private upper-floor master suite with loft and balcony

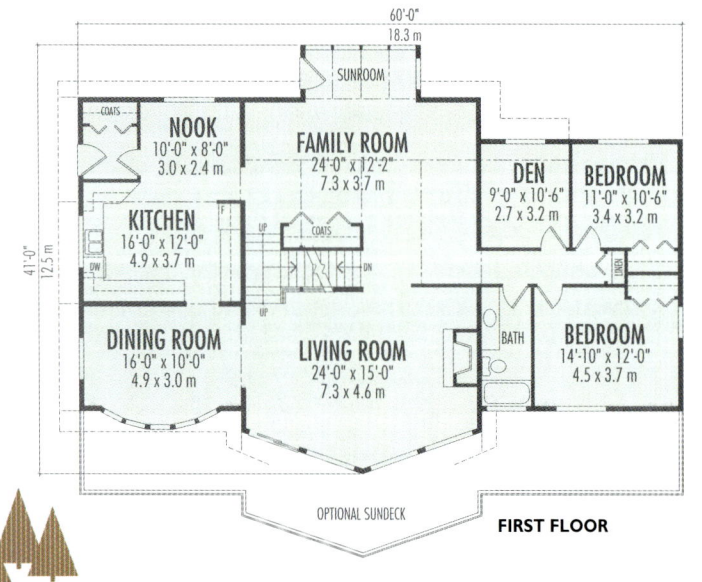

FIRST FLOOR

60'-0"
18.3 m

41'-0"
12.5 m

SUNROOM

COATS

NOOK
10'-0" x 8'-0"
3.0 x 2.4 m

FAMILY ROOM
24'-0" x 12'-2"
7.3 x 3.7 m

DEN
9'-0" x 10'-6"
2.7 x 3.2 m

BEDROOM
11'-0" x 10'-6"
3.4 x 3.2 m

KITCHEN
16'-0" x 12'-0"
4.9 x 3.7 m

UP
COATS
DN
UP

DINING ROOM
16'-0" x 10'-0"
4.9 x 3.0 m

LIVING ROOM
24'-0" x 15'-0"
7.3 x 4.6 m

BATH

LINEN

BEDROOM
14'-10" x 12'-0"
4.5 x 3.7 m

OPTIONAL SUNDECK

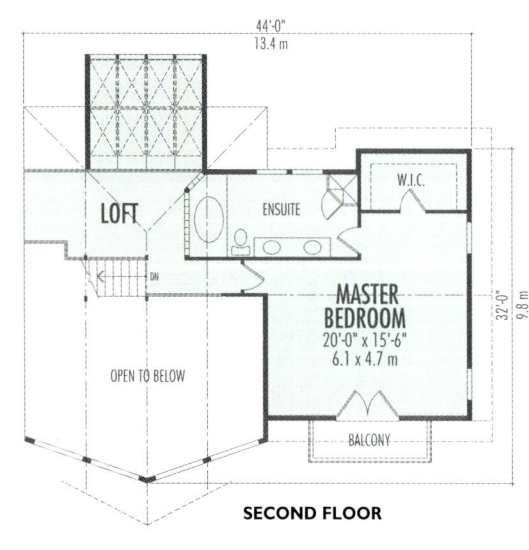

SECOND FLOOR

44'-0"
13.4 m

32'-0"
9.8 m

LOFT

ENSUITE

W.I.C.

DN

OPEN TO BELOW

MASTER BEDROOM
20'-0" x 15'-6"
6.1 x 4.7 m

BALCONY

~ MILLCREEK ~

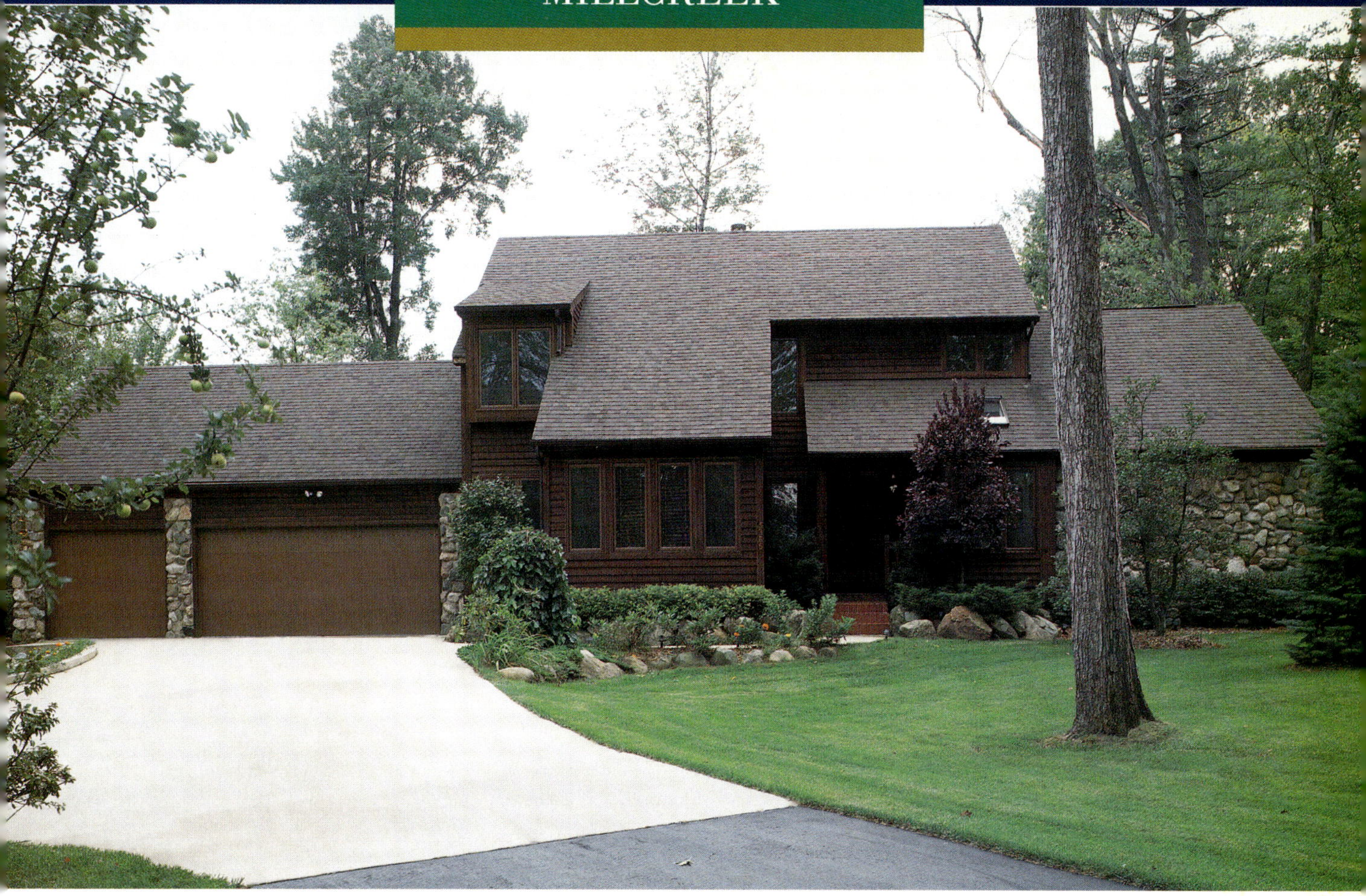

PHOTOGRAPHY: BETH SINGER

1,487 sq. ft.

- This compact contemporary three-bedroom home has a large deck which provides extra living space and brings in the outdoors.
- One of the bedrooms on the second floor features a deck, and the second floor landing balcony overlooks the living room.
- The versatility of the basic design is shown in the above photograph by the addition of a two-car garage and a large family room.

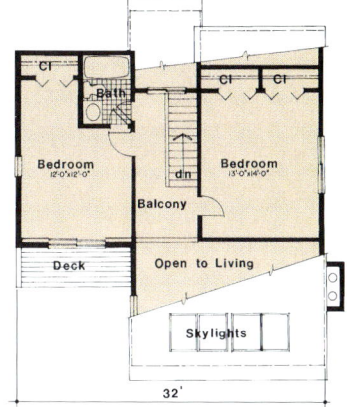

SECOND FLOOR

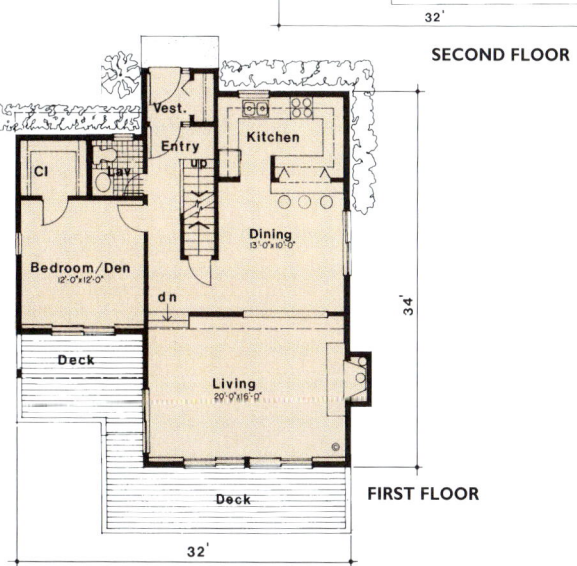

FIRST FLOOR

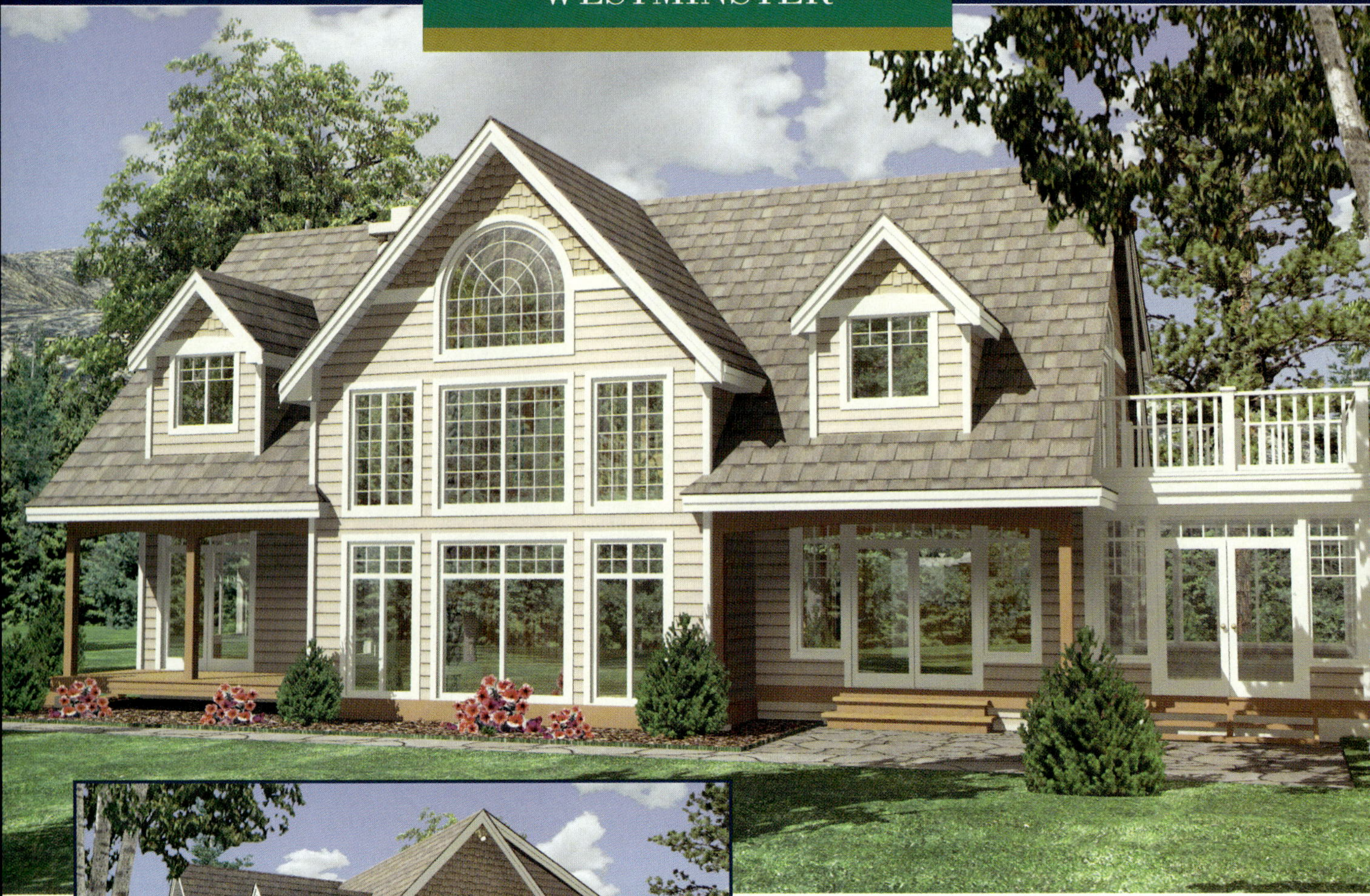

3,004 sq. ft.

- large open living areas including a vaulted great-room
- master suite with 5-piece ensuite on the main floor
- large bedrooms with vaulted ceilings and a shared private balcony
- 4 bedrooms, 2½ bathrooms
- large screen porch for comfort outdoors

(see front cover)

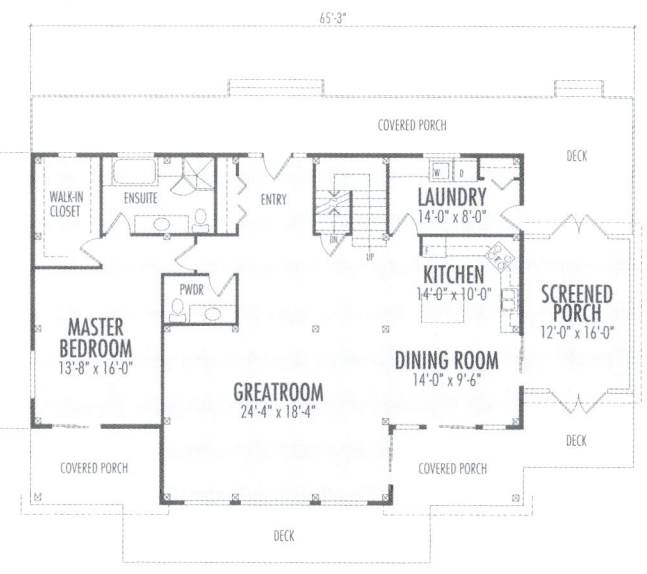

FIRST FLOOR

65'-3"

COVERED PORCH

DECK

WALK-IN CLOSET

ENSUITE

ENTRY

W D

LAUNDRY
14'-0" x 8'-0"

KITCHEN
14'-0" x 10'-0"

SCREENED PORCH
12'-0" x 16'-0"

PWDR

MASTER BEDROOM
13'-8" x 16'-0"

GREATROOM
24'-4" x 18'-4"

DINING ROOM
14'-0" x 9'-6"

COVERED PORCH

COVERED PORCH

DECK

DECK

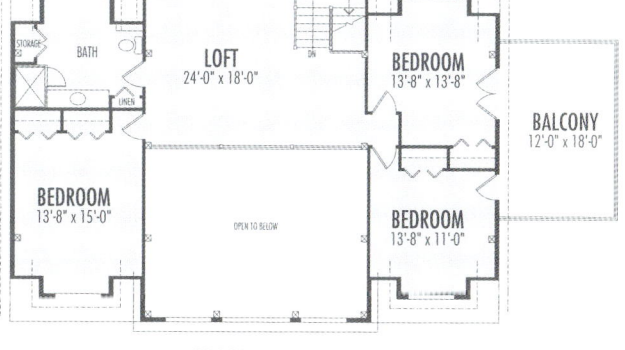

SECOND FLOOR

STORAGE

BATH

LINEN

LOFT
24'-0" x 18'-0"

BEDROOM
13'-8" x 13'-8"

BALCONY
12'-0" x 18'-0"

BEDROOM
13'-8" x 15'-0"

OPEN TO BELOW

BEDROOM
13'-8" x 11'-0"

1,653 sq. ft.

- exterior dimensions 52' x 40'
- vaulted living room, kitchen, and dining room
- 3 bedrooms, 2 bathrooms
- covered porch

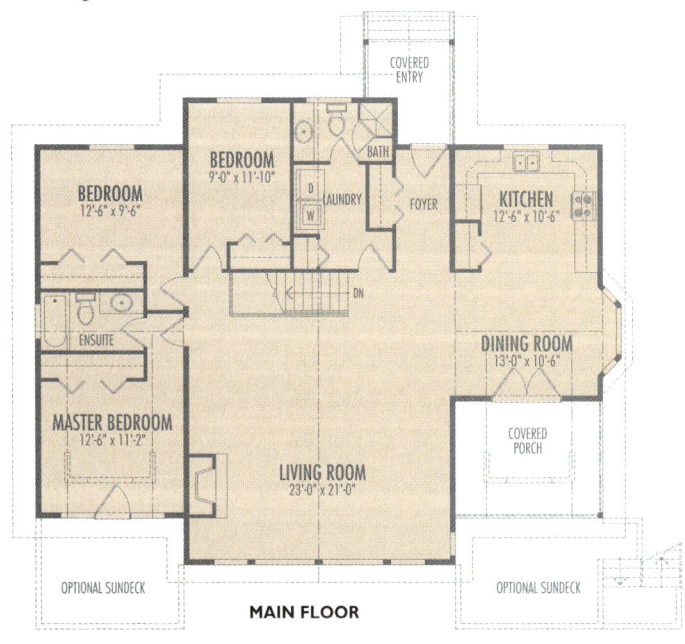

COVERED ENTRY

BEDROOM 9'-0" x 11'-10"

BATH

BEDROOM 12'-6" x 9'-6"

D W LAUNDRY

FOYER

KITCHEN 12'-6" x 10'-6"

DN

ENSUITE

DINING ROOM 13'-0" x 10'-6"

MASTER BEDROOM 12'-6" x 11'-2"

COVERED PORCH

LIVING ROOM 23'-0" x 21'-0"

OPTIONAL SUNDECK

OPTIONAL SUNDECK

MAIN FLOOR

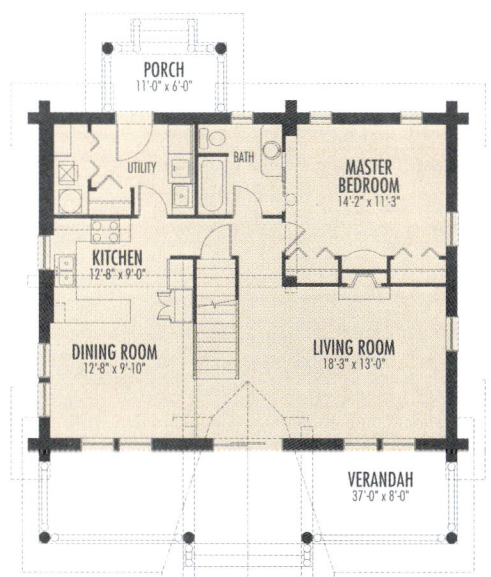

1,465 sq. ft.

- exterior dimensions 36' x 42'
- large covered verandah
- vaulted living areas and master bedroom
- 3 bedrooms, 2 bathrooms, back porch off laundry room

FIRST FLOOR

PORCH
11'-0" x 6'-0"

UTILITY

BATH

MASTER BEDROOM
14'-2" x 11'-3"

KITCHEN
12'-8" x 9'-0"

DINING ROOM
12'-8" x 9'-10"

LIVING ROOM
18'-3" x 13'-0"

VERANDAH
37'-0" x 8'-0"

SECOND FLOOR

BEDROOM
12'-10" x 11'-2"

BATH

BEDROOM
12'-10" x 9'-8"/13'-8"

OPEN TO BELOW

PHOTOGRAPHY: JOHN EHRENCLOU

3,440 sq. ft.

- An impressive courtyard leads up to the covered porch in front, while the back is graced with a patio and private court with hot tub.

- The first floor caters to just about every need with its living and dining rooms, kitchen, bar, and morning room. The master suite is also located on this floor.

- Bedrooms with plenty of closet space share the second floor and each have direct access to a full bath.

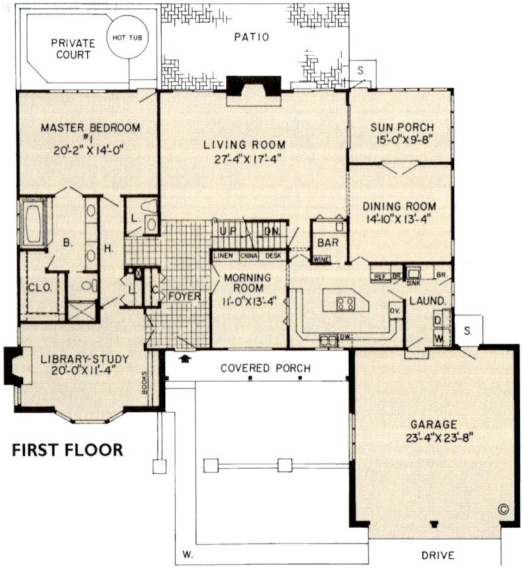

FIRST FLOOR

PRIVATE COURT
HOT TUB
PATIO
MASTER BEDROOM 20'-2" X 14'-0"
LIVING ROOM 27'-4" X 17'-4"
SUN PORCH 15'-0" X 9'-8"
DINING ROOM 14'-10" X 13'-4"
BAR
LINEN CHINA DESK
MORNING ROOM 11'-0" X 13'-4"
LAUND.
FOYER
LIBRARY-STUDY 20'-0" X 11'-4"
COVERED PORCH
GARAGE 23'-4" X 23'-8"
W.
DRIVE

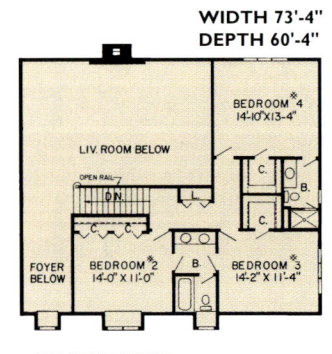

WIDTH 73'-4"
DEPTH 60'-4"

LIV. ROOM BELOW
OPEN RAIL
BEDROOM #4 14'-10" X 13'-4"
FOYER BELOW
BEDROOM #2 14'-0" X 11'-0"
BEDROOM #3 14'-2" X 11'-4"

SECOND FLOOR

2,078 sq. ft.

- Unique roof lines and the use of glass add warmth and character to this elegant two-bedroom, chalet-style home.

- The enormous second-floor master bedroom offers a large walk-in closet and full ensuite with separate shower.

- The main level features comfortable open-plan living and dining areas, a gourmet kitchen with exceptionally large island, the second bedroom, another full bath, and utility room with access to the garden.

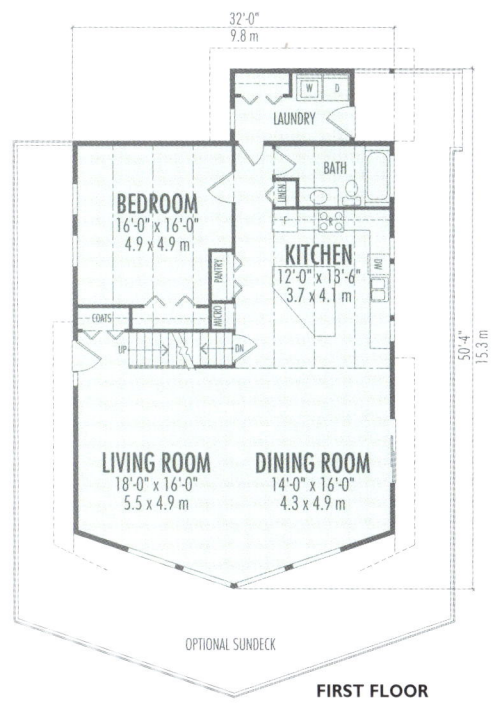

FIRST FLOOR

32'-0"
9.8 m

50'-4"
15.3 m

LAUNDRY

W | D

BATH

LINEN

BEDROOM
16'-0" x 16'-0"
4.9 x 4.9 m

KITCHEN
12'-0" x 18'-6"
3.7 x 4.1 m

PANTRY

MICRO

COATS

UP

DN

LIVING ROOM
18'-0" x 16'-0"
5.5 x 4.9 m

DINING ROOM
14'-0" x 16'-0"
4.3 x 4.9 m

OPTIONAL SUNDECK

SECOND FLOOR

32'-0"
9.8 m

22'-0"
6.7 m

MASTER BEDROOM
22'-10" x 18'-6"
6.9 x 5.6 m

ENSUITE

W.I.C.

DN

OPEN TO BELOW

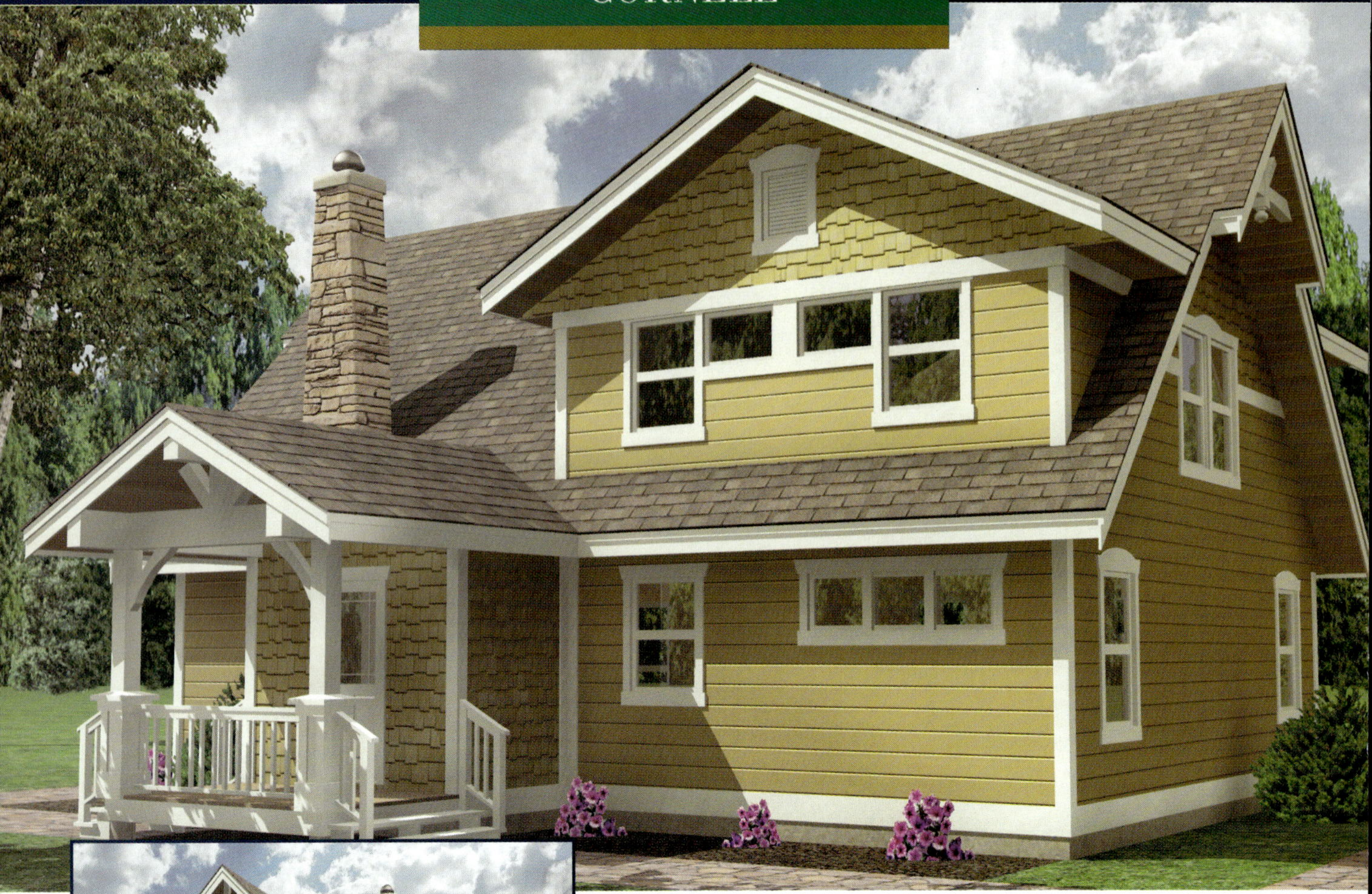

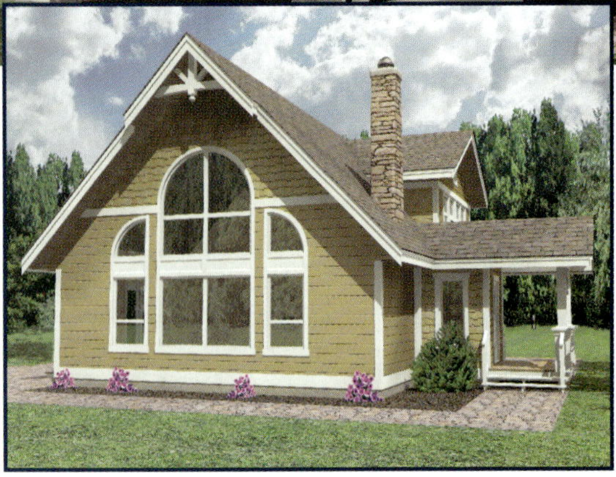

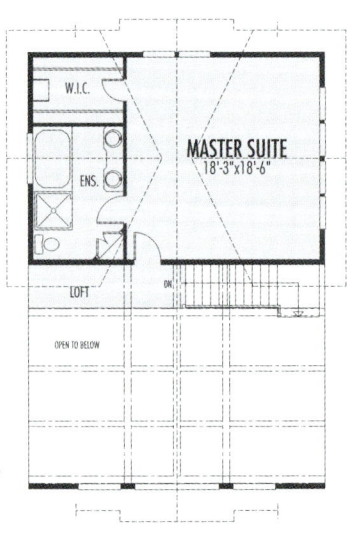

1,783 sq. ft.

- exterior dimensions 40' x 40'
- private upper-floor master suite
- 3 bedrooms, 2 bathrooms

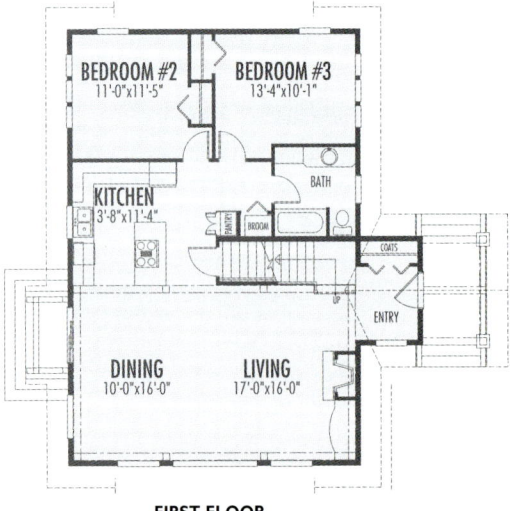

BEDROOM #2
11'-0"x11'-5"

BEDROOM #3
13'-4"x10'-1"

BATH

KITCHEN
13'-8"x11'-4"

PANTRY

BROOM

COATS

UP

ENTRY

DINING
10'-0"x16'-0"

LIVING
17'-0"x16'-0"

FIRST FLOOR

W.I.C.

MASTER SUITE
18'-3"x18'-6"

ENS.

LOFT

DN

OPEN TO BELOW

SECOND FLOOR

1,262 sq. ft.

- The vaulted living area and kitchen act as the hub of this open-plan bungalow, with natural light streaming in through the splendid solarium and the majestic windows.

- Each of the two bedrooms is situated in a separate wing for maximum privacy, and the master bedroom features magnificent prow windows.

- A utility room and a full bath on the main level round out the elegant floor plan. Log siding adds to the visual appeal of this practical and appealing home.

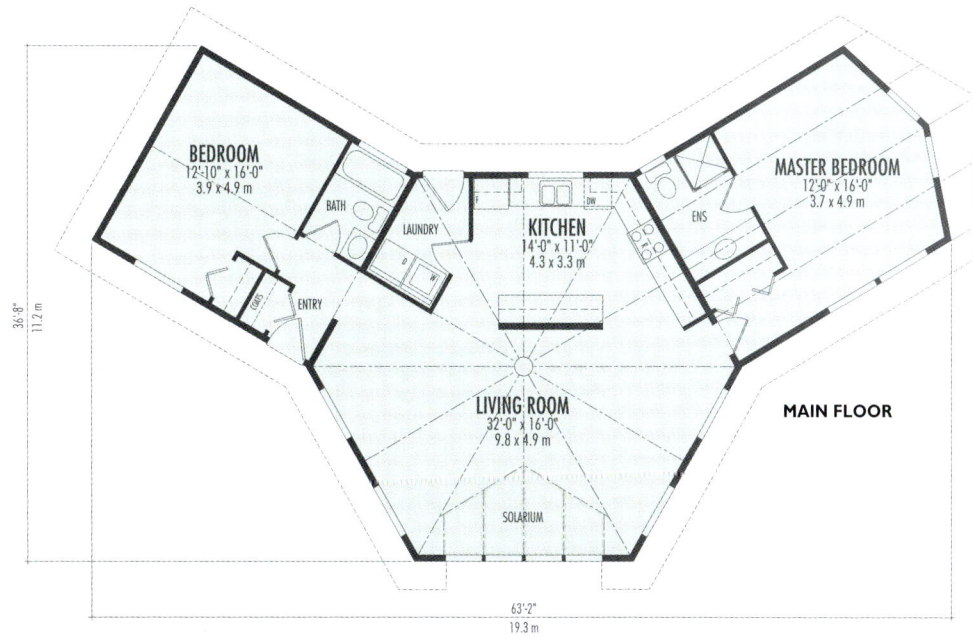

BEDROOM
12'-10" x 16'-0"
3.9 x 4.9 m

BATH

LAUNDRY

KITCHEN
14'-0" x 11'-0"
4.3 x 3.3 m

ENS

MASTER BEDROOM
12'-0" x 16'-0"
3.7 x 4.9 m

ENTRY

LIVING ROOM
32'-0" x 16'-0"
9.8 x 4.9 m

MAIN FLOOR

SOLARIUM

36'-8"
11.2 m

63'-2"
19.3 m

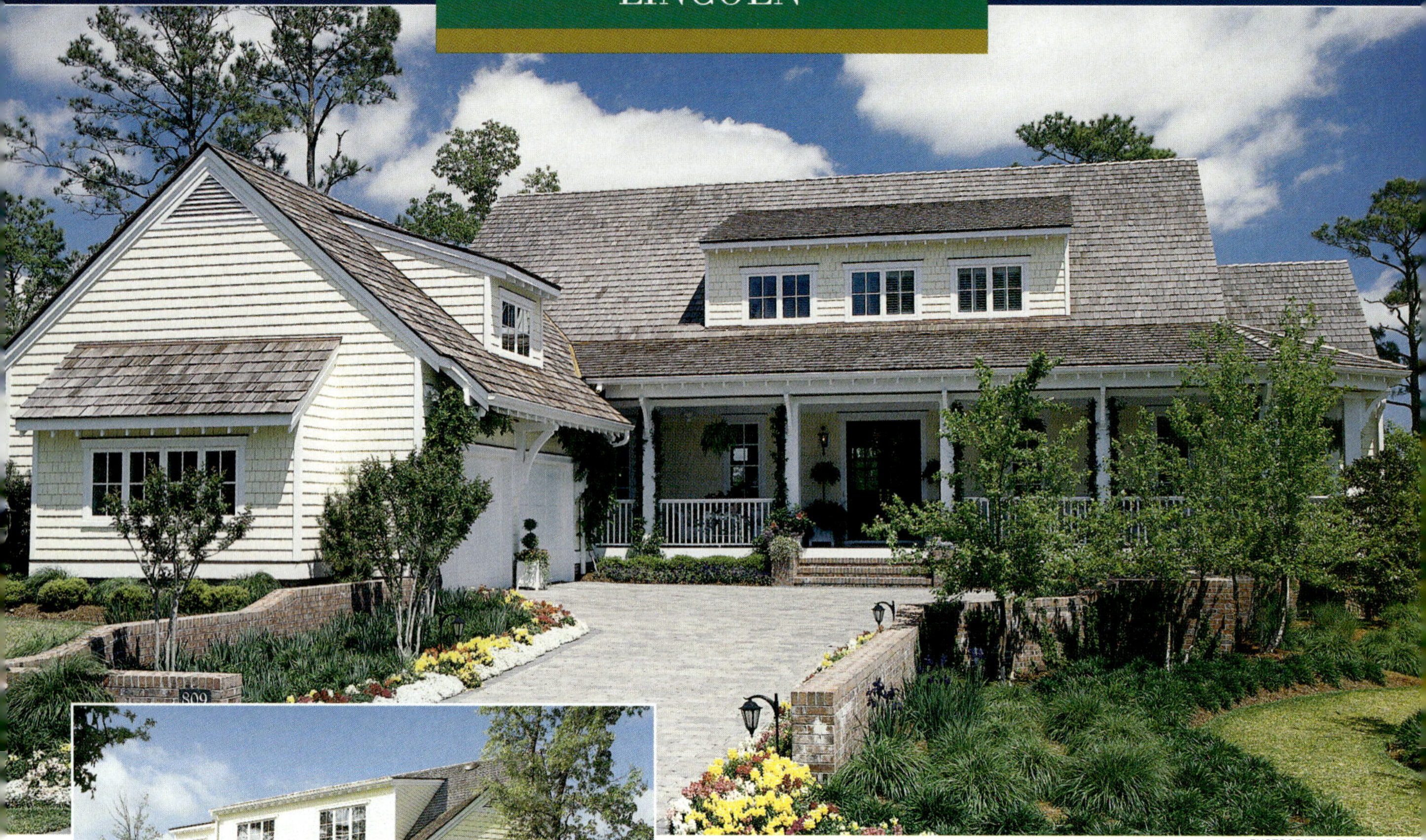

PHOTOGRAPHY: DAVID W. BROWN

4,205 sq. ft.

- The garage wraps around to create a courtyard atmosphere in the front yard, while the wide dormers over the porch and garage fill the interior with light.

- The center and left wings of the home hold the open common areas, while the right wing and second floor are reserved for the more private spaces.

- While the front porch graces the front and side of the home, the rear deck adds additional outdoor living area.

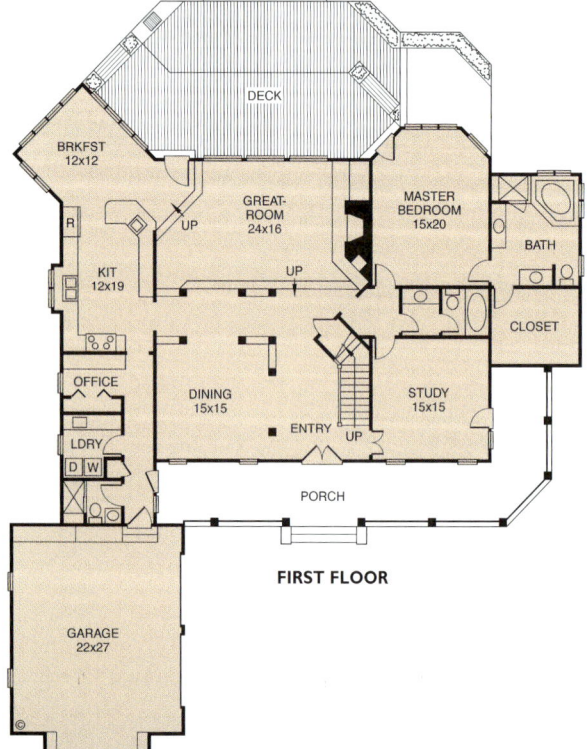

FIRST FLOOR

DECK

BRKFST 12x12

KIT 12x19

OFFICE

LDRY

DINING 15x15

ENTRY

GREAT-ROOM 24x16

MASTER BEDROOM 15x20

BATH

CLOSET

STUDY 15x15

PORCH

GARAGE 22x27

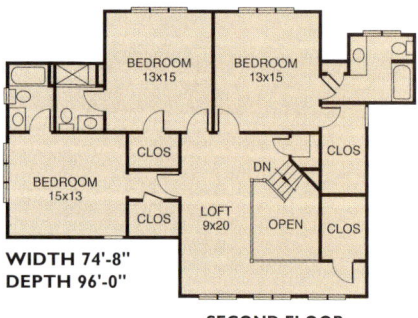

SECOND FLOOR

BEDROOM 13x15

BEDROOM 13x15

BEDROOM 15x13

CLOS

CLOS

CLOS

LOFT 9x20

OPEN

CLOS

DN

WIDTH 74'-8"
DEPTH 96'-0"

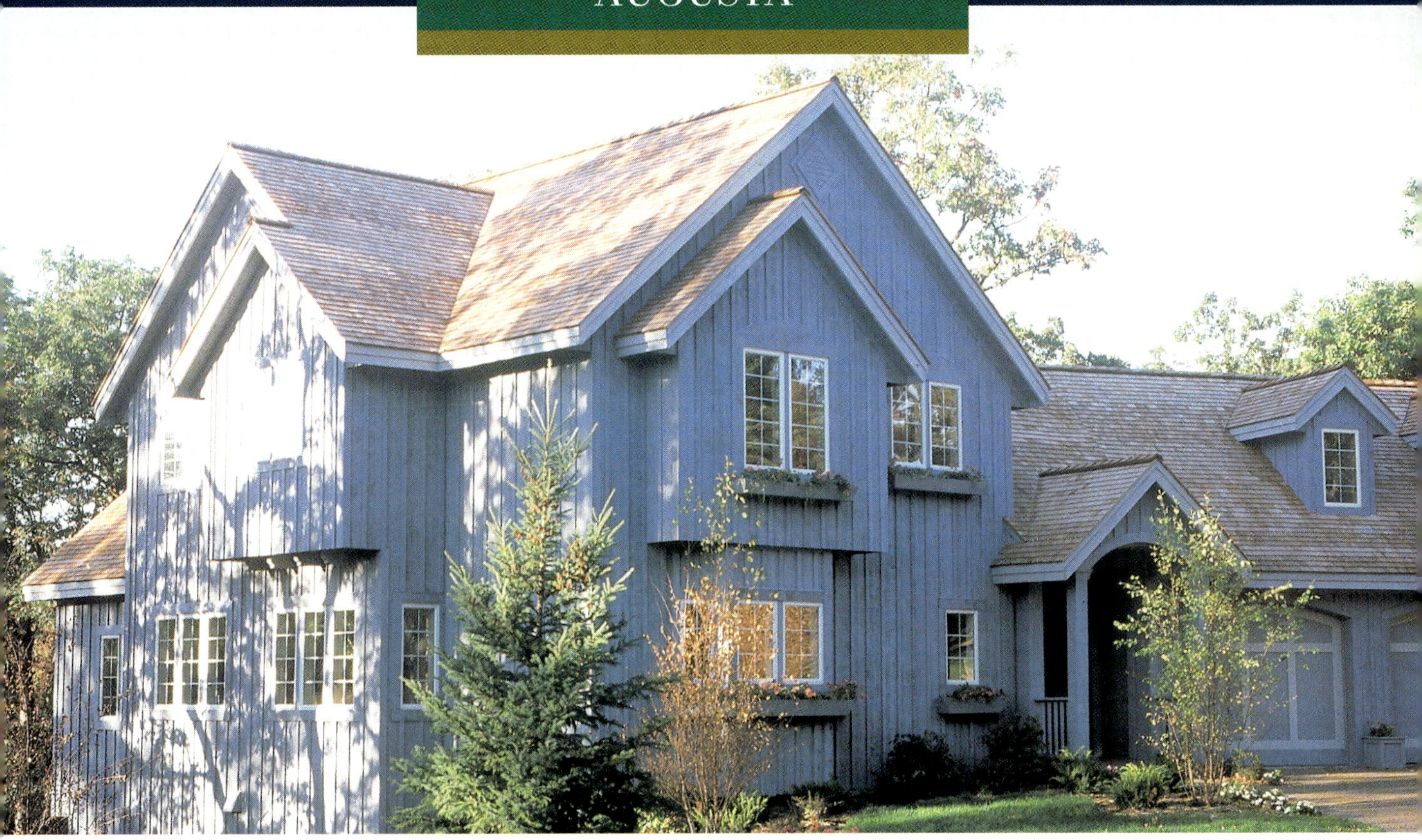

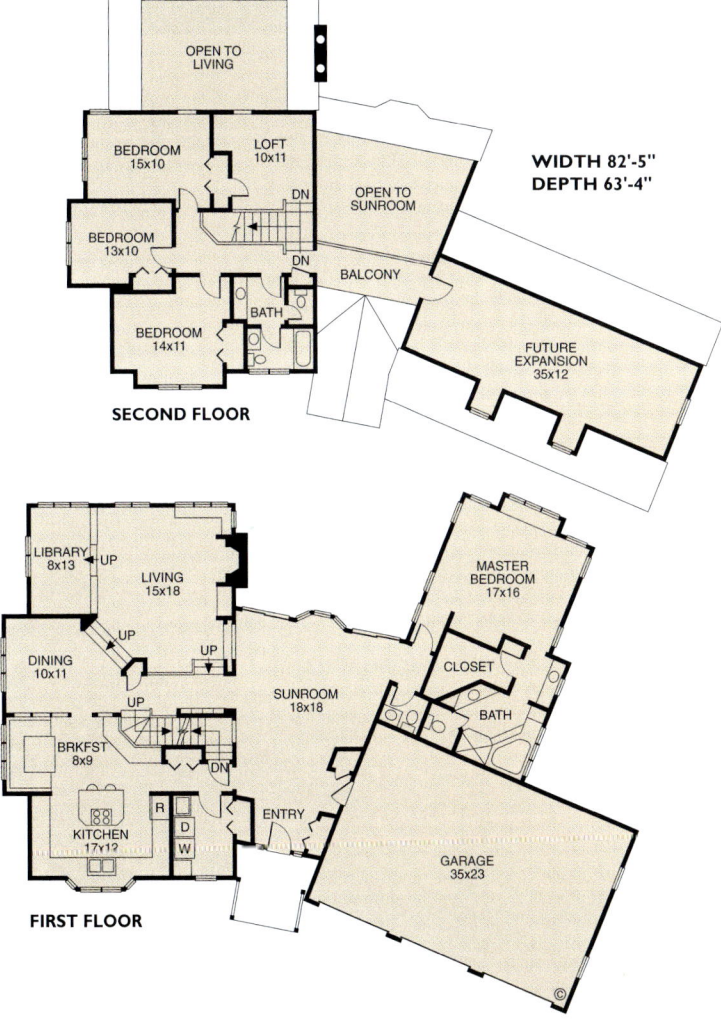

PHOTOGRAPHY: SUSAN GILMORE

3,859 sq. ft.

- This large and comfortable four-bedroom home offers an unusual but appealing floor plan. The main entry opens to a large sunroom that divides the home's living area from the private, main-floor master bedroom.
- The sunken living room has a fireplace with built-in bookcases and leads to a small, secluded library and formal dining room.
- The U-shape kitchen with cooktop island and plentiful counter/cupboard space, is an epicure's delight. A multi-windowed breakfast nook and separate laundry room complete the kitchen area.
- The sizeable, airy upper floor offers three additional bedrooms, a loft, and a unique full and half-bath combination. A balcony walkway leads to a large bonus room.

WIDTH 82'-5"
DEPTH 63'-4"

SECOND FLOOR

FIRST FLOOR

~ SPRUCE ~

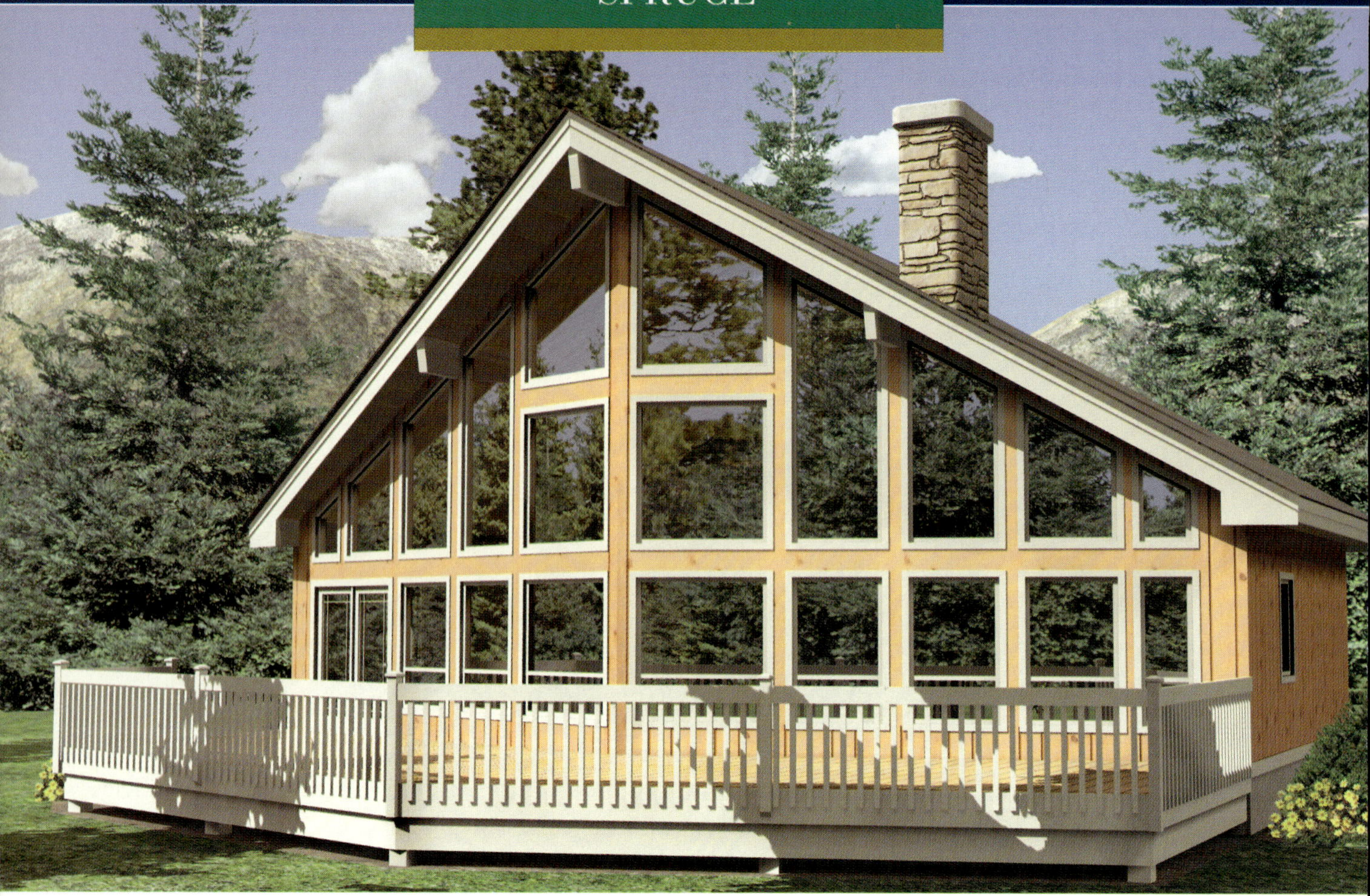

1,513 sq. ft.

- exterior dimensions 44' x 32'
- expansive vaulted living, dining, and kitchen area
- 3 bedrooms, 2 bathrooms
- large vaulted master bedroom with ensuite

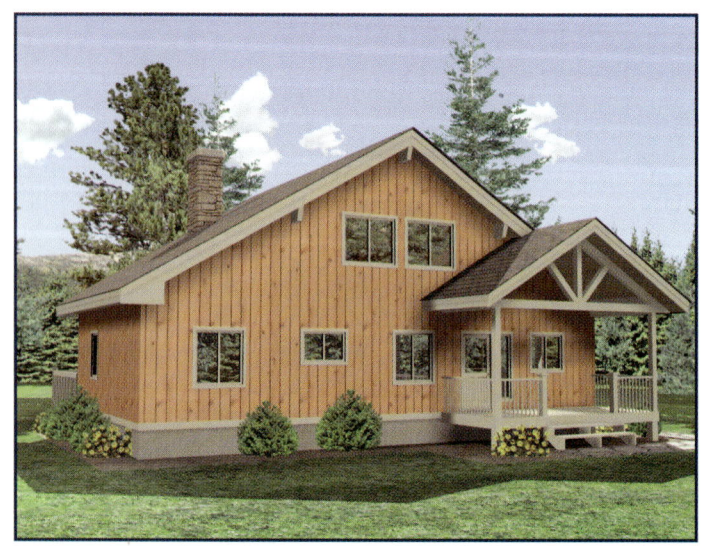

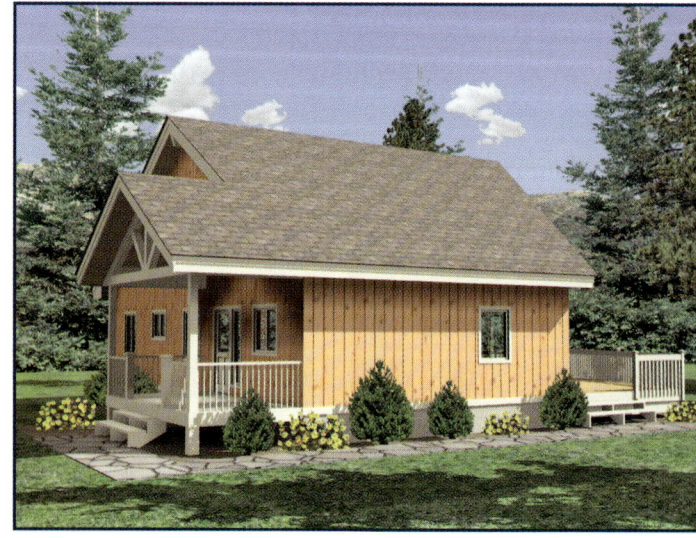

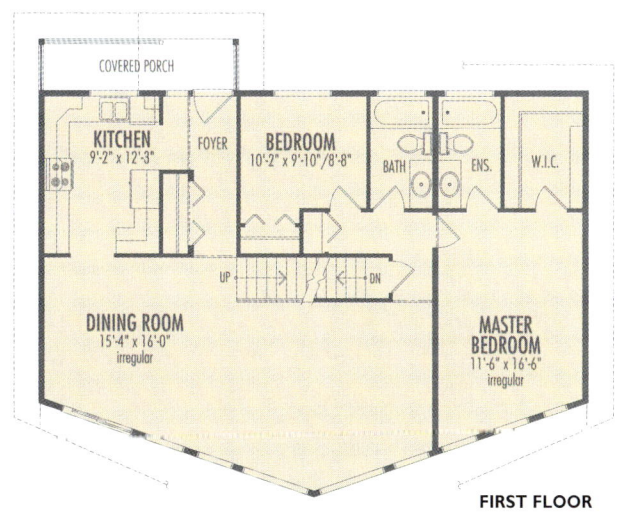

COVERED PORCH

KITCHEN
9'-2" x 12'-3"

FOYER

BEDROOM
10'-2" x 9'-10"/8'-8"

BATH

ENS.

W.I.C.

UP

DN

DINING ROOM
15'-4" x 16'-0"
irregular

MASTER
BEDROOM
11'-6" x 16'-6"
irregular

FIRST FLOOR

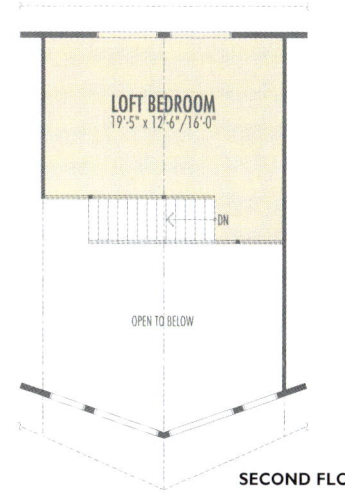

LOFT BEDROOM
19'-5" x 12'-6"/16'-0"

DN

OPEN TO BELOW

SECOND FLOOR

~ GENEVA ~

1,579 sq. ft.

- An impressive foyer leads into this spectacular three-bedroom home, with a front-oriented, upper master bedroom, highlighted by a dazzling cathedral window, private ensuite, and walk-in closet.

- The second level is completed by a second bedroom and a cozy loft.

- The main floor features a delightful open-plan living room, dining area, and fantastic kitchen; a third bedroom, full bath, mudroom, and a utility area complete the plan.

FIRST FLOOR

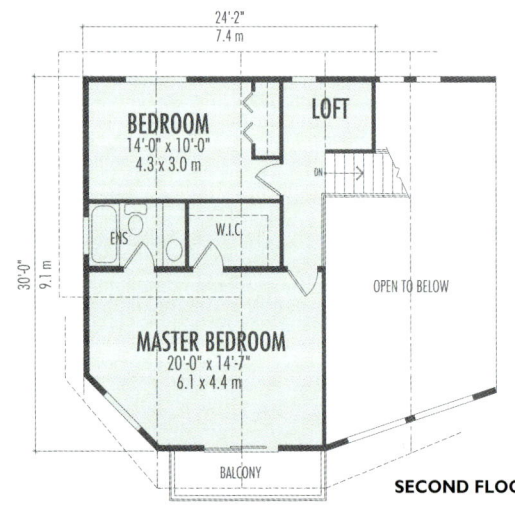

SECOND FLOOR

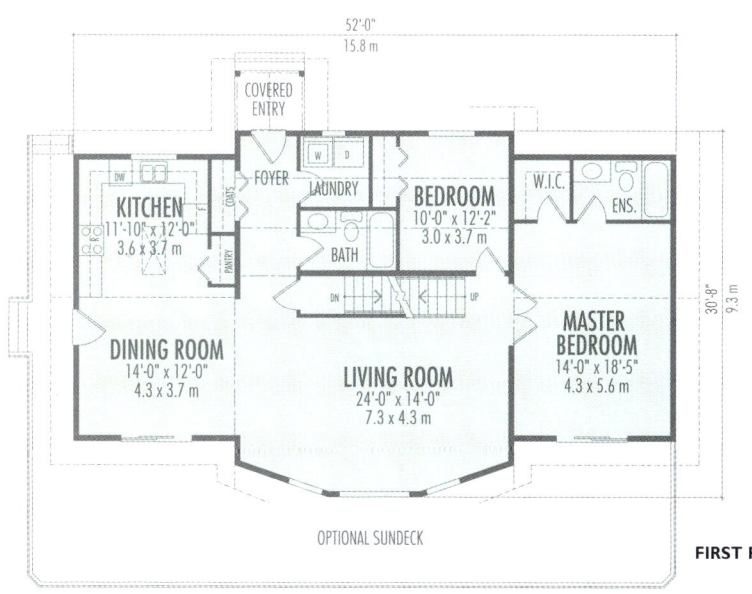

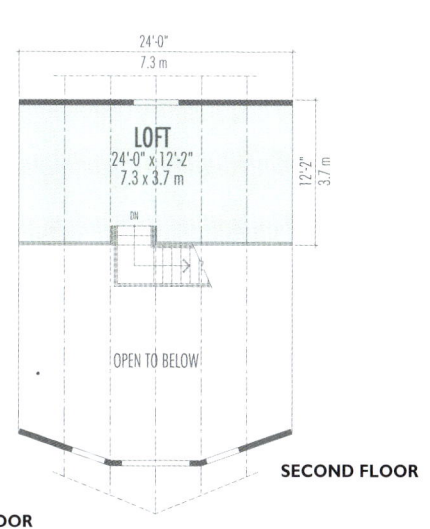

1,673 sq. ft.

- exterior dimensions 52' x 31'
- large vaulted living room
- 2 bedrooms, 2 bathrooms
- open loft on upper floor

FIRST FLOOR

- 52'-0" / 15.8 m
- COVERED ENTRY
- KITCHEN 11'-10" x 12'-0" 3.6 x 3.7 m
- FOYER
- LAUNDRY
- W
- D
- COATS
- PANTRY
- BATH
- BEDROOM 10'-0" x 12'-2" 3.0 x 3.7 m
- W.I.C.
- ENS.
- DINING ROOM 14'-0" x 12'-0" 4.3 x 3.7 m
- LIVING ROOM 24'-0" x 14'-0" 7.3 x 4.3 m
- DN
- UP
- MASTER BEDROOM 14'-0" x 18'-5" 4.3 x 5.6 m
- 30'-8" / 9.3 m
- OPTIONAL SUNDECK

SECOND FLOOR

- 24'-0" / 7.3 m
- LOFT 24'-0" x 12'-2" 7.3 x 3.7 m
- 12'-2" / 3.7 m
- DN
- OPEN TO BELOW

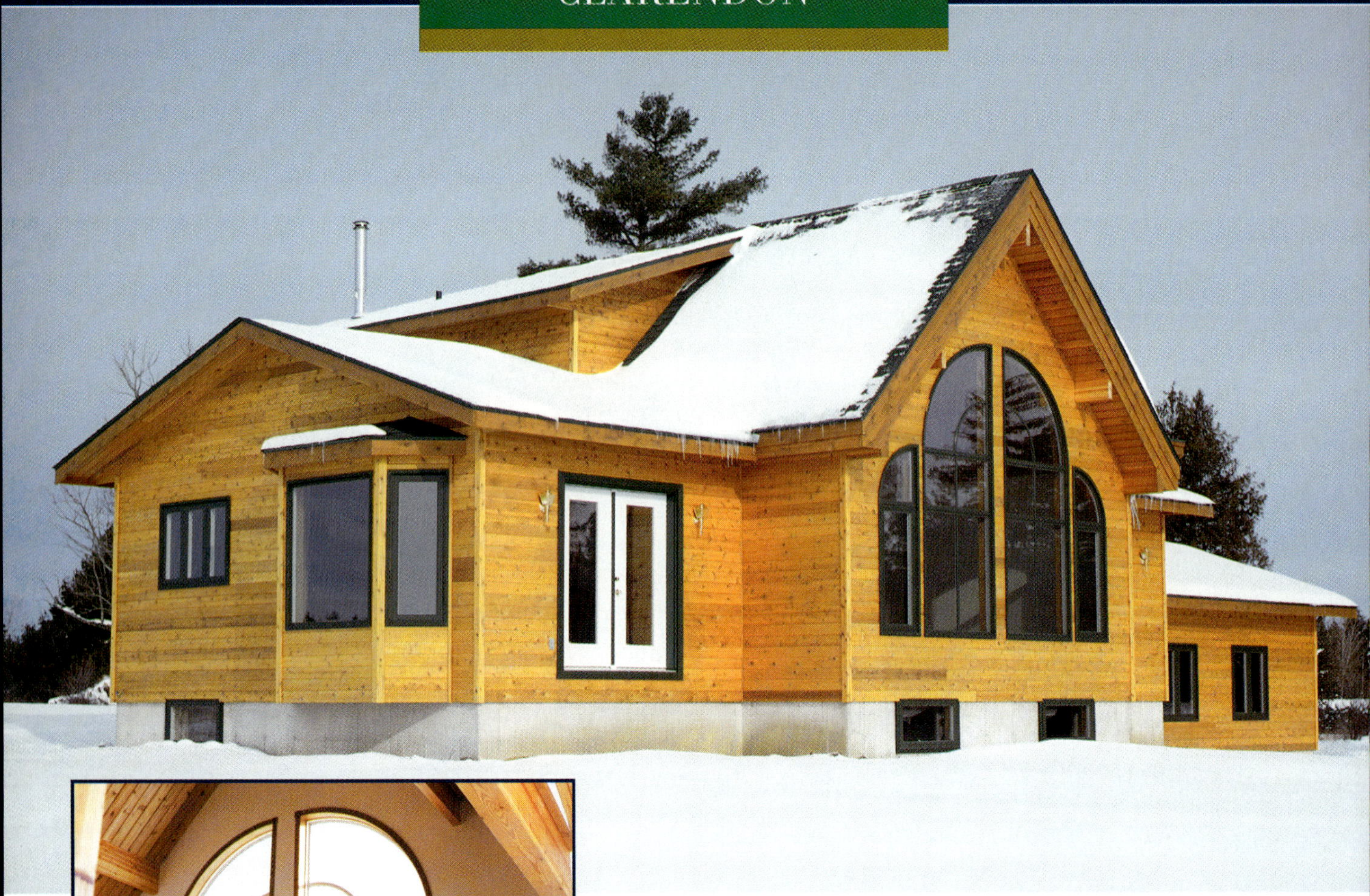

1,684 sq. ft.

- exterior dimensions 50' x 31'6"
- dining room has beautiful bay windows and French doors to an optional deck
- 3 bedrooms, 2 bathrooms
- gourmet kitchen has a large walk-in pantry

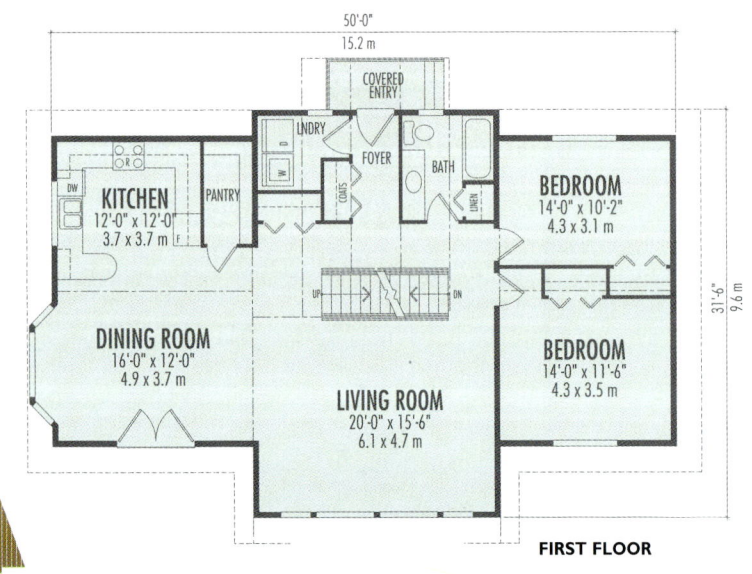

FIRST FLOOR

SECOND FLOOR

~ CASCADE ~

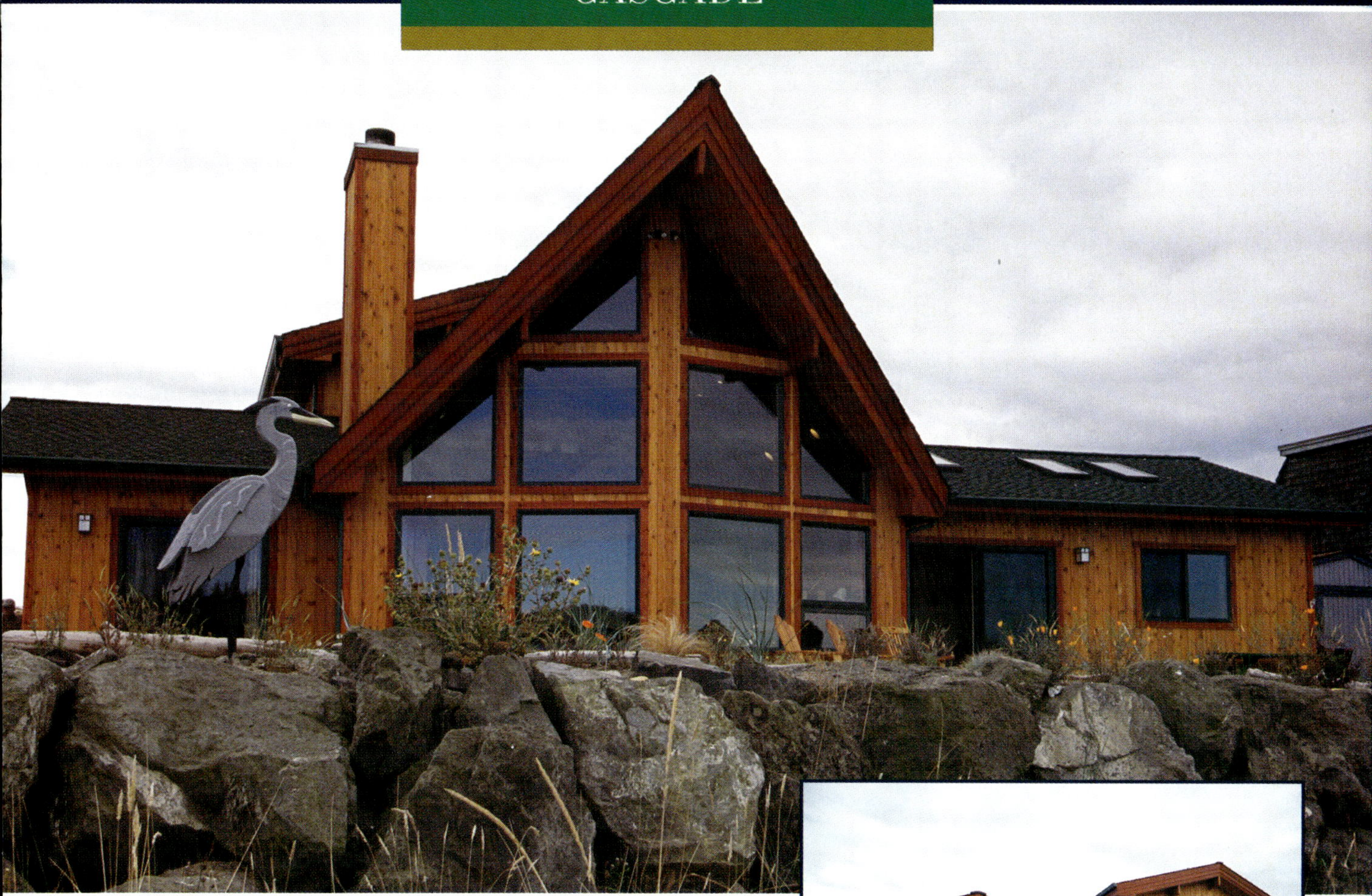

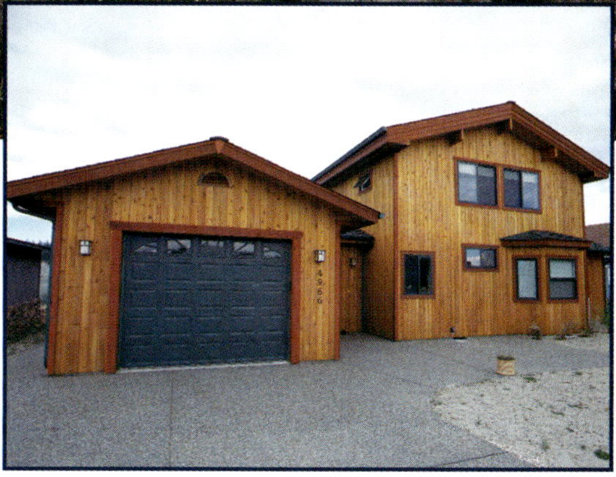

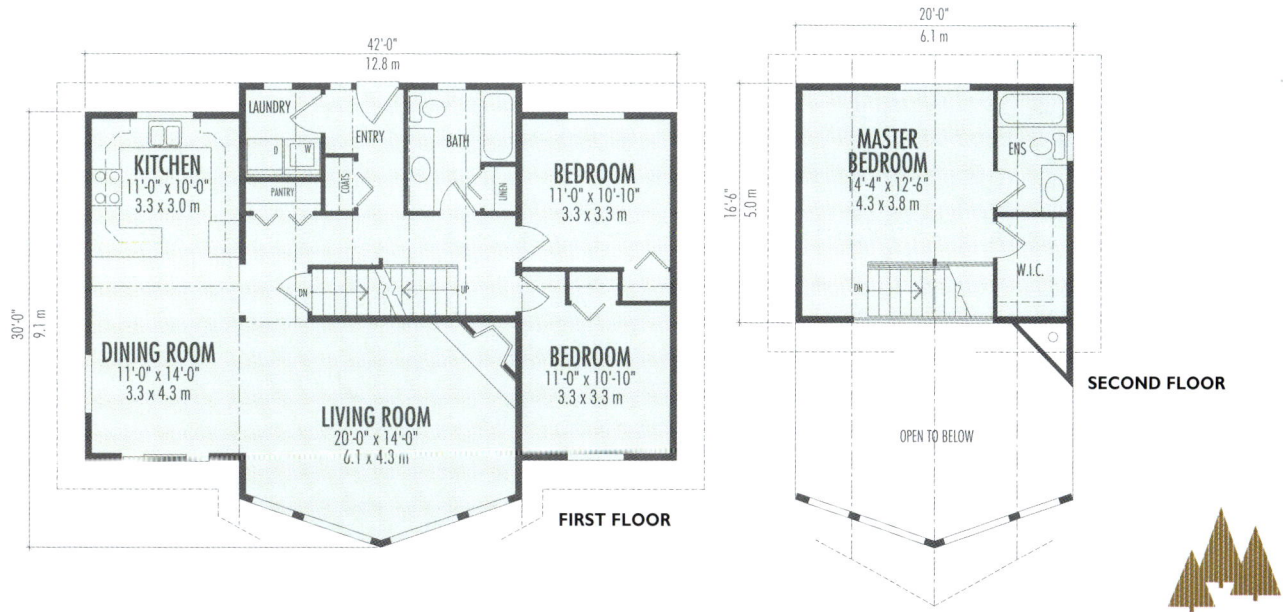

1,465 sq. ft.

- exterior dimensions 42' x 32'
- upper floor contains large, private master suite
- 3 bedrooms, 2 bathrooms
- spacious prow-front living room

42'-0"
12.8 m
LAUNDRY
ENTRY
BATH
KITCHEN
11'-0" x 10'-0"
3.3 x 3.0 m
PANTRY
COATS
LINEN
BEDROOM
11'-0" x 10'-10"
3.3 x 3.3 m
DN
UP
30'-0"
9.1 m
DINING ROOM
11'-0" x 14'-0"
3.3 x 4.3 m
LIVING ROOM
20'-0" x 14'-0"
6.1 x 4.3 m
BEDROOM
11'-0" x 10'-10"
3.3 x 3.3 m

FIRST FLOOR

20'-0"
6.1 m
MASTER
BEDROOM
14'-4" x 12'-6"
4.3 x 3.8 m
ENS
16'-6"
5.0 m
W.I.C.
DN
OPEN TO BELOW

SECOND FLOOR

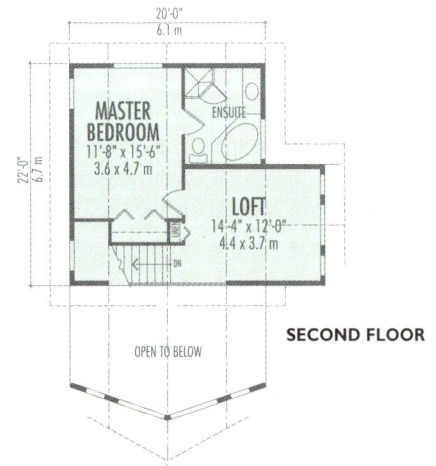

~ CARLYLE ~

1,860 sq. ft.

- Broad, projecting roof lines distinguish the design of this gorgeous three-bedroom home. Both stone and a wide profile cedar siding have been used to create a striking exterior effect.

- The master bedroom, with corner-tub ensuite and adjacent loft, is located on the private second level.

- The huge country kitchen, separate dining area, vaulted living room with prow front, and wraparound sundeck ensure comfortable living on the main level.

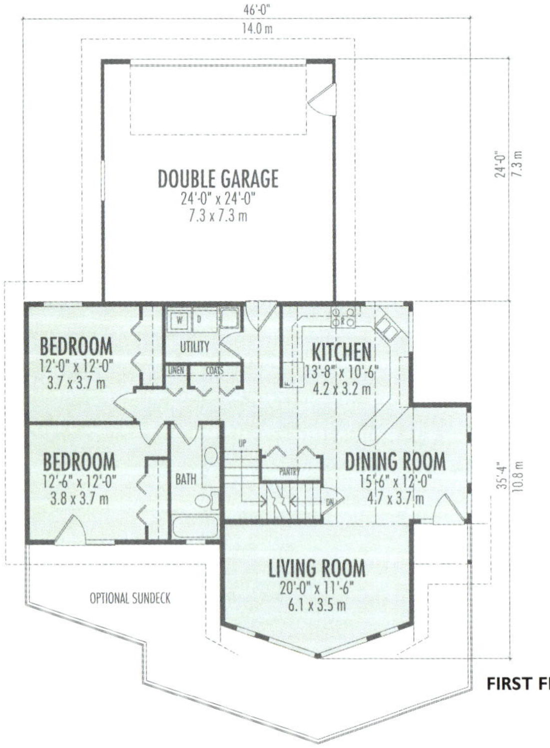

FIRST FLOOR

46'-0"
14.0 m

24'-0"
7.3 m

35'-4"
10.8 m

DOUBLE GARAGE
24'-0" x 24'-0"
7.3 x 7.3 m

BEDROOM
12'-0" x 12'-0"
3.7 x 3.7 m

W | D
UTILITY
LINEN | COATS

KITCHEN
13'-8" x 10'-6"
4.2 x 3.2 m

BEDROOM
12'-6" x 12'-0"
3.8 x 3.7 m

BATH
UP
PANTRY

DINING ROOM
15'-6" x 12'-0"
4.7 x 3.7 m

OPTIONAL SUNDECK

LIVING ROOM
20'-0" x 11'-6"
6.1 x 3.5 m

SECOND FLOOR

20'-0"
6.1 m

22'-0"
6.7 m

MASTER BEDROOM
11'-8" x 15'-6"
3.6 x 4.7 m

ENSUITE

LOFT
14'-4" x 12'-0"
4.4 x 3.7 m

DN

OPEN TO BELOW

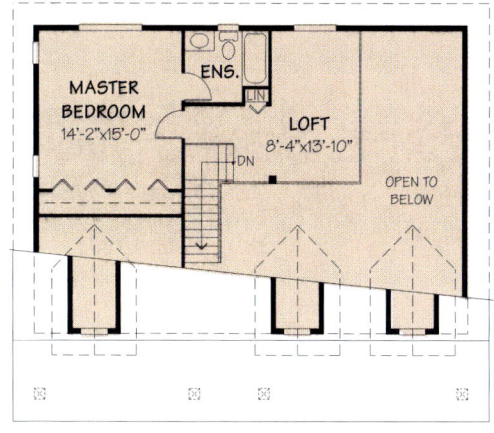

1,752 sq. ft.

- This luxurious three-bedroom log home has the added appeal of a covered front porch and a covered deck at the rear. The large, bright kitchen features an L-shape island and opens to both the living room, with its cozy fireplace, and the dining room.

- Two bedrooms or a bedroom and den share a full bathroom on one side of the house.

- Upstairs, the master suite also boasts a private loft area to allow for some space away from the family, or room to curl up with a good book.

MASTER BEDROOM 14'-2"x15'-0"

ENS.

LOFT 8'-4"x13'-10"

OPEN TO BELOW

DN

SECOND FLOOR

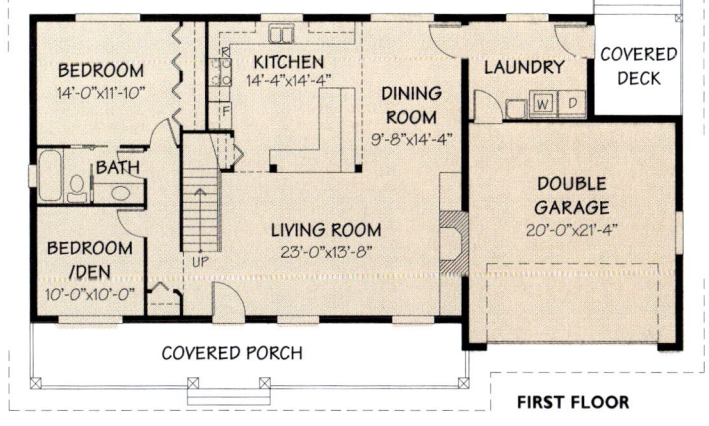

BEDROOM 14'-0"x11'-10"

KITCHEN 14'-4"x14'-4"

DINING ROOM 9'-8"x14'-4"

LAUNDRY

COVERED DECK

BATH

DOUBLE GARAGE 20'-0"x21'-4"

BEDROOM /DEN 10'-0"x10'-0"

LIVING ROOM 23'-0"x13'-8"

UP

COVERED PORCH

FIRST FLOOR

PHOTOGRAPHY: BETH SINGER

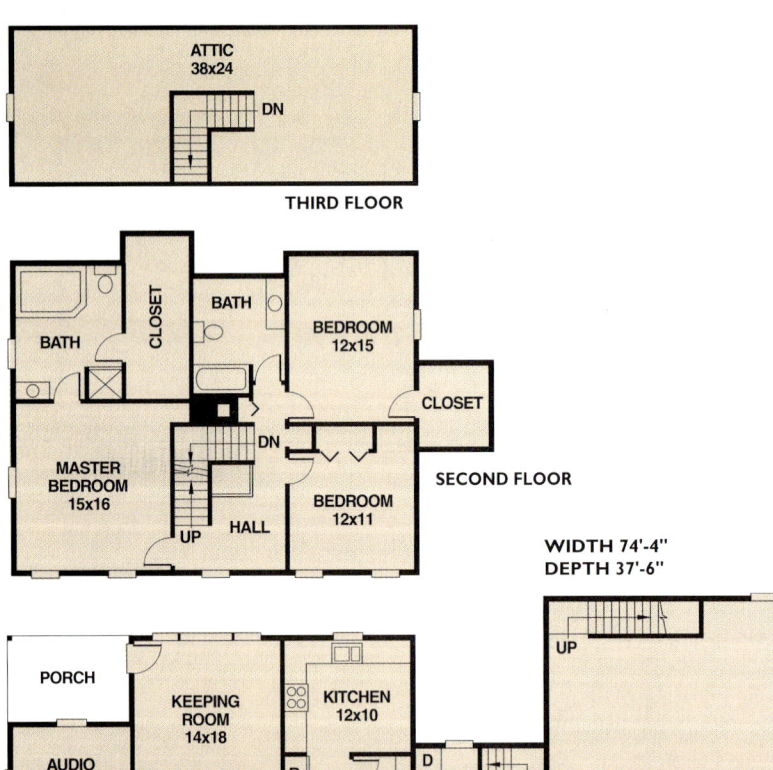

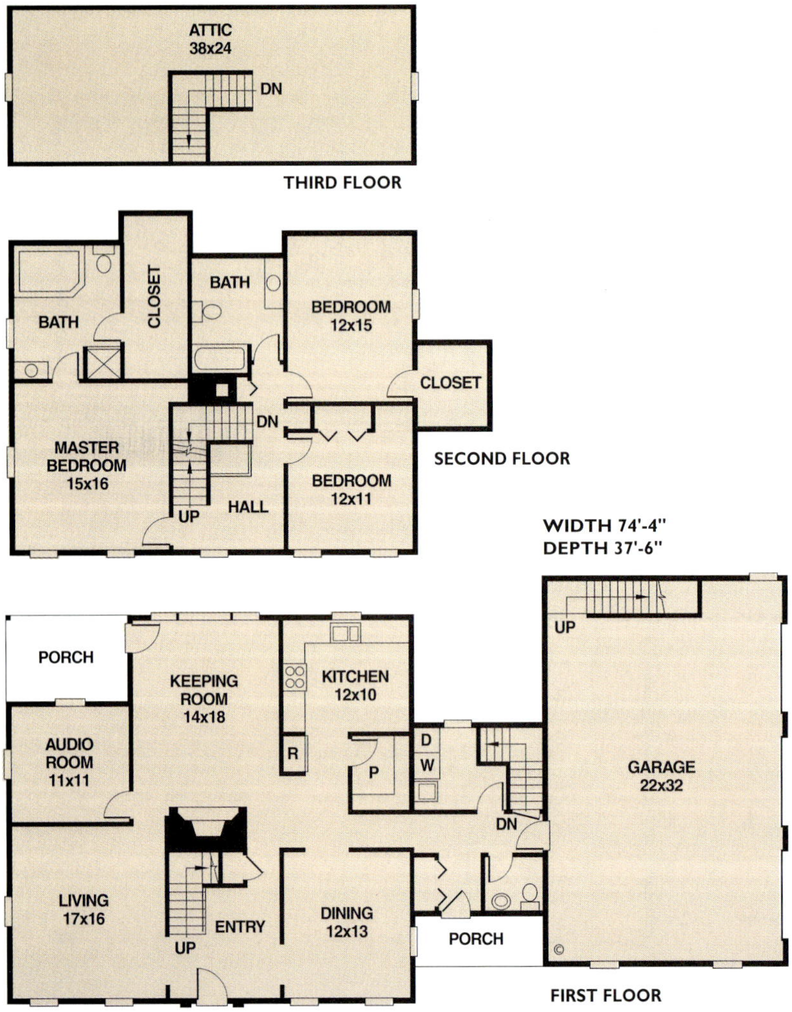

THIRD FLOOR

ATTIC
38x24

DN

SECOND FLOOR

BATH

CLOSET

BATH

BEDROOM
12x15

CLOSET

MASTER
BEDROOM
15x16

DN

UP HALL

BEDROOM
12x11

WIDTH 74'-4"
DEPTH 37'-6"

FIRST FLOOR

PORCH

KEEPING
ROOM
14x18

KITCHEN
12x10

UP

AUDIO
ROOM
11x11

R

P

D
W

GARAGE
22x32

DN

LIVING
17x16

ENTRY

UP

DINING
12x13

PORCH

2,752 sq. ft.

- This home is all about simplicity and style.

- Formal dining and living rooms, as well as a more casual audio room, are ideal for entertaining. The L-shape kitchen is ideal for food preparation for these occasions.

- On the second floor, two bedrooms sit near the master suite, all of which have ample closet space.

- Vast attic space and a three-car garage offer plenty of storage.

1,778 sq. ft.

- exterior dimensions 92' x 31'
- stunning vaulted living room and dining room
- 2 bedrooms, 2 bathrooms
- enormous master suite opens onto optional sundeck

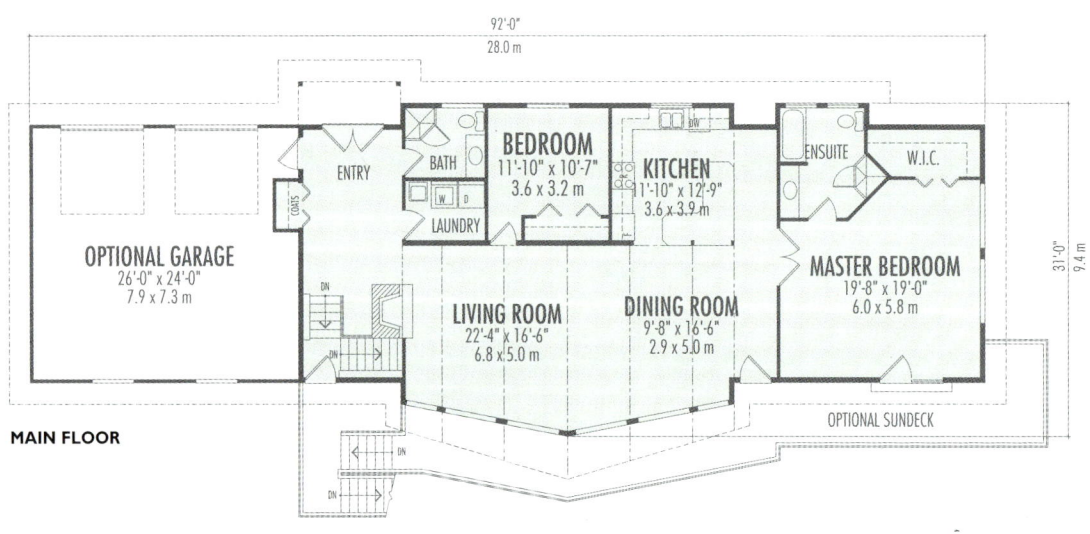

MAIN FLOOR

92'-0"
28.0 m

31'-0"
9.4 m

OPTIONAL GARAGE
26'-0" x 24'-0"
7.9 x 7.3 m

ENTRY

BATH

LAUNDRY

W D

COATS

BEDROOM
11'-10" x 10'-7"
3.6 x 3.2 m

KITCHEN
11'-10" x 12'-9"
3.6 x 3.9 m

ENSUITE

W.I.C.

MASTER BEDROOM
19'-8" x 19'-0"
6.0 x 5.8 m

LIVING ROOM
22'-4" x 16'-6"
6.8 x 5.0 m

DINING ROOM
9'-8" x 16'-6"
2.9 x 5.0 m

DN

DN

DN

OPTIONAL SUNDECK

~ FRANKLIN ~

2,722 sq. ft.

- exterior dimensions 64' x 44'
- large front covered verandah
- 3 bedrooms, 2½ bathrooms
- magnificent great-room

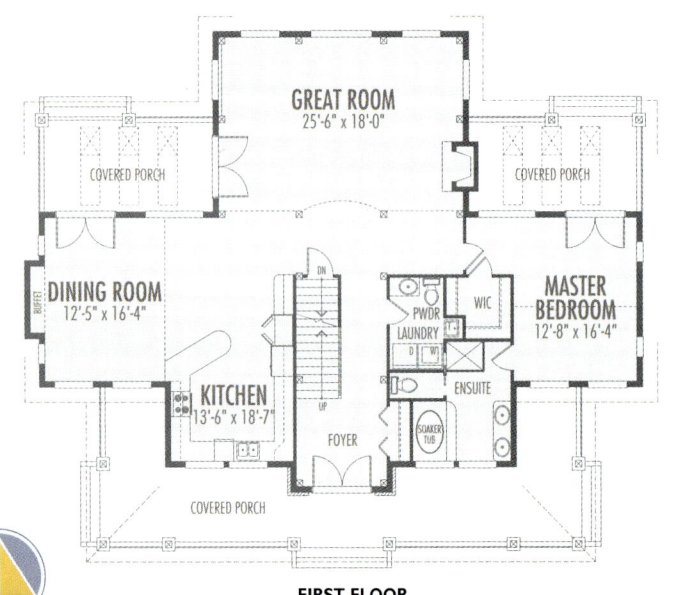

FIRST FLOOR

GREAT ROOM
25'-6" x 18'-0"

COVERED PORCH

COVERED PORCH

DINING ROOM
12'-5" x 16'-4"

DN

PWDR

WIC

MASTER BEDROOM
12'-8" x 16'-4"

LAUNDRY

D W

KITCHEN
13'-6" x 18'-7"

UP

ENSUITE

FOYER

SOAKER TUB

COVERED PORCH

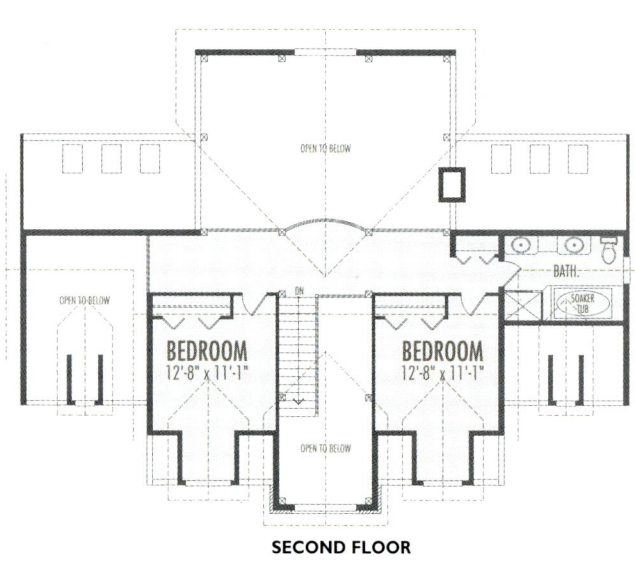

SECOND FLOOR

OPEN TO BELOW

OPEN TO BELOW

OPEN TO BELOW

DN

BATH.

SOAKER TUB

BEDROOM
12'-8" x 11'-1"

BEDROOM
12'-8" x 11'-1"

837 sq. ft.

- spacious and attractive three-car garage
- large bonus room with dormers
- 2-piece bathroom
- generous storage space

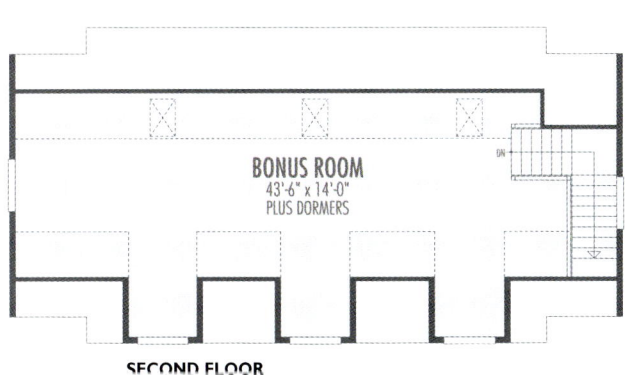

SECOND FLOOR

BONUS ROOM
43'-6" x 14'-0"
PLUS DORMERS

DN

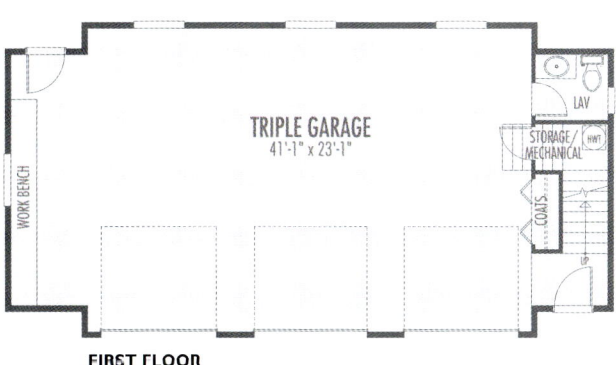

FIRST FLOOR

TRIPLE GARAGE
41'-1" x 23'-1"

WORK BENCH

LAV

STORAGE /
MECHANICAL

HWT

COATS

UP

3,559 sq. ft.

- a beautiful home and garage combination with enough space and versatility to satisfy just about everyone

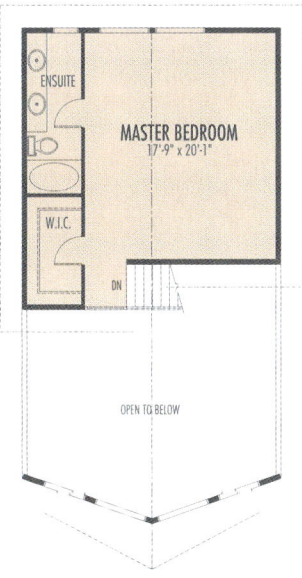

2,279 sq. ft.

- exterior dimensions 52' x 44'
- spacious vaulted living room and kitchen with walk-in pantry
- 4 bedrooms, 2 bathrooms
- huge master bedroom with ensuite and walk-in closet

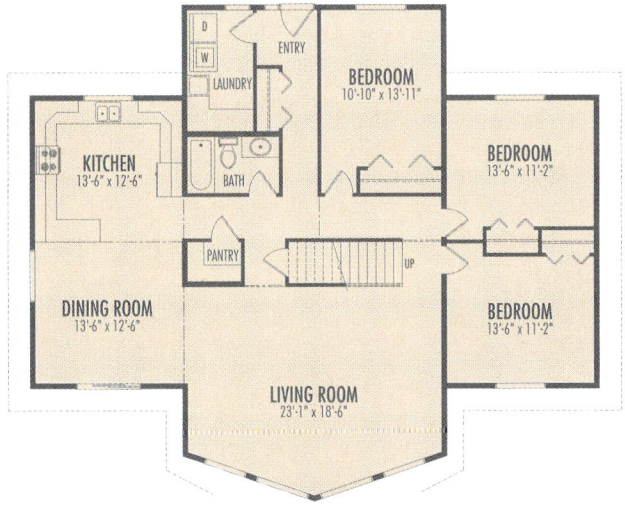

FIRST FLOOR

SECOND FLOOR

3,080 sq. ft.

- Gables and arches add to this home's facade's curb appeal, while well-designed rooms add interest to the interior.

- Windows line the entire first floor, offering a sense of openness and light to the distinctly separated areas.

- On the second floor, each bedroom has it's own special touches, one of which is a private porch.

WIDTH 56'-0"
DEPTH 99'-8"

OPEN TO GREAT-RM

OPEN   CLOS

DN   PORCH

BEDRM 13x18

BEDRM 13x18

BATH

SECOND FLOOR

SUN-RM 11x20

GREAT-RM 19½x25

KIT 9x16

BAR   UP   PORCH

BEDRM 12½x12½

W/D

UTIL

DN

ENTRY

MASTER BEDRM 17x16

BATH

GARAGE 21½x21

BATH

STUDY 13½x16   BATH

FIRST FLOOR

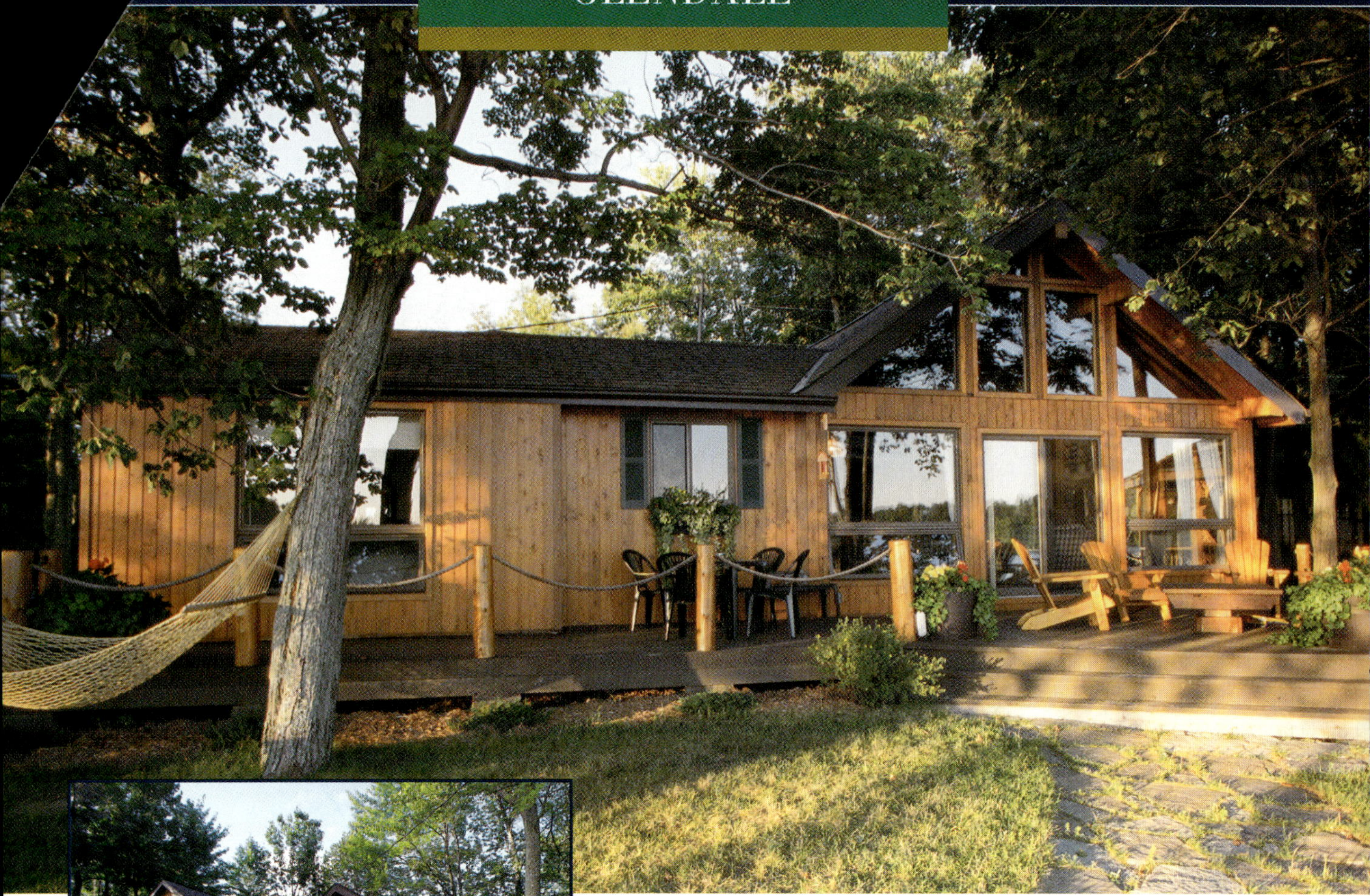

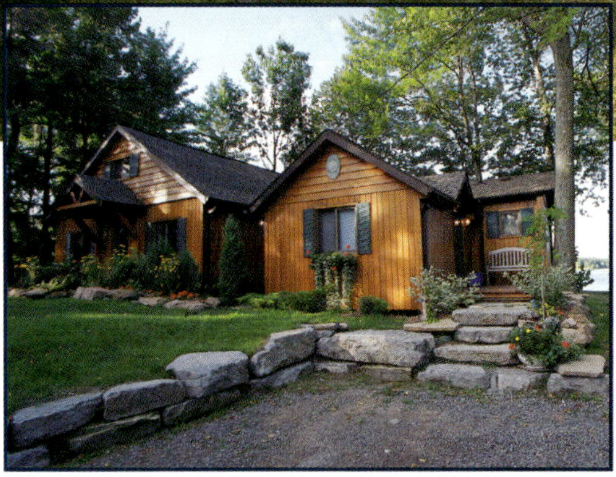

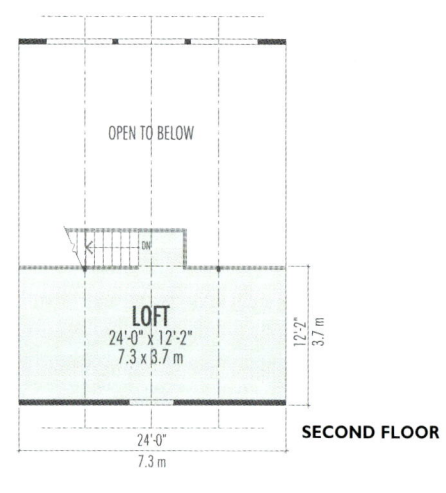

1,645 sq. ft.

- exterior dimensions 49' x 34'
- private, front facing master suite
- 3 bedrooms, 2 bathrooms
- large upper-floor loft

FIRST FLOOR

49'-0"
14.9 m

34'-0"
10.4 m

GREAT ROOM
24'-0" x 14'-0"
7.3 x 4.3 m

KITCHEN
10'-0" x 10'-0"
3.0 x 3.0 m

MASTER BEDROOM
15'-0" x 10'-5"
4.6 x 3.2 m

ENS.

W   D

MUD ROOM

BATH

BEDROOM
10'-0" x 9'-8"
3.0 x 2.9 m

FOYER

BEDROOM
10'-0" x 9'-8"
3.0 x 2.9 m

UP

DW

CL

COVERED ENTRY

SECOND FLOOR

OPEN TO BELOW

DN

LOFT
24'-0" x 12'-2"
7.3 x 3.7 m

12'-2"
3.7 m

24'-0"
7.3 m

~ YORK ~

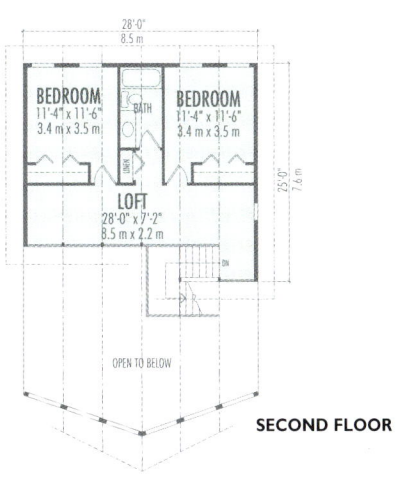

1,759 sq. ft.

- exterior dimensions 72' x 62', including the optional double garage
- 3 bedrooms, 2 bathrooms

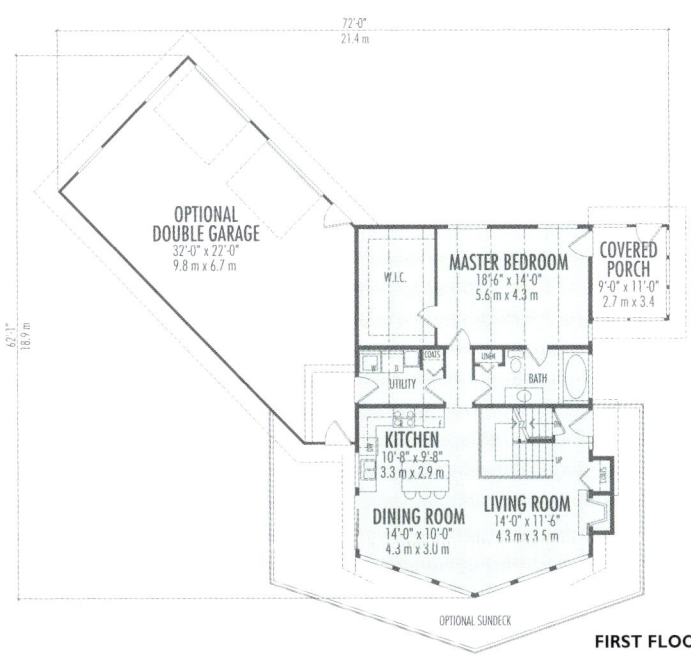

FIRST FLOOR

72'-0"
21.4 m

62'-1"
18.9 m

OPTIONAL
DOUBLE GARAGE
32'-0" x 22'-0"
9.8 m x 6.7 m

W.I.C.

MASTER BEDROOM
18'-6" x 14'-0"
5.6 m x 4.3 m

COVERED
PORCH
9'-0" x 11'-0"
2.7 m x 3.4

UTILITY

LINEN

BATH

KITCHEN
10'-8" x 9'-8"
3.3 m x 2.9 m

DINING ROOM
14'-0" x 10'-0"
4.3 m x 3.0 m

LIVING ROOM
14'-0" x 11'-6"
4.3 m x 3.5 m

OPTIONAL SUNDECK

SECOND FLOOR

28'-0"
8.5 m

BEDROOM
11'-4" x 11'-6"
3.4 m x 3.5 m

BATH

BEDROOM
11'-4" x 11'-6"
3.4 m x 3.5 m

LOFT
28'-0" x 7'-2"
8.5 m x 2.2 m

25'-0"
7.6 m

OPEN TO BELOW

TIMBER CRAFTED HOMES

75

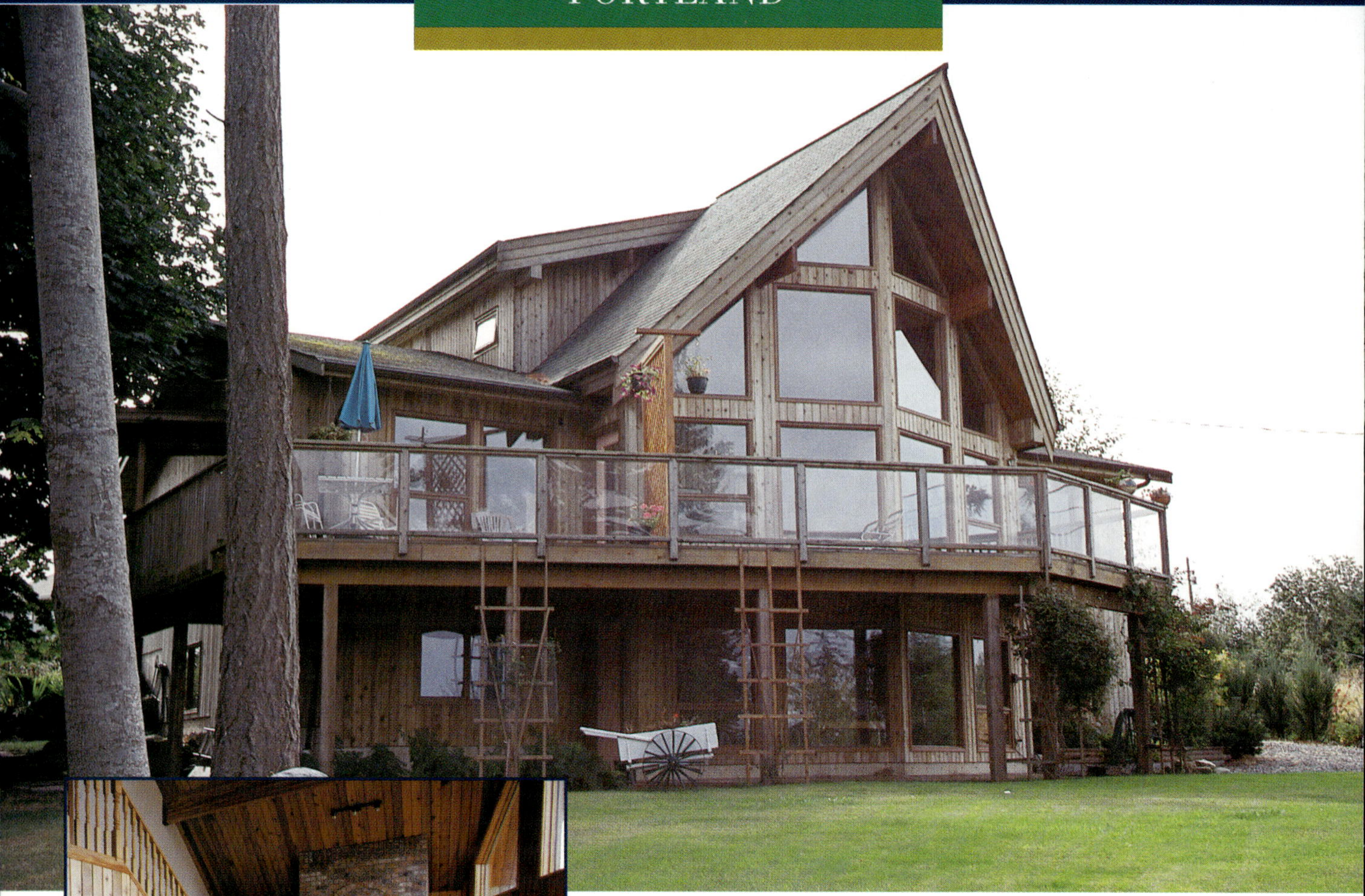

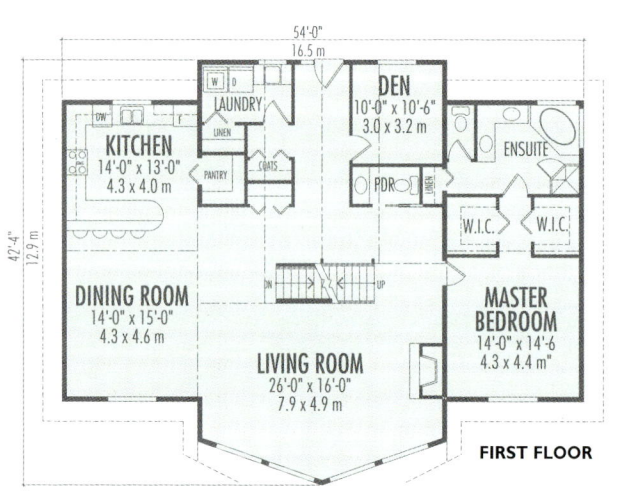

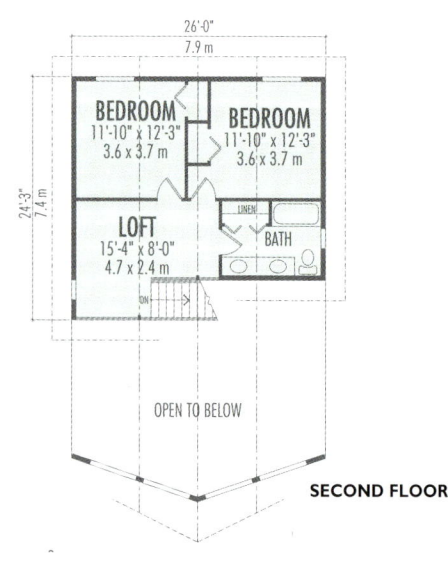

2,443 sq. ft.

- exterior dimensions 54' x 42'4"
- large open-plan living and entertaining area
- 4 bedrooms, 2½ bathrooms
- 2 bedrooms on second floor, with additional loft space

FIRST FLOOR

54'-0"
16.5 m

42'-4"
12.9 m

W D

LAUNDRY

LINEN

DEN
10'-0" x 10'-6"
3.0 x 3.2 m

ENSUITE

KITCHEN
14'-0" x 13'-0"
4.3 x 4.0 m

PANTRY

COATS

PDR

LINEN

DW

W.I.C.   W.I.C.

DINING ROOM
14'-0" x 15'-0"
4.3 x 4.6 m

IN   UP

MASTER BEDROOM
14'-0" x 14'-6
4.3 x 4.4 m

LIVING ROOM
26'-0" x 16'-0"
7.9 x 4.9 m

FIRST FLOOR

SECOND FLOOR

26'-0"
7.9 m

24'-3"
7.4 m

BEDROOM
11'-10" x 12'-3"
3.6 x 3.7 m

BEDROOM
11'-10" x 12'-3"
3.6 x 3.7 m

LINEN

LOFT
15'-4" x 8'-0"
4.7 x 2.4 m

BATH

DN

OPEN TO BELOW

SECOND FLOOR

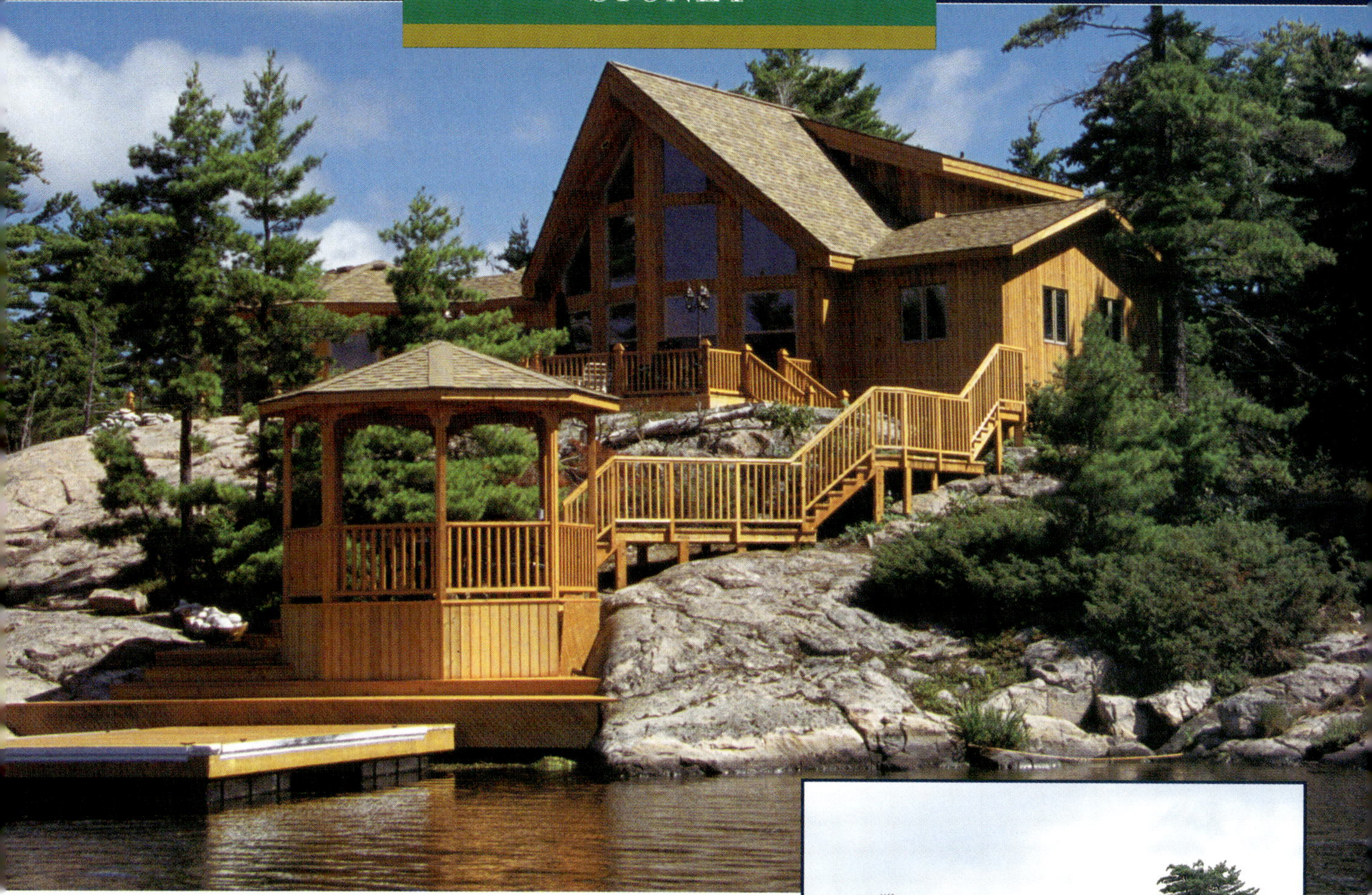

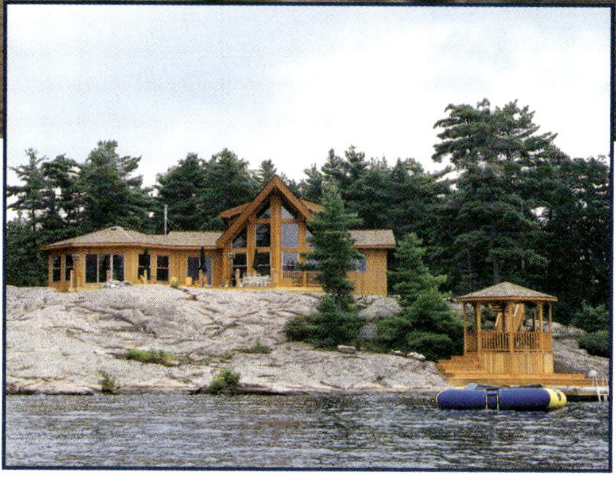

2,562 sq. ft.

- exterior dimensions 76'6" x 38'6"
- magnificent octagonal great-room
- 4 bedrooms, 2 bathrooms
- vaulted living room and enormous open-plan entertaining areas

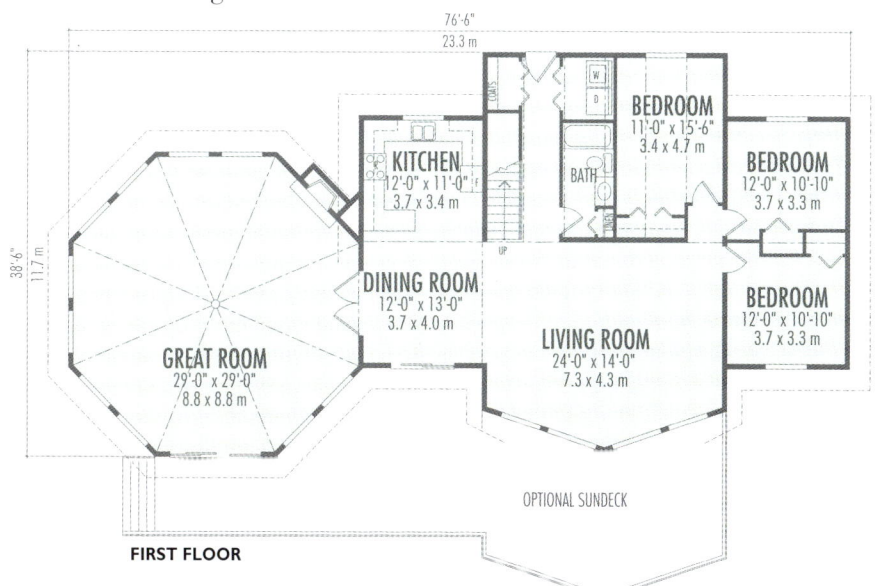

FIRST FLOOR

GREAT ROOM
29'-0" x 29'-0"
8.8 x 8.8 m

KITCHEN
12'-0" x 11'-0"
3.7 x 3.4 m

DINING ROOM
12'-0" x 13'-0"
3.7 x 4.0 m

LIVING ROOM
24'-0" x 14'-0"
7.3 x 4.3 m

BEDROOM
11'-0" x 15'-6"
3.4 x 4.7 m

BEDROOM
12'-0" x 10'-10"
3.7 x 3.3 m

BEDROOM
12'-0" x 10'-10"
3.7 x 3.3 m

BATH

76'-6"
23.3 m

38'-6"
11.7 m

OPTIONAL SUNDECK

SECOND FLOOR

MASTER BEDROOM
18'-0" x 18'-0"
5.5 x 5.5 m

ENS.

W.I.C.

OPEN TO BELOW

24'-0"
7.3 m

18'-0"
5.5 m

1,637 sq. ft.

- This spacious, three-bedroom home demonstrates elegance and charm, accentuated by a large open-plan dining and kitchen area.

- The dazzling combination of vaulted living areas, extensive use of glass, and wraparound balcony provides an outdoor feeling throughout the home.

- The upper master bedroom offers absolute privacy, with the luxury of an ensuite and walk-in closet.

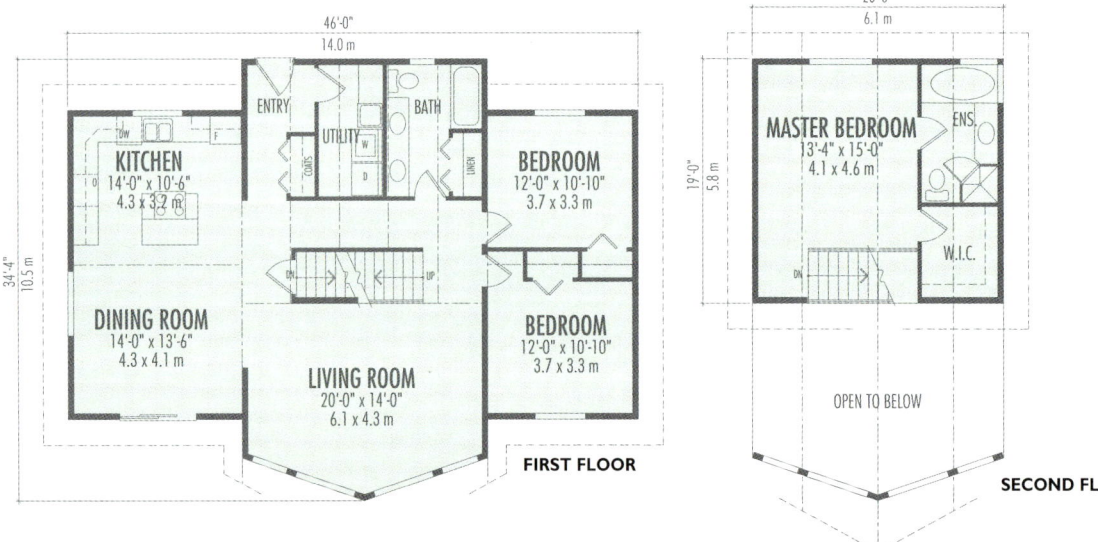

FIRST FLOOR

46'-0"
14.0 m

34'-4"
10.5 m

ENTRY

UTILITY

BATH

KITCHEN
14'-0" x 10'-6"
4.3 x 3.2 m

BEDROOM
12'-0" x 10'-10"
3.7 x 3.3 m

LINEN

DINING ROOM
14'-0" x 13'-6"
4.3 x 4.1 m

LIVING ROOM
20'-0" x 14'-0"
6.1 x 4.3 m

BEDROOM
12'-0" x 10'-10"
3.7 x 3.3 m

SECOND FLOOR

20'-0"
6.1 m

19'-0"
5.8 m

MASTER BEDROOM
13'-4" x 15'-0"
4.1 x 4.6 m

ENS.

W.I.C.

OPEN TO BELOW

~ SELKIRK ~

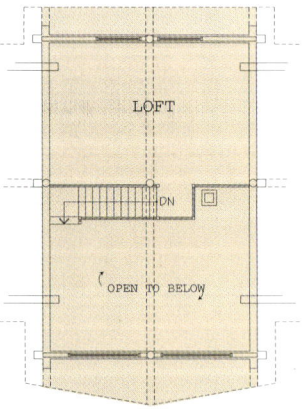

2,875 sq. ft.

- Large windows, impressive decks and porches, a stunning great-room, a beautiful loft and large beam accents make this design the epitome of log home style. A large kitchen is tucked conveniently away from the more formal living areas of the great-room.

- The master suite and secondary bedroom, each complete with ensuite, are isolated in separate wings. A spacious third room can be used for home office, den, or family room.

LOFT

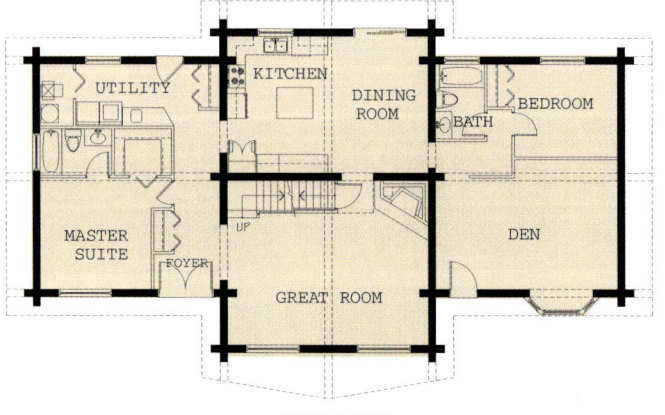

MAIN FLOOR

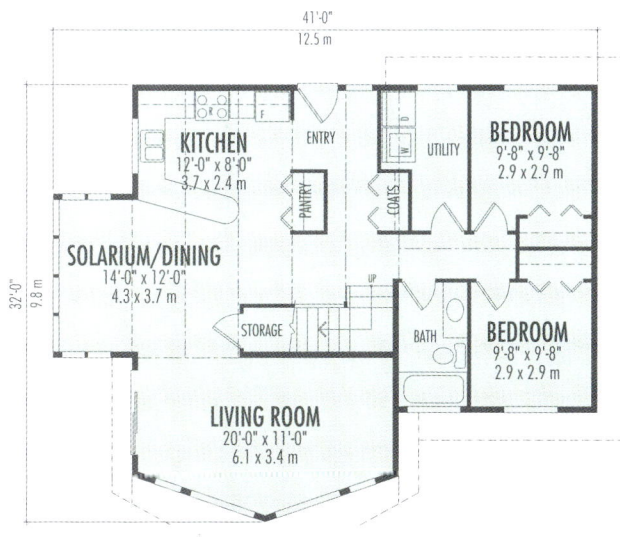

1,439 sq. ft.

- exterior dimensions 41' x 32'
- two-story solarium windows illuminate both the main floor and the master suite
- 3 bedrooms, 2 bathrooms

FIRST FLOOR

41'-0"
12.5 m

32'-0"
9.8 m

KITCHEN
12'-0" x 8'-0"
3.7 x 2.4 m

ENTRY

F

UTILITY

W D

BEDROOM
9'-8" x 9'-8"
2.9 x 2.9 m

PANTRY

COATS

SOLARIUM/DINING
14'-0" x 12'-0"
4.3 x 3.7 m

UP

STORAGE

BATH

BEDROOM
9'-8" x 9'-8"
2.9 x 2.9 m

LIVING ROOM
20'-0" x 11'-0"
6.1 x 3.4 m

SECOND FLOOR

26'-0"
7.9 m

20'-0"
6.1 m

MASTER BEDROOM
13'-6" x 16'-0"
4.1 x 4.9 m

ENSUITE

OPEN TO BELOW

W.I.C.

DN

OPEN TO BELOW

~ WILLOW ~

1,585 sq. ft.

- exterior dimensions 35' x 38'
- open vaulted living, dining, and kitchen area
- 3 bedrooms, 2 bathrooms
- large wraparound verandah

FIRST FLOOR

SECOND FLOOR

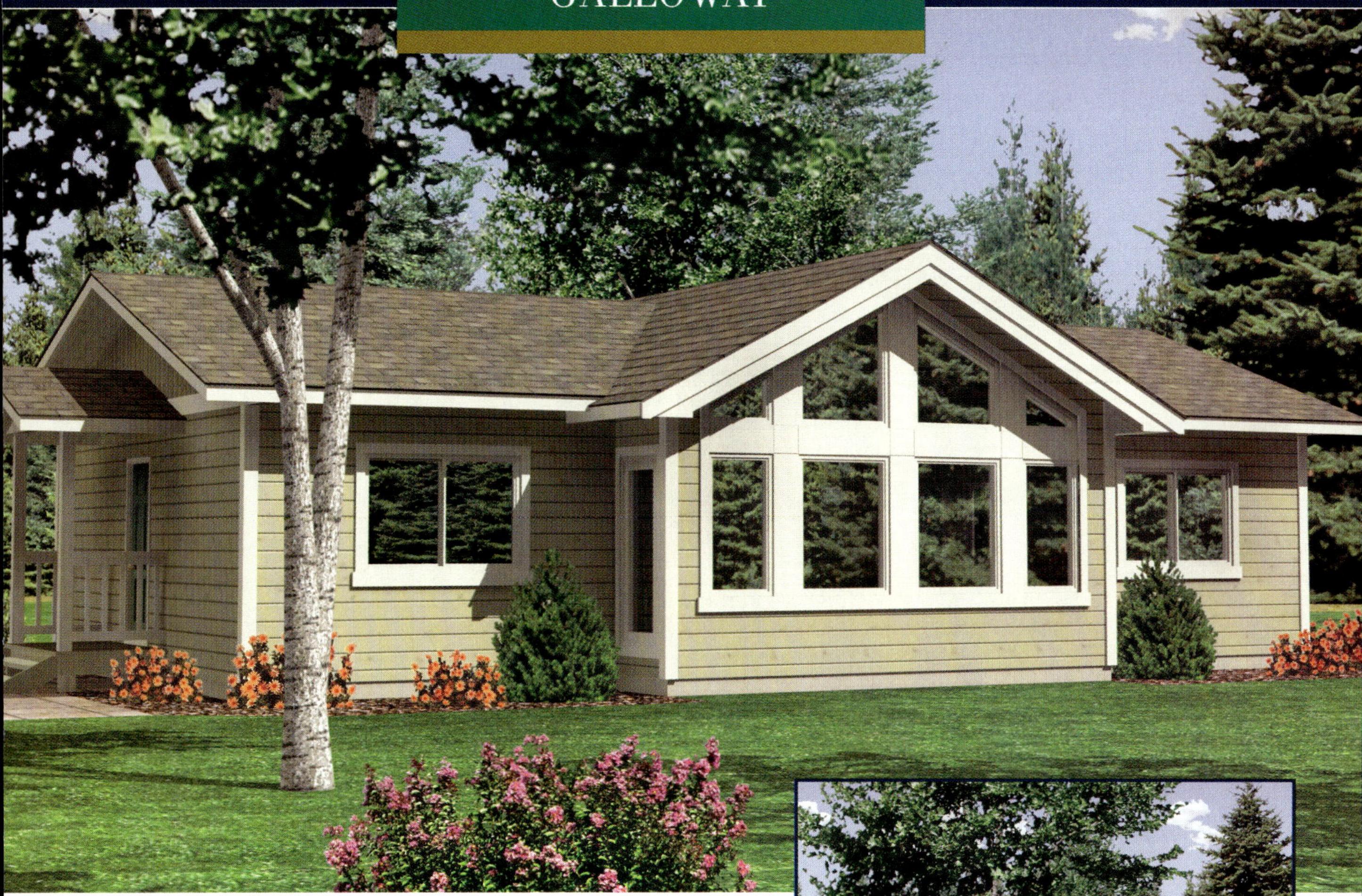

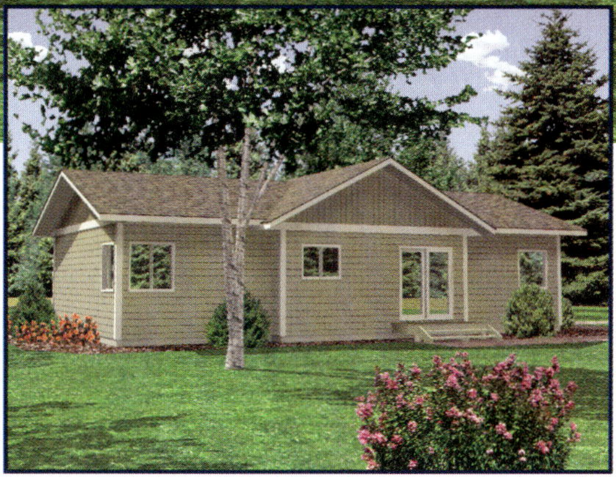

1,368 sq. ft.

- exterior dimensions 48' x 32'
- vaulted master bedroom with 4-piece ensuite
- 2 bedrooms, 2 bathrooms
- spacious central living, dining, and kitchen area

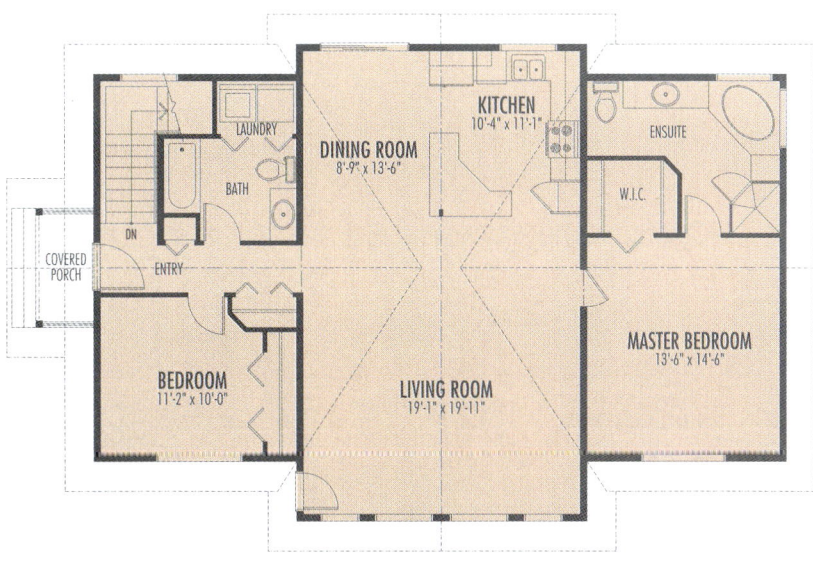

MAIN FLOOR

LAUNDRY

BATH

DN

COVERED PORCH

ENTRY

KITCHEN
10'-4" x 11'-1"

DINING ROOM
8'-9" x 13'-6"

ENSUITE

W.I.C.

MASTER BEDROOM
13'-6" x 14'-6"

BEDROOM
11'-2" x 10'-0"

LIVING ROOM
19'-1" x 19'-11"

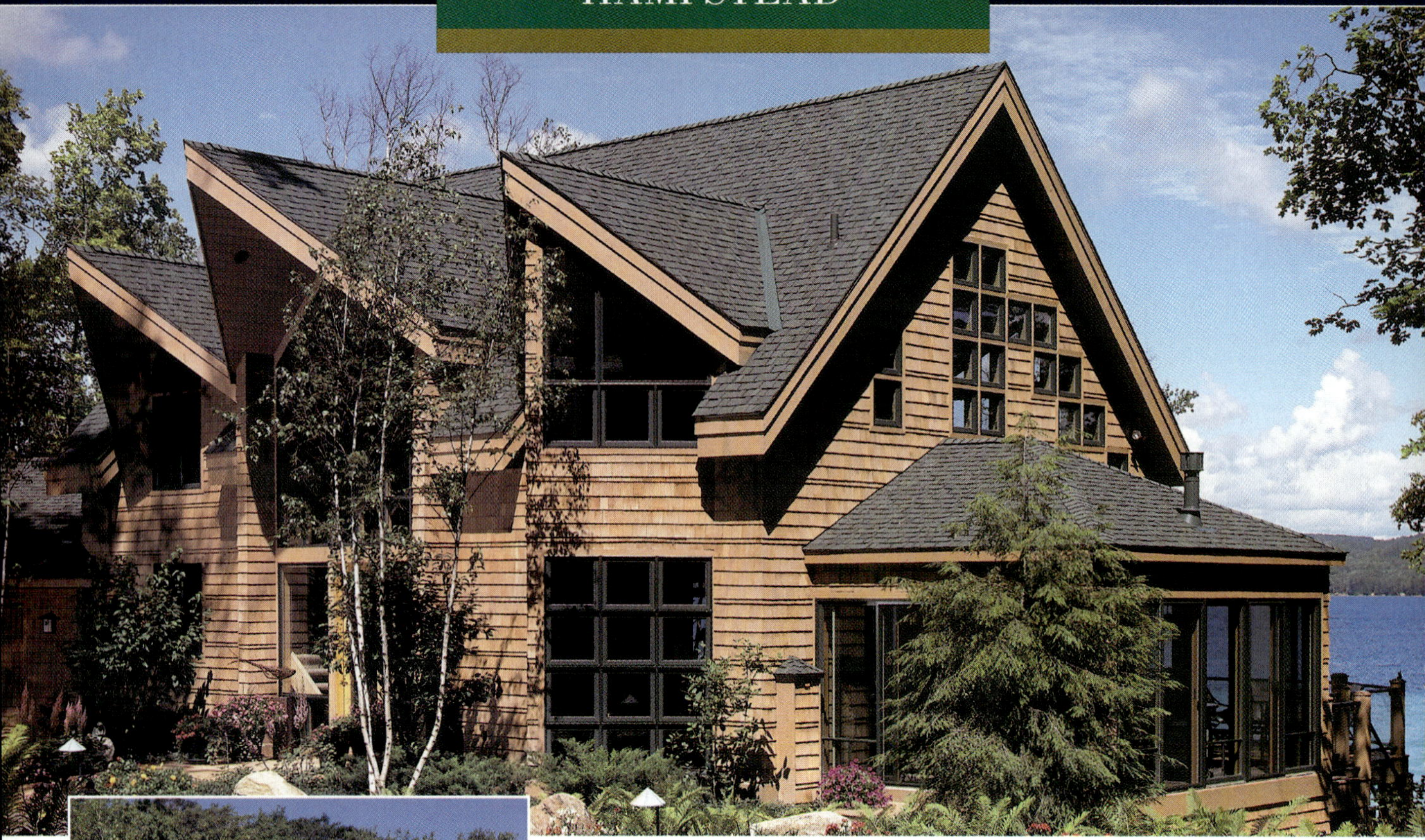

PHOTOGRAPHY: BETH SINGER

2,329 sq. ft.

- Angles form the theme of this home, from angled decks to massive prow windows that add light and elegance to the design.

- The first floor is the picture of efficiency with a large, counter-lined kitchen, separate dining area, mudroom, private study and open great-room.

- A loft connects the upper-level bedrooms, each with its own bath.

WIDTH 91'-6"
DEPTH 65'-0"

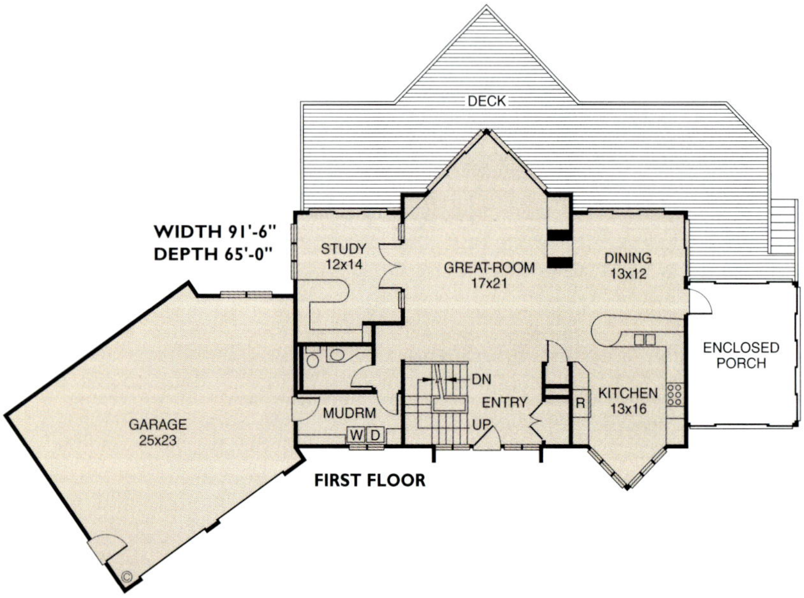

STUDY 12x14

GREAT-ROOM 17x21

DINING 13x12

DECK

ENCLOSED PORCH

GARAGE 25x23

MUDRM

W D

DN ENTRY UP

KITCHEN 13x16

R

FIRST FLOOR

BEDROOM 12x15

OPEN TO GREAT-ROOM

MASTER BEDROOM 13x14

LOFT

DN

OPEN TO ENTRY

SECOND FLOOR

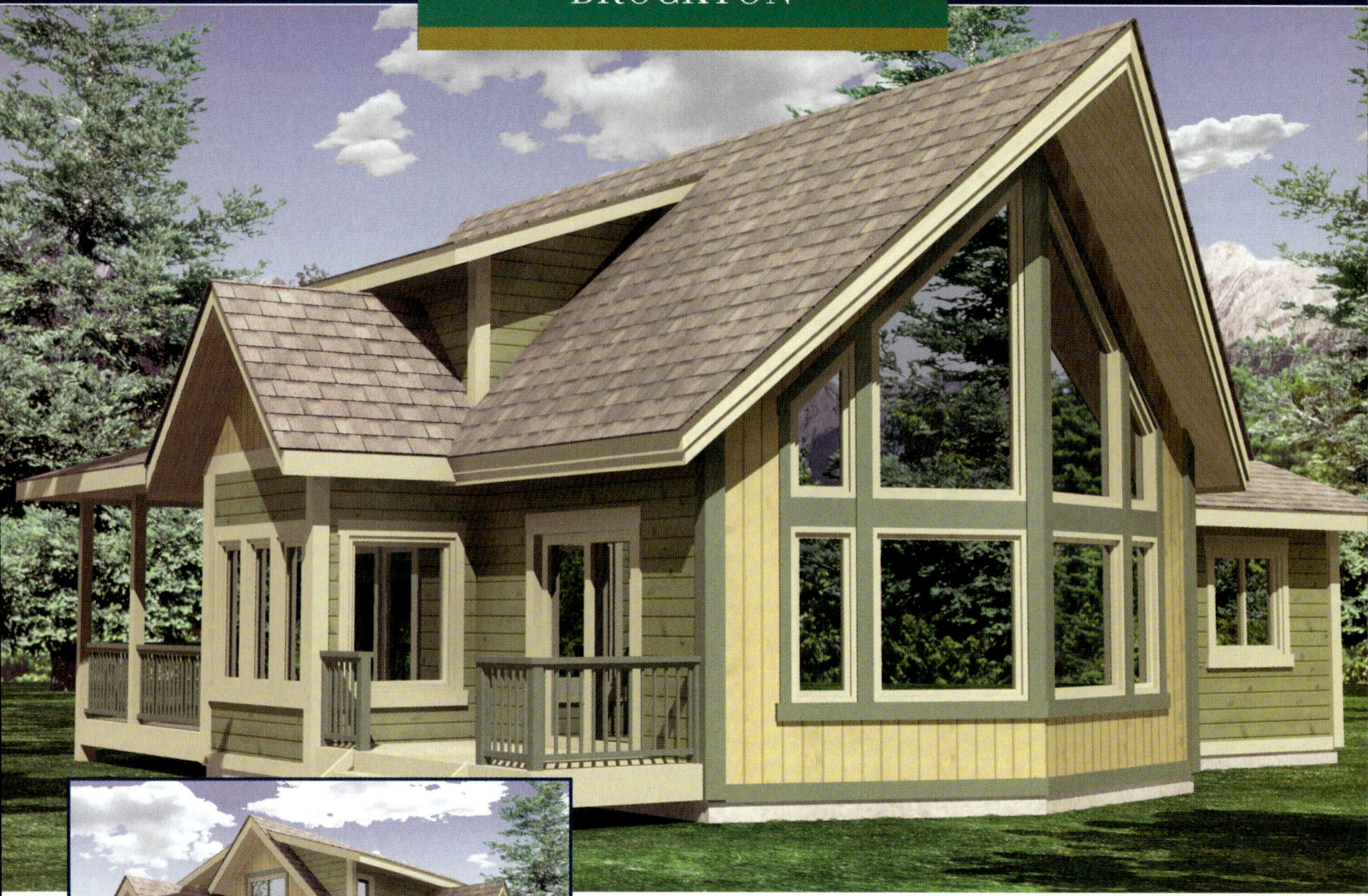

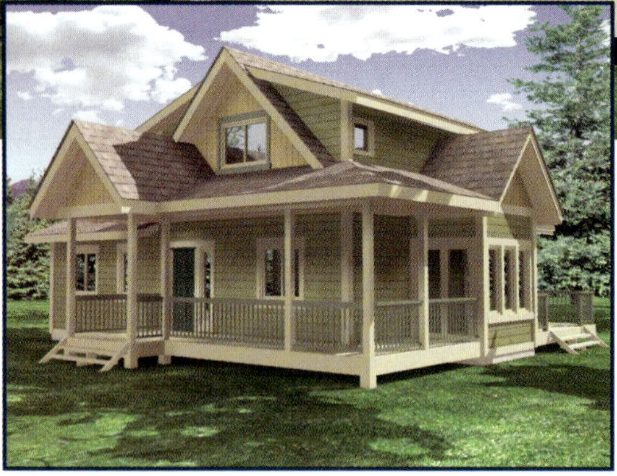

1,444 sq. ft.

- exterior dimensions 42' x 35'
- vaulted great-room and master suite
- large open kitchen and dining room with sunroom
- 3 bedrooms, 2 bathrooms

FIRST FLOOR

VERANDAH

KITCHEN
12'-0" x 10'-9"

FOYER

BEDROOM
9'-4" x 8'-8"

LAUNDRY

DINING ROOM
13'-4" x 8'-0"

UP

BATH

BEDROOM
9'-4" x 8'-8"

GREAT ROOM
19'-0" x 13'-4"

SECOND FLOOR

MASTER BEDROOM
12'-8" x 16'-0"

ENSUITE

W.I.C.

DN

OPEN TO BELOW

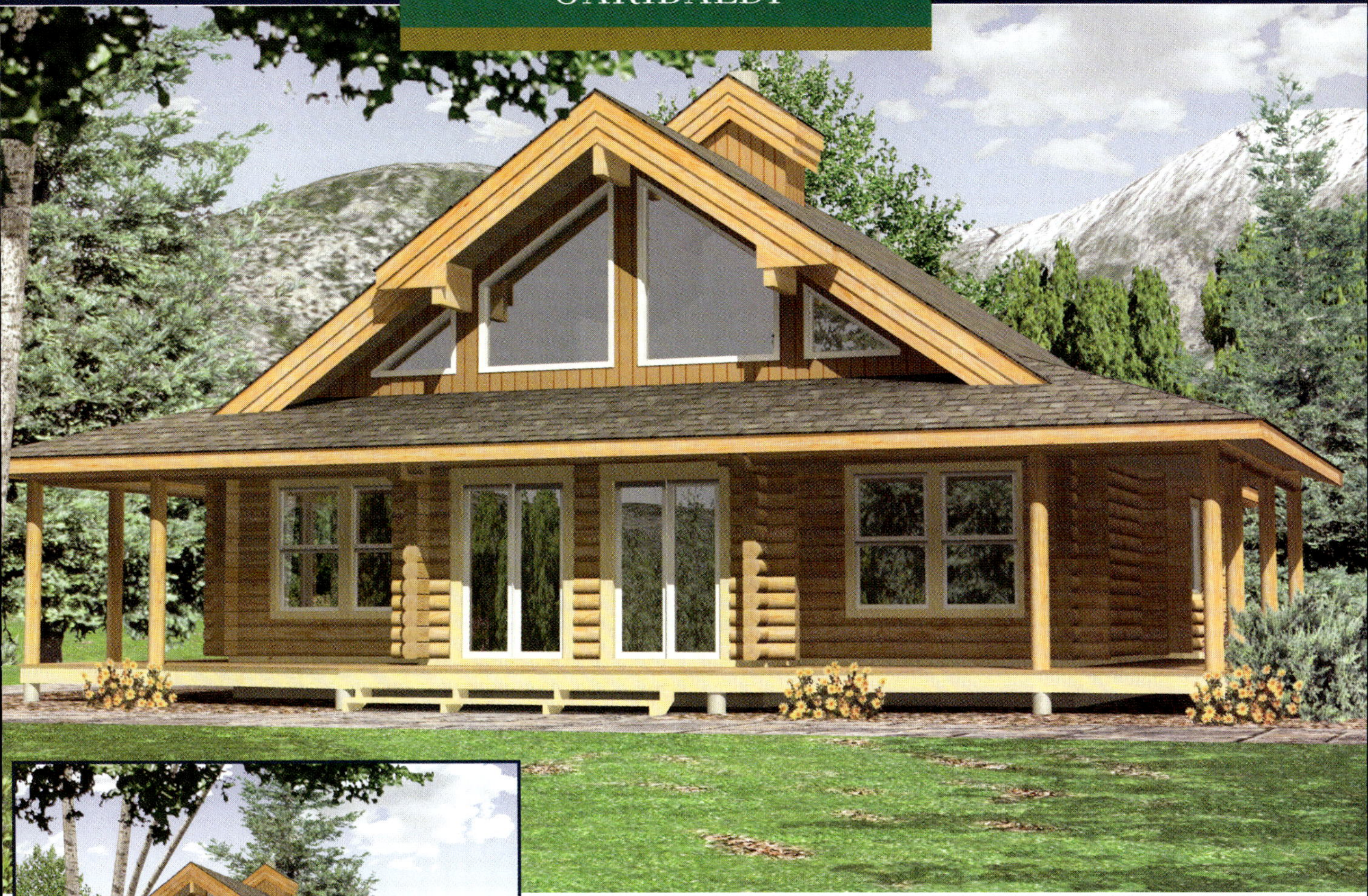

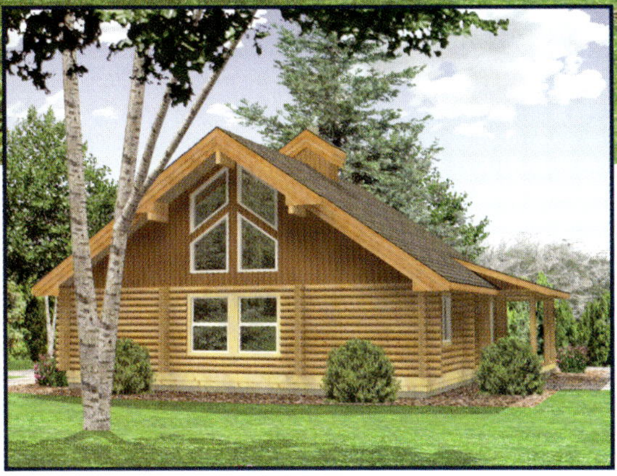

1,352 sq. ft.

- exterior dimensions 49' x 46'
- master bedroom with full ensuite
- entire floor area vaulted
- extra large great-room
- 3 bedrooms, 2 bathrooms
- wraparound covered verandah

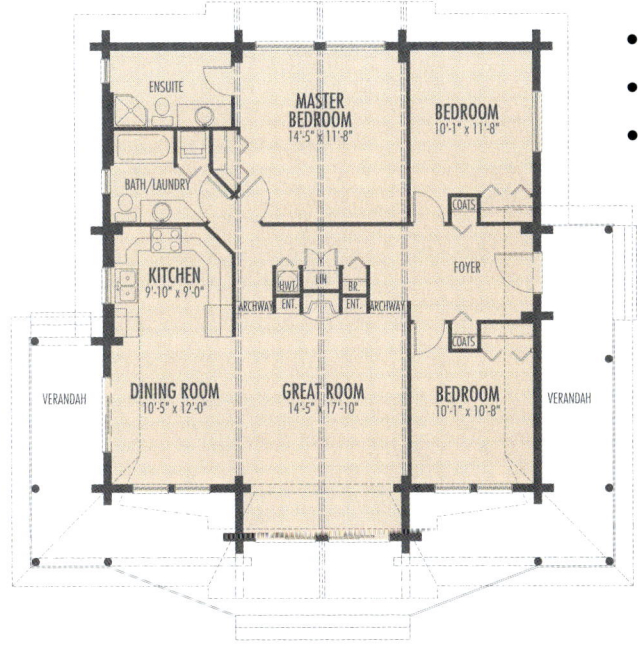

ENSUITE

MASTER BEDROOM
14'-5" x 11'-8"

BEDROOM
10'-1" x 11'-8"

BATH/LAUNDRY

COATS

FOYER

KITCHEN
9'-10" x 9'-0"

HWT LIN BR ENT. ARCHWAY

ENT. ARCHWAY

COATS

VERANDAH

DINING ROOM
10'-5" x 12'-0"

GREAT ROOM
14'-5" x 17'-10"

BEDROOM
10'-1" x 10'-8"

VERANDAH

MAIN FLOOR

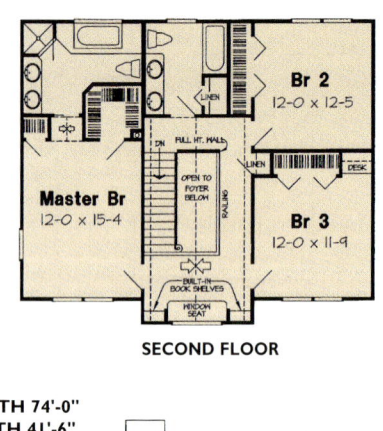

SECOND FLOOR

Master Br
12-0 x 15-4

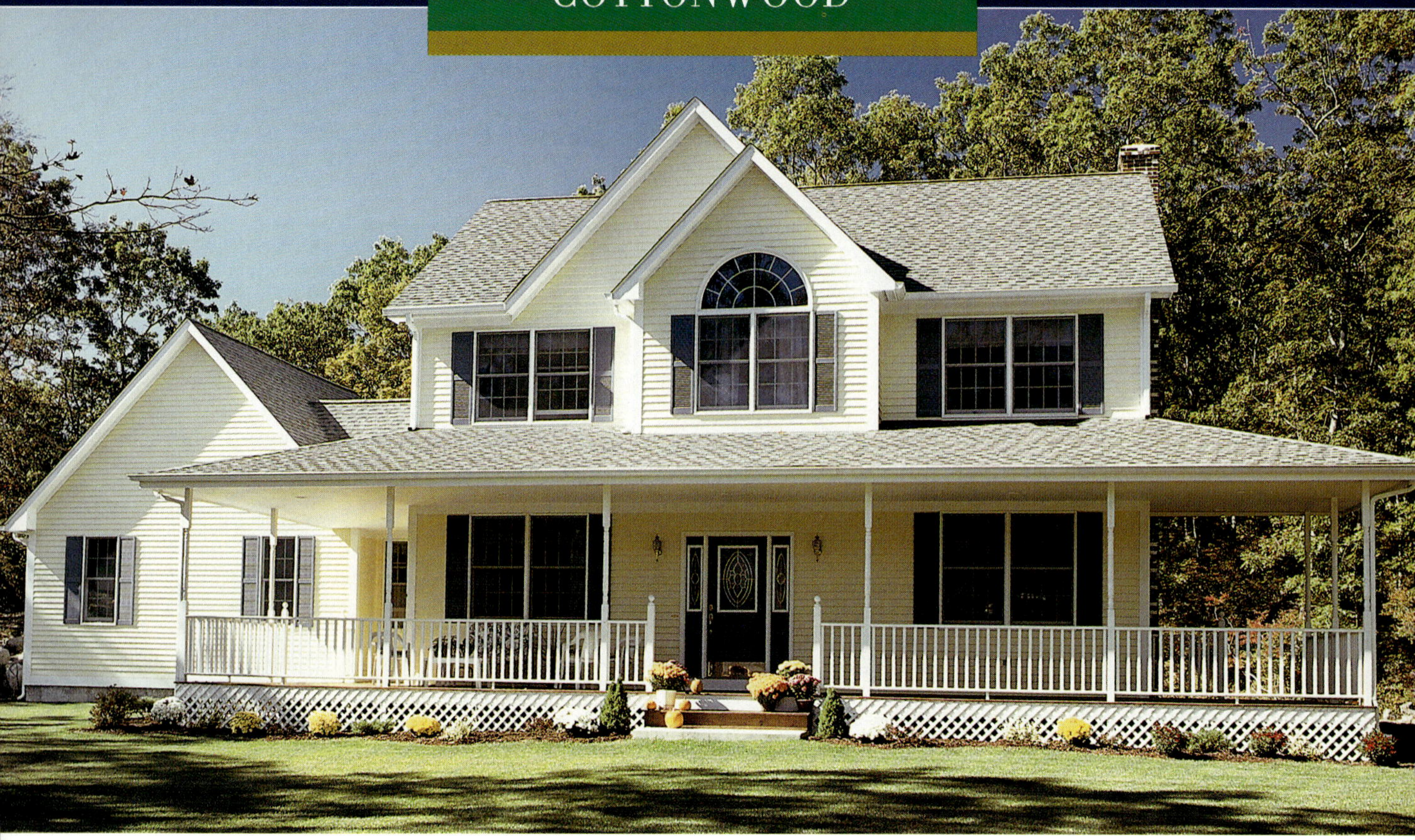

Br 2
12-0 x 12-5

Br 3
12-0 x 11-9

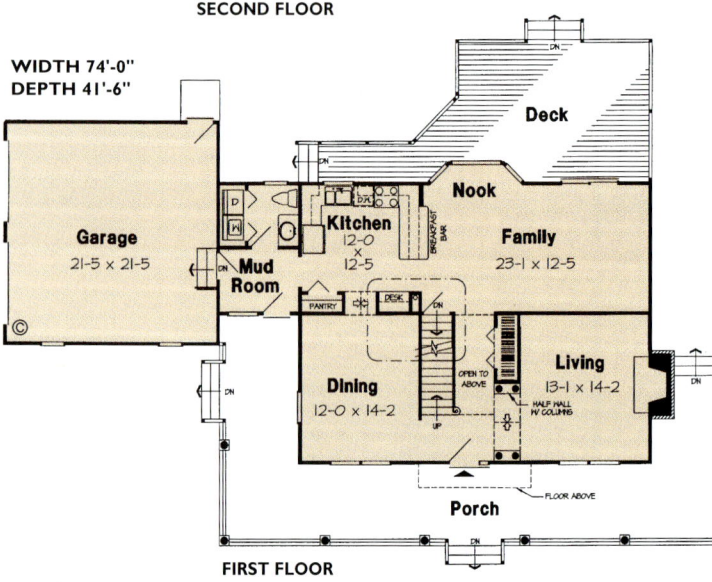

WIDTH 74'-0"
DEPTH 41'-6"

Garage
21-5 x 21-5

Mud Room

Kitchen
12-0 x 12-5

Nook

Family
23-1 x 12-5

Deck

Dining
12-0 x 14-2

Living
13-1 x 14-2

Porch

FIRST FLOOR

2,047 sq. ft.

- Picture a porch swing, cozy rocking chairs, and a pitcher of lemonade on this country veranda. The formal areas of this traditional three-bedroom home flank the entry hall.

- The well-appointed kitchen is divided from the family room by a breakfast bar. A mudroom with garden and garage access, laundry room, and guest bathroom complete the main floor.

- In addition to the three bedrooms, the upper floor features a window seat framed by built-in bookshelves, providing a cozy place to curl up with a book.

PHOTOGRAPHY: JOHN EHRENCLOU

1,668 sq. ft.

- This cozy three-bedroom home has immediate appeal with its charming old-fashioned country porch.

- A first-floor master suite, including a luxurious master bath, ensures privacy as the two additional bedrooms are located on the second floor. These second-floor bedrooms are both large and have ample closet space. Additional roof storage is accessible on each side of both bedrooms.

- The well-designed floor space efficiently combines an open-plan living and dining area, accented by a welcoming fireplace. The kitchen and breakfast room open to a rear sundeck, expanding into outdoor living space.

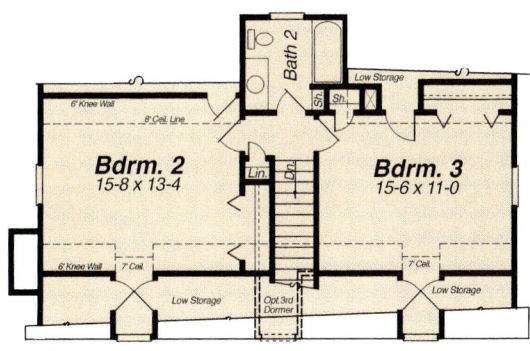

SECOND FLOOR

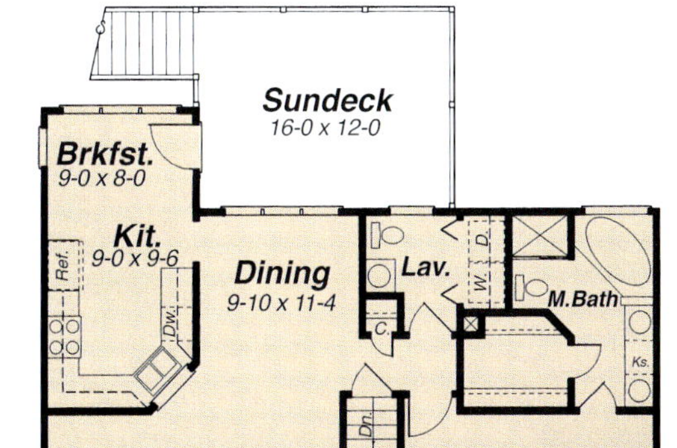

6' Knee Wall
8' Ceil. Line
Bath 2
Low Storage
Sh. Sh.

Bdrm. 2
15-8 x 13-4

Lin. Dn.

Bdrm. 3
15-6 x 11-0

6' Knee Wall   7' Ceil.
Low Storage   Opt 3rd Dormer   7' Ceil.   Low Storage

FIRST FLOOR

Sundeck
16-0 x 12-0

Brkfst.
9-0 x 8-0

Ref.

Kit.
9-0 x 9-6

Dw.

Dining
9-10 x 11-4

Lav.   W. D.

C

M.Bath

Ks.

Dn.

Living Area
18-0 x 13-6

Up

Master Bdrm.
15-6 x 13-6

Porch

1,732 sq. ft.

- A spectacular chalet with multi-gabled roof.

- The dramatic entry way with high ceilings and an impressive open staircase is one of the features of this popular design.

- This home offers all this with a feeling of coziness in keeping with a desire to retain a casual lifestyle.

- The open-plan kitchen is part of the living space and has become a focal point for both family life and informal parties.

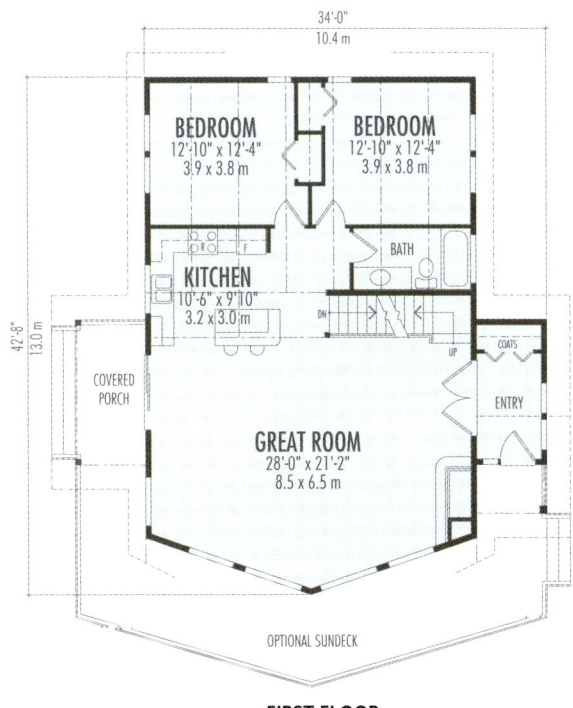

FIRST FLOOR

34'-0"
10.4 m

BEDROOM
12'-10" x 12'-4"
3.9 x 3.8 m

BEDROOM
12'-10" x 12'-4"
3.9 x 3.8 m

BATH

KITCHEN
10'-6" x 9'10"
3.2 x 3.0 m

DN

UP

COATS

ENTRY

COVERED PORCH

GREAT ROOM
28'-0" x 21'-2"
8.5 x 6.5 m

42'-8"
13.0 m

OPTIONAL SUNDECK

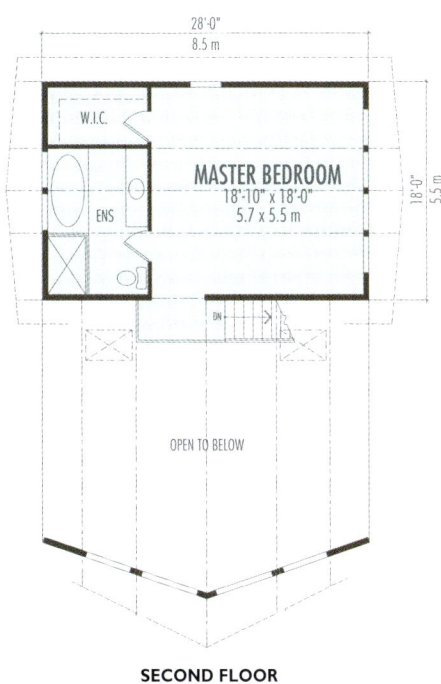

SECOND FLOOR

28'-0"
8.5 m

W.I.C.

ENS

MASTER BEDROOM
18'-10" x 18'-0"
5.7 x 5.5 m

18'-0"
5.5 m

DN

OPEN TO BELOW

~ SIERRA ~

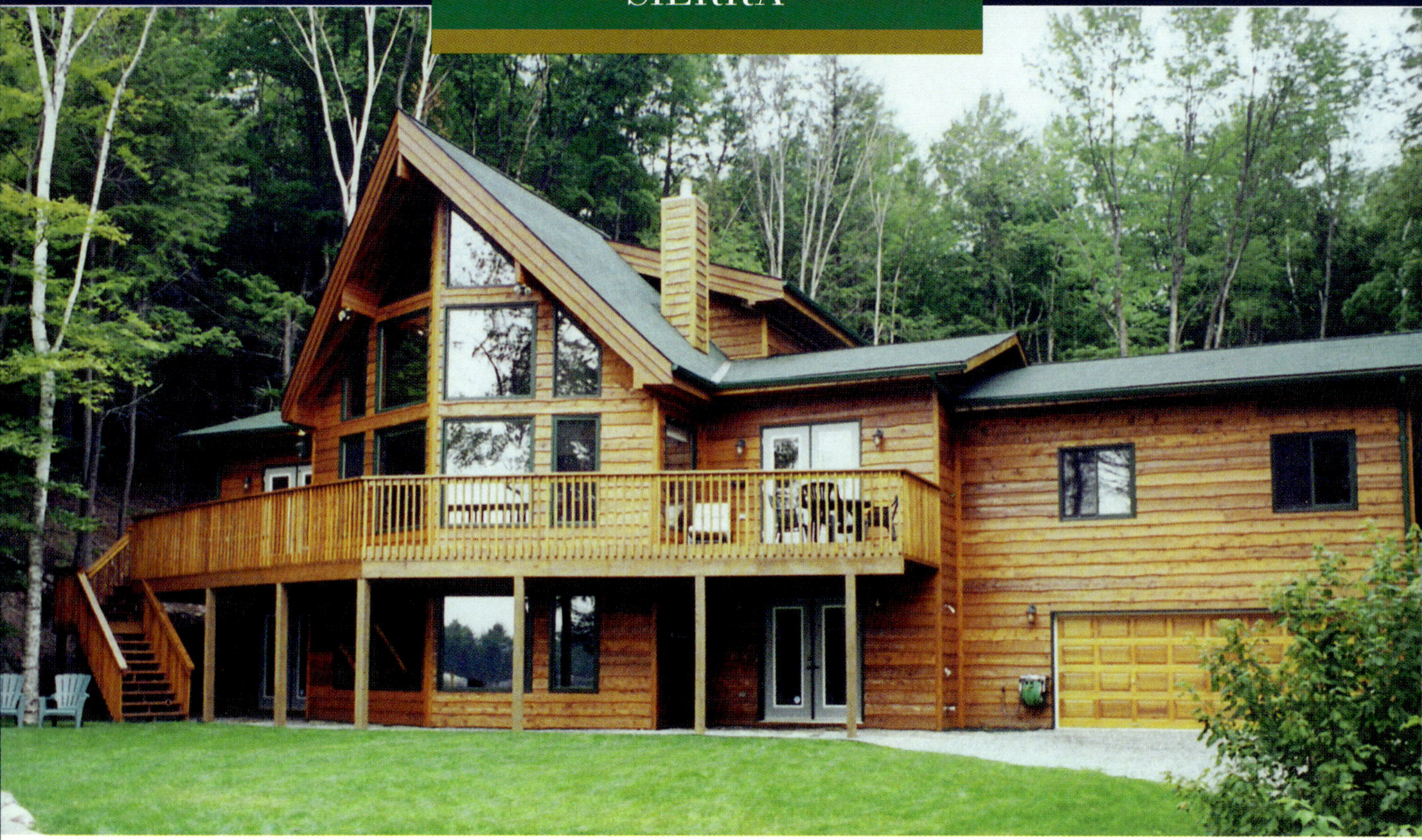

1,911 sq. ft.

- A popular design, this distinctive four-bedroom home features the exceptional use of glass and the privacy of a second-floor master bedroom with walk-in closet and full ensuite.
- Amenities on the main level include the vaulted living room, open-plan dining area, and a delightfully large kitchen.
- Three bedrooms, another full bath, and the utility/mudroom complete this superb floor plan.

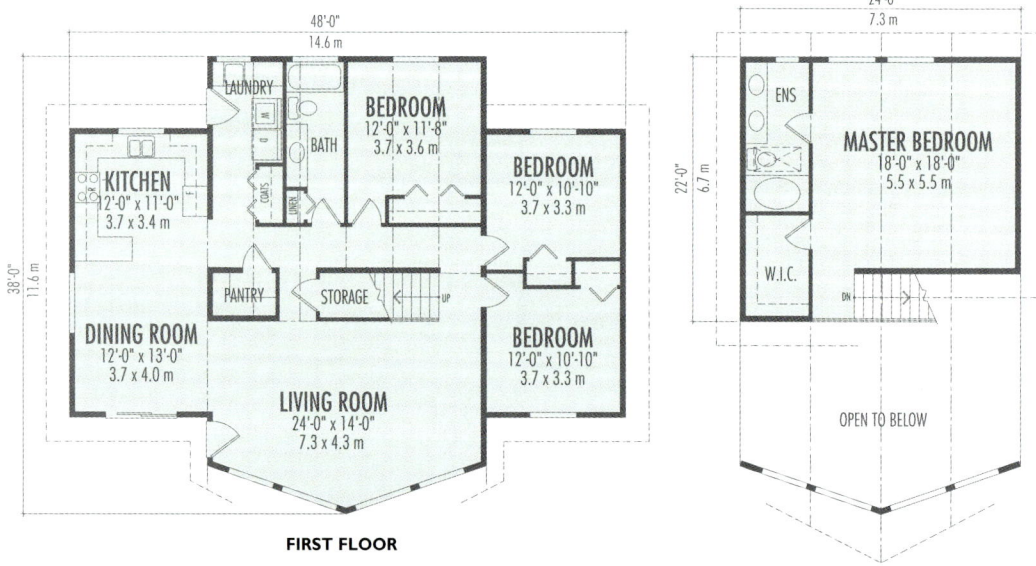

48'-0"
14.6 m
38'-0"
11.6 m
LAUNDRY
BATH
COATS
LINEN
BEDROOM
12'-0" x 11'-8"
3.7 x 3.6 m
KITCHEN
12'-0" x 11'-0"
3.7 x 3.4 m
BEDROOM
12'-0" x 10'-10"
3.7 x 3.3 m
PANTRY
STORAGE
UP
DINING ROOM
12'-0" x 13'-0"
3.7 x 4.0 m
BEDROOM
12'-0" x 10'-10"
3.7 x 3.3 m
LIVING ROOM
24'-0" x 14'-0"
7.3 x 4.3 m

FIRST FLOOR

24'-0"
7.3 m
22'-0"
6.7 m
ENS
MASTER BEDROOM
18'-0" x 18'-0"
5.5 x 5.5 m
W.I.C.
DN
OPEN TO BELOW

SECOND FLOOR

2,190 sq. ft.

- A very distinctive roof line and windows, two covered porches, and a charming optional gazebo distinguish this spectacular four-bedroom residence.

- The master bedroom, featuring a spacious walk-in closet and full ensuite with corner shower, plus two additional private bedrooms and bath, are situated on the second floor.

- Main floor amenities include an impressive entry, laundry/storage room, and a large bedroom with walk-in closet adjacent to a full bath. The superb U-shape kitchen, living, and dining areas are designed for family or entertaining.

SECOND FLOOR

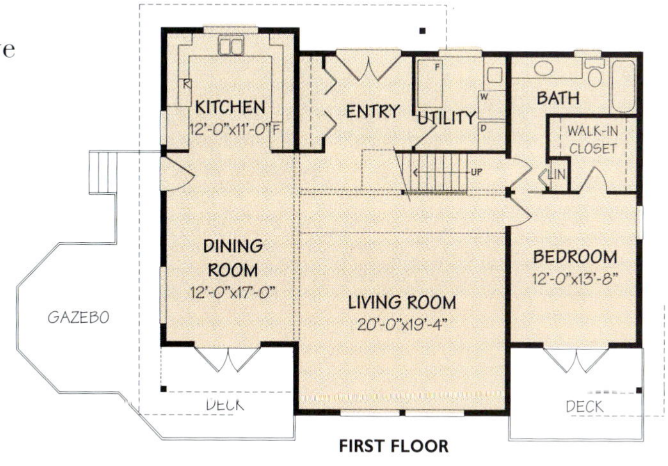

ENSUITE
WALK-IN CLOSET
BEDROOM 13'-6"x8'-10"
BATH
BEDROOM 12'-0"x13'-6"
BEDROOM 12'-0"x15'-0"
DN
OPEN TO BELOW

FIRST FLOOR

KITCHEN 12'-0"x11'-0"
ENTRY
UTILITY
BATH
WALK-IN CLOSET
DINING ROOM 12'-0"x17'-0"
LIVING ROOM 20'-0"x19'-4"
BEDROOM 12'-0"x13'-8"
GAZEBO
DECK
DECK

2,520 sq. ft.

- Exterior dimensions 83'10" x 62'6"
- Large and gracious great-room, dining room, and kitchen
- Extensive covered verandah
- 4 bedrooms and den, 2½ bathrooms

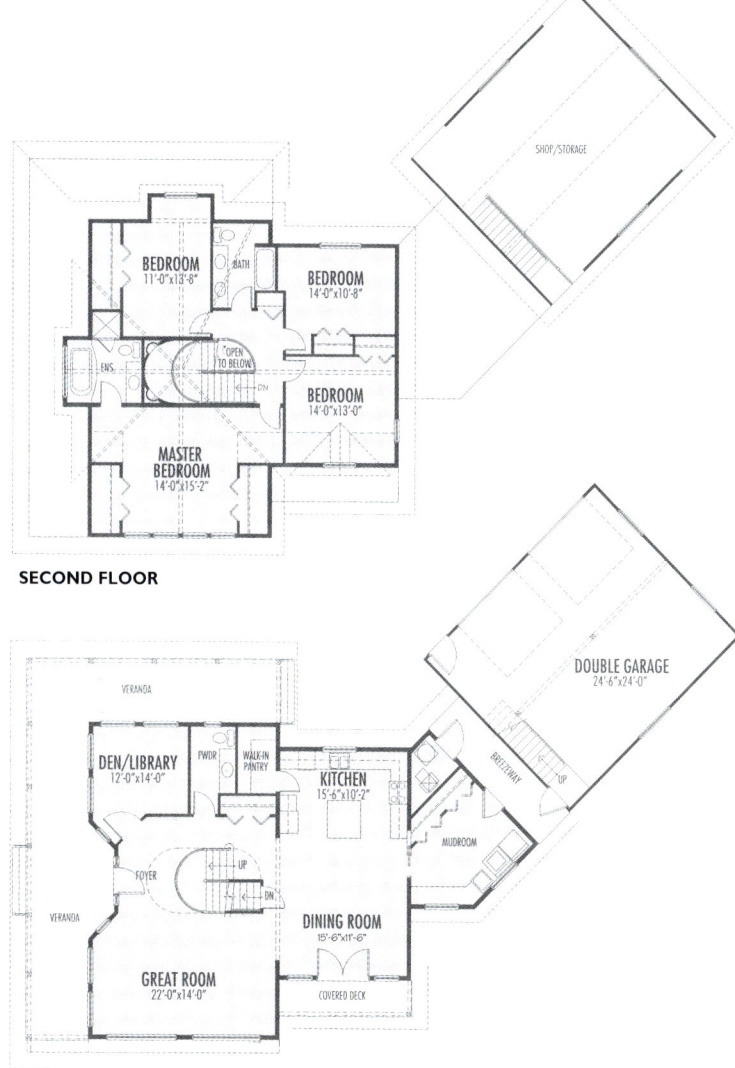

SECOND FLOOR

FIRST FLOOR

2,035 sq. ft.

- exterior dimensions 52' x 40'
- large vaulted great-room
- 3 bedrooms, 2 bathrooms
- two covered porches at back of house

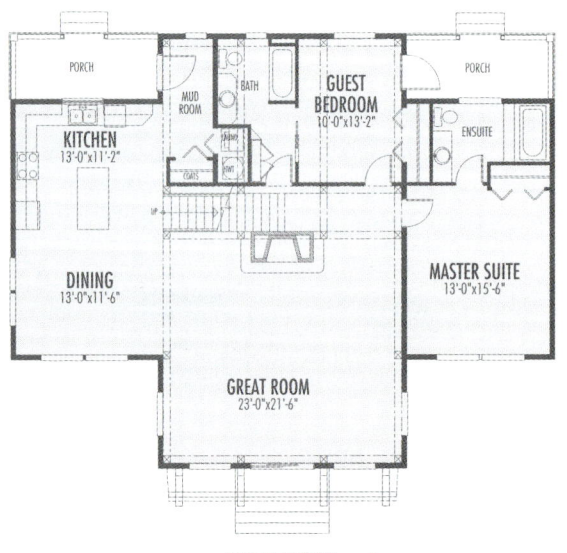

FIRST FLOOR

PORCH

MUD ROOM

BATH

GUEST BEDROOM
10'-0"x13'-2"

PORCH

ENSUITE

KITCHEN
13'-0"x11'-2"

CLOS.

DINING
13'-0"x11'-6"

MASTER SUITE
13'-0"x15'-6"

GREAT ROOM
23'-0"x21'-6"

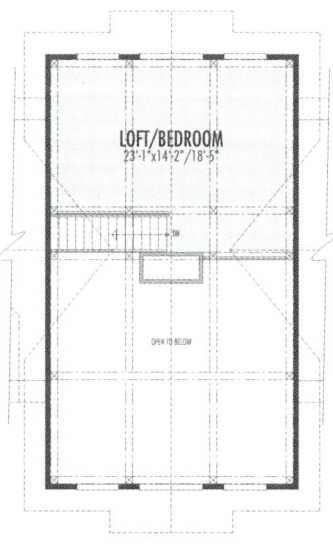

SECOND FLOOR

LOFT/BEDROOM
23'-1"x14'-2"/18'-5"

OPEN TO BELOW

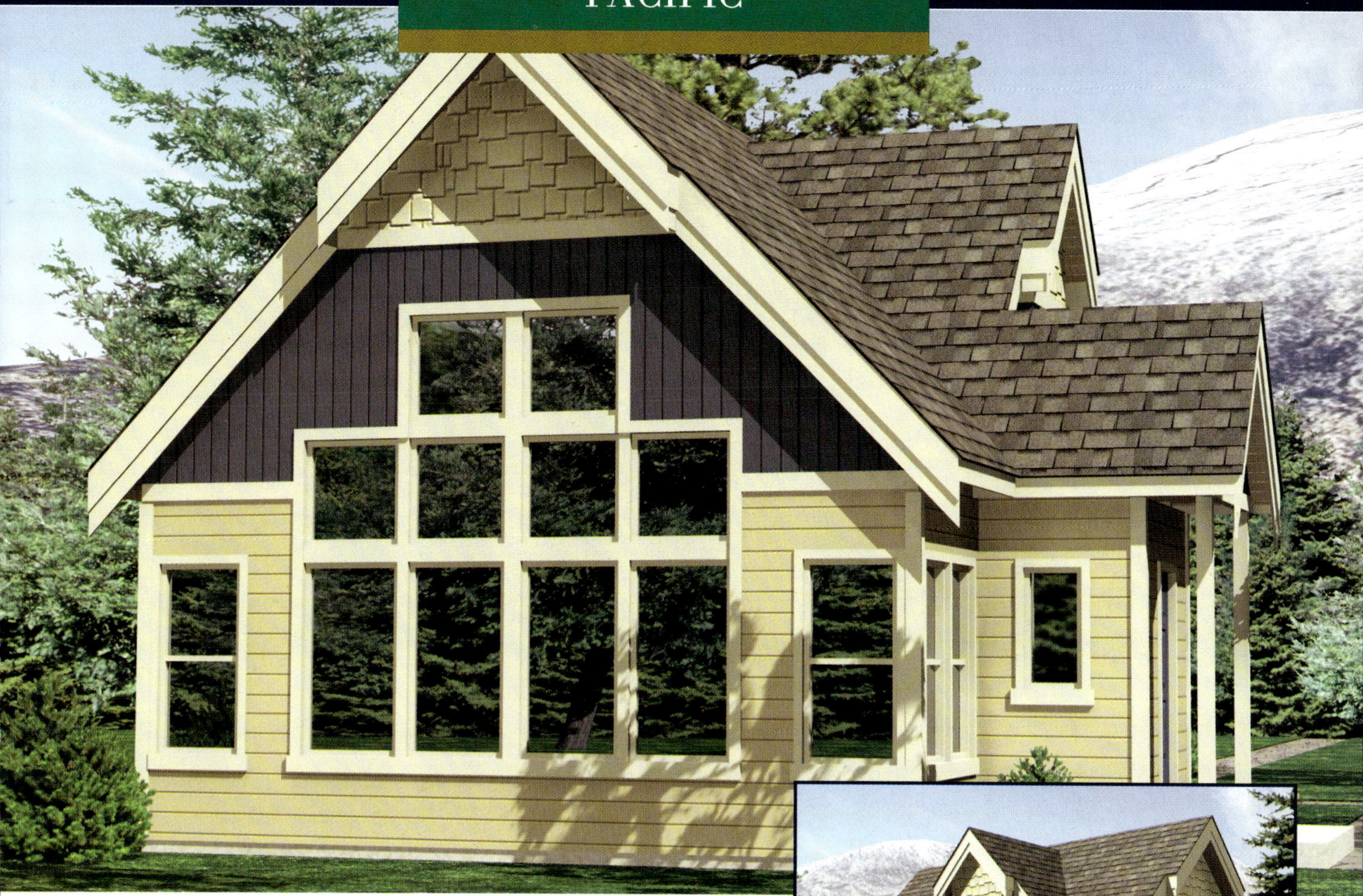

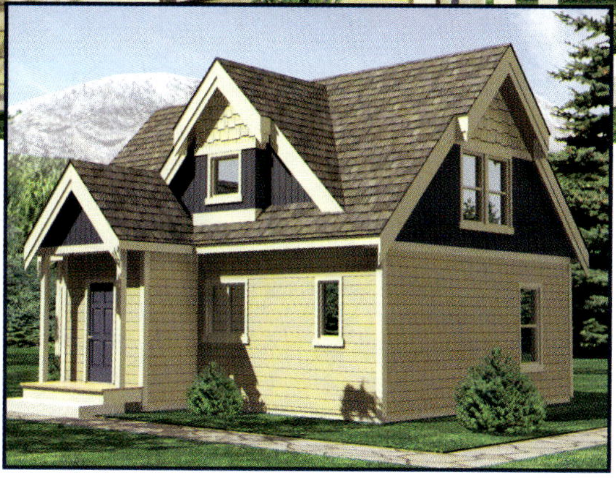

1,116 sq. ft.

- exterior dimensions 29' x 33'
- vaulted open-plan living/dining area
- 2 bedrooms, 2 bathrooms
- large vaulted master bedroom with ensuite

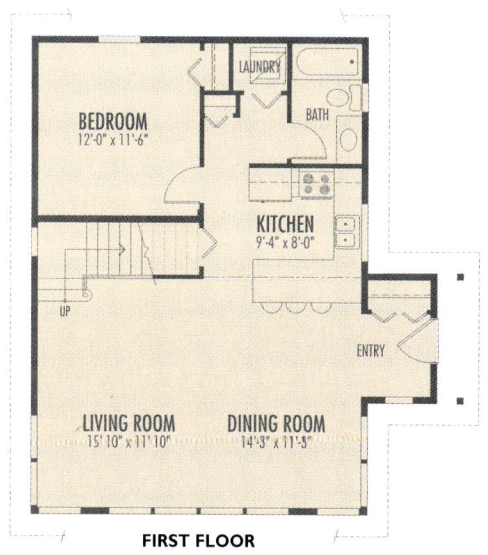

FIRST FLOOR

BEDROOM
12'-0" x 11'-6"

LAUNDRY

BATH

KITCHEN
9'-4" x 8'-0"

UP

ENTRY

LIVING ROOM
15'-10" x 11'-10"

DINING ROOM
14'-3" x 11'-5"

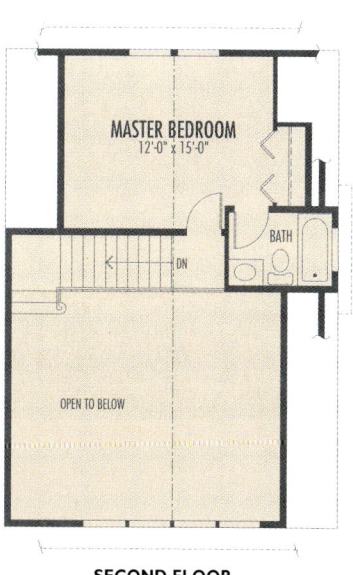

SECOND FLOOR

MASTER BEDROOM
12'-0" x 15'-0"

BATH

DN

OPEN TO BELOW

4,277 sq. ft.

- This large and distinctive five-bedroom home features an expansive vaulted dining and living area, with fireplace and enormous windows—perfect for entertaining.

- Located in its own private wing, the huge master bedroom offers a corner fireplace, full ensuite with windowed-alcove tub, very generous walk-in closet, and secluded balcony.

- Other highlights include a superb island kitchen adjacent to the family room (with a third fireplace), covered porch, mudroom, two bedrooms on the main level, and two more bedrooms up, with a full bath and roomy loft.

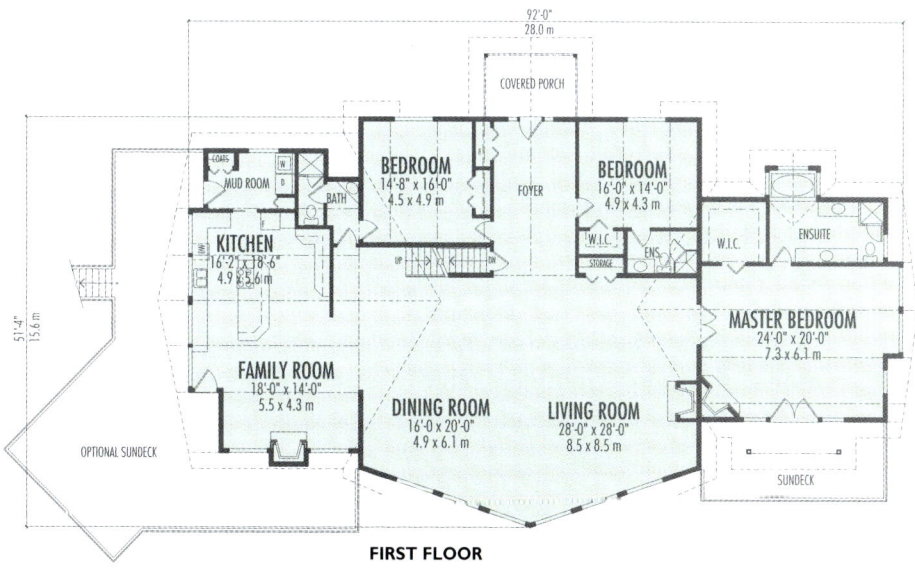

FIRST FLOOR

SECOND FLOOR

PHOTOGRAPHY: PHIL MUELLER

3,256 sq. ft.

- The gracious open-plan main floor of this unique and appealing three-bedroom home offers generous great-room, dining, kitchen, and breakfast areas, all with deck access. A cozy den/library, laundry room, half-bath, and breezeway complete the main floor.

- A central staircase leads to the second floor which includes a well-appointed master suite and two secondary bedrooms, each with private bath.

- A steeply pitched roof line and deep eaves, along with rounded windows, dormers, and Craftsman-style details contribute to the outstanding curb appeal of this home.

INTERIOR PHOTOGRAPHY: SUSAN GILMORE

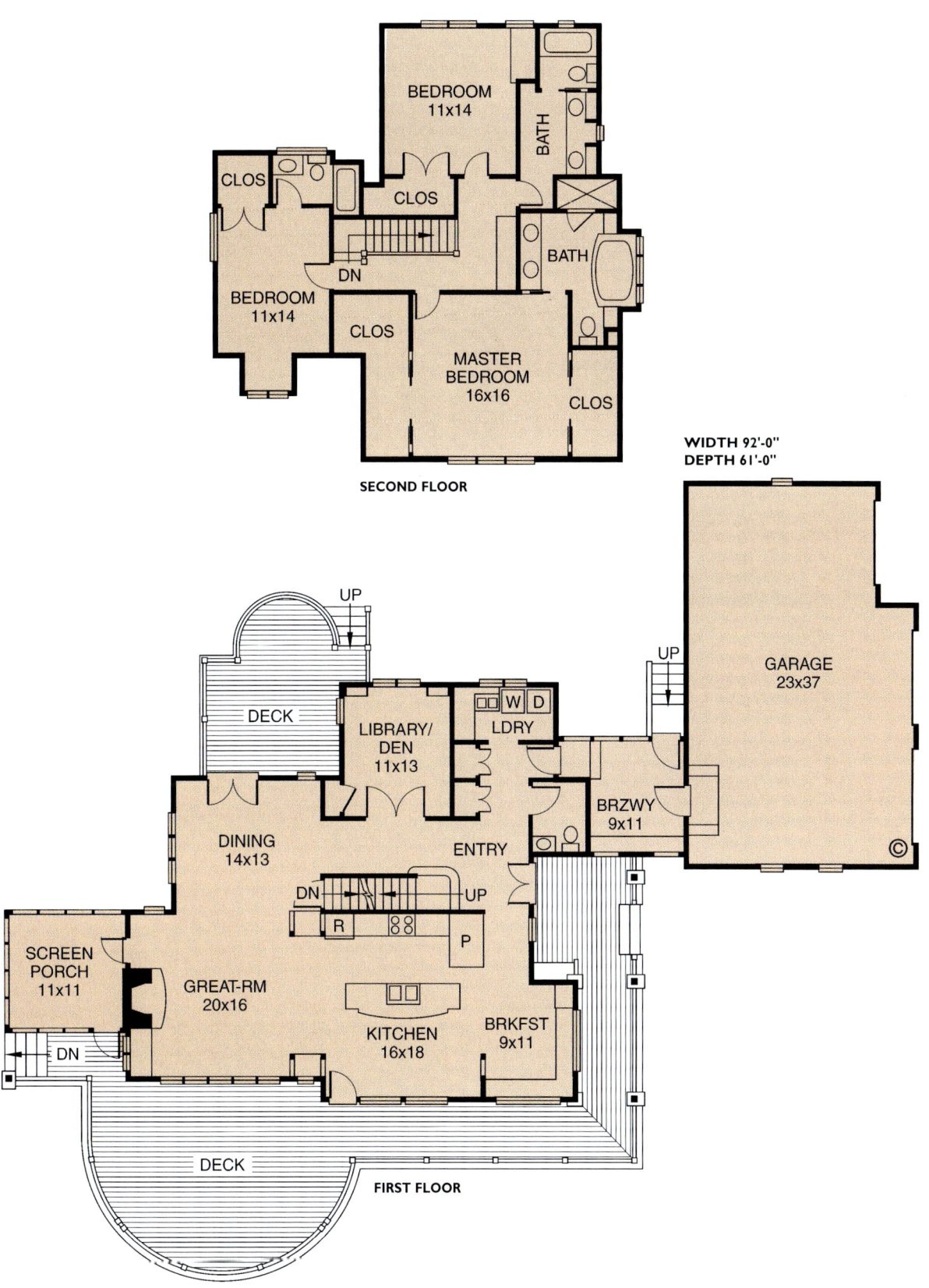

SECOND FLOOR

BEDROOM
11x14

BATH

CLOS

CLOS

BATH

DN

BEDROOM
11x14

CLOS

MASTER
BEDROOM
16x16

CLOS

WIDTH 92'-0"
DEPTH 61'-0"

UP

DECK

LIBRARY/
DEN
11x13

W D

LDRY

UP

GARAGE
23x37

DINING
14x13

BRZWY
9x11

ENTRY

DN

UP

R

P

SCREEN
PORCH
11x11

GREAT-RM
20x16

KITCHEN
16x18

BRKFST
9x11

DN

DECK

FIRST FLOOR

~ CORBIN ~

1,089 sq. ft.

- exterior dimensions 28' x 24'
- generous two-car garage
- multipurpose loft with dormer windows

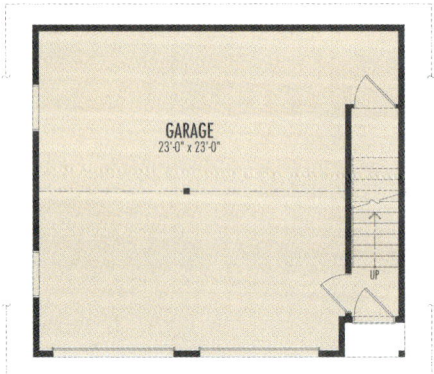

GARAGE

GARAGE
23'-0" x 23'-0"

UP

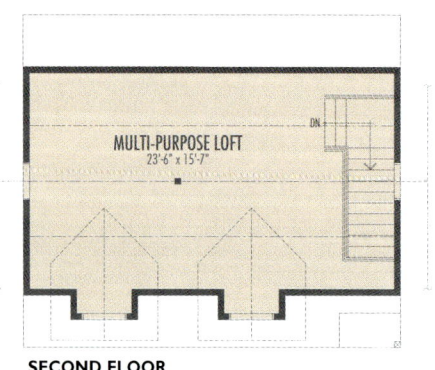

SECOND FLOOR

MULTI-PURPOSE LOFT
23'-6" x 15'-7"

DN

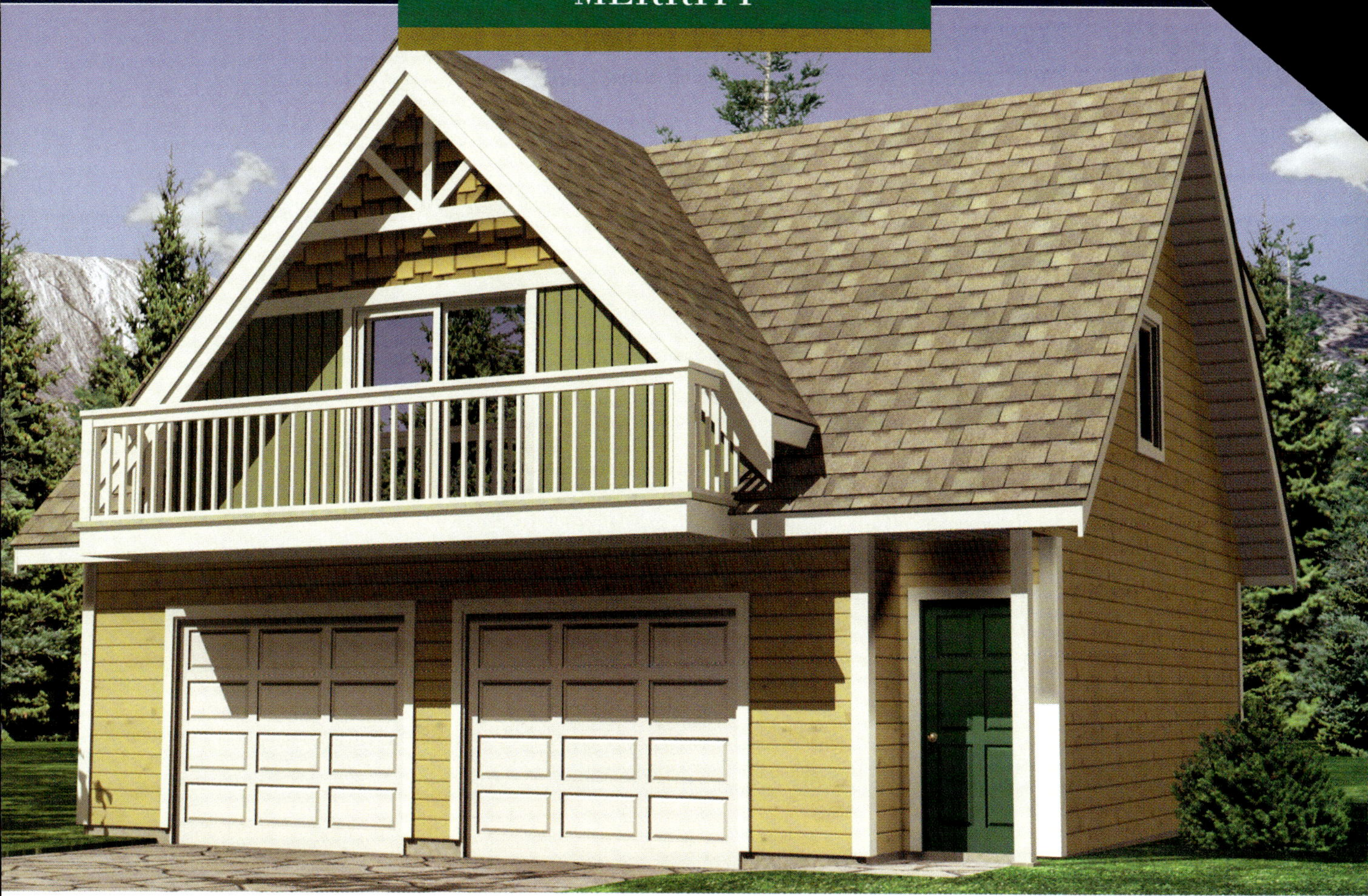

1,547 sq. ft.

- exterior dimensions 32' x 26'
- generous two-car garage with storage
- vaulted studio suite with full bathroom and balcony

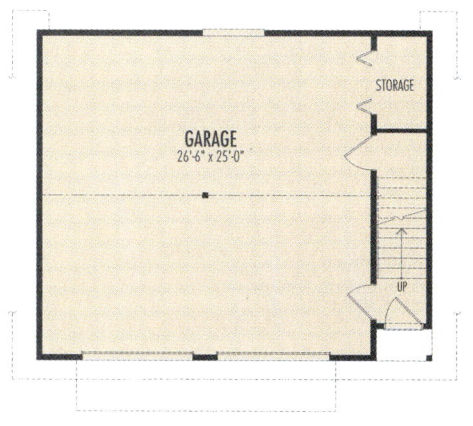

GARAGE

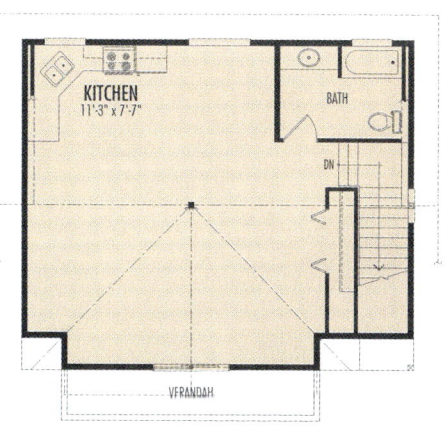

SECOND FLOOR-STUDIO SUITE

2,346 sq. ft.

- This outstanding three-bedroom home features a totally private master bedroom wing with full ensuite, generous walk-in closet, and additional space.

- A feature fireplace stands between the vaulted living and dining areas with their magnificent prow windows.

- The large kitchen has ample cupboards, counter space, and a nook.

105'-10"
32.3 m

48'-10"
14.9 m

OPTIONAL GARAGE
24'-0" x 24'-0"
7.3 m x 7.3 m

BEDROOM
11'-2" x 12'-0"
3.4 m x 3.7 m

BATH

BEDROOM
11'-2" x 12'-0"
3.4 m x 3.7 m

FOYER

FAMILY ROOM
13'-6" x 14'-6"
4.1 m x 4.4 m

ENSUITE

W.I.C.

MASTER BEDROOM
19'-0" x 16'-4"
5.8 m x 5.0 m

COATS

UTILITY

NOOK
10'-0" x 12'-8"
3.0 m x 3.9 m

KITCHEN
13'-8" x 12'-8"
4.2 m x 3.9 m

DINING ROOM
14'-0" x 18'-0"
4.3 m x 5.5 m

LIVING ROOM
22'-0" x 20'-0"
6.7 m x 6.1 m

D   W

OPTIONAL SUNDECK

MAIN FLOOR

1,450 sq. ft.

- Get back to the basics with this charming log design. Enjoy the expansive open-living concept of this dwelling. A large gourmet kitchen is conveniently located within the spacious, light-filled great-room, making this the ideal home for entertaining.

- A bedroom/office, full bath, and complete laundry facilities round off the main floor, while an impressive master bedroom with full ensuite is secluded in the privacy of the second level. This home features large walls of glass and ample wraparound deck space, so whether you are inside or out, you will always be treated to a spectacular view.

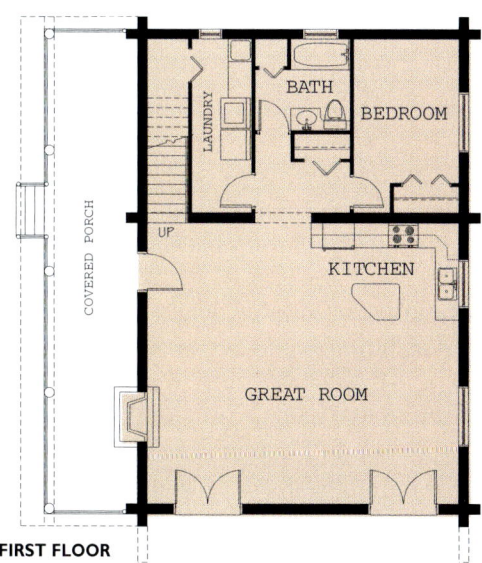

FIRST FLOOR

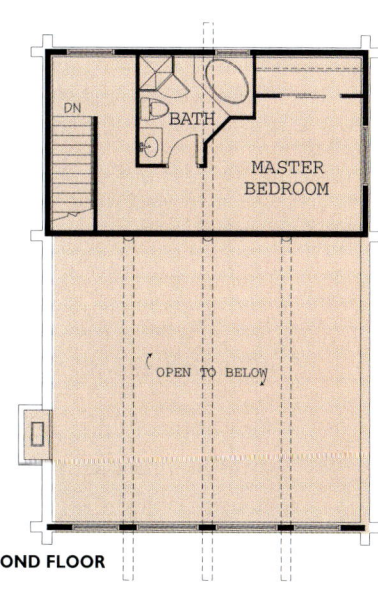

SECOND FLOOR

PHOTOGRAPHY: COURTESY OF THE DESIGNER

4,768 sq. ft.

- An impressive four-bedroom home, designed with imagination and style: ideal for formal entertaining or busy family life.

- A two-story ceiling and an awesome stone fireplace lend grandeur to a truly great room. The bank of windows allows enjoyment of all the seasons. A second cozy fireplace is found in the comfortable bookshelf-lined study.

- Elegant columns separate the formal dining room with its beautiful decorative ceiling, custom cabinetry, and gleaming hardwood floors.

- The kitchen, with its island and peninsula counter, leads to a breakfast room that accesses both the rear porch and enclosed sunroom.

- The upper floor is as exciting as the main floor. A breathtaking master suite has its own fireplace, private deck, and a magnificently appointed ensuite, which includes two very generous walk-in closets.

WIDTH 76'-6"
DEPTH 68'-6"

SECOND FLOOR

FIRST FLOOR

912 sq. ft.

- exterior dimensions 28' x 36'
- vaulted living, dining, and kitchen area
- 2 bedrooms, 1 bathroom
- covered porch

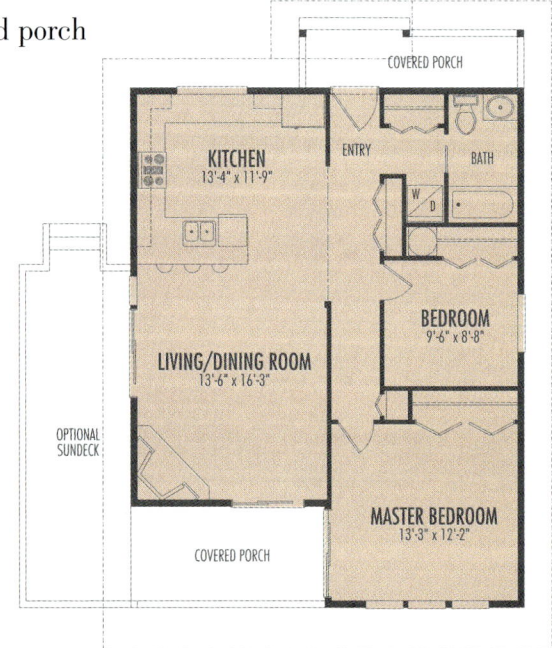

COVERED PORCH

KITCHEN
13'-4" x 11'-9"

ENTRY

BATH

W D

BEDROOM
9'-6" x 8'-8"

LIVING/DINING ROOM
13'-6" x 16'-3"

OPTIONAL
SUNDECK

MASTER BEDROOM
13'-3" x 12'-2"

COVERED PORCH

MAIN FLOOR

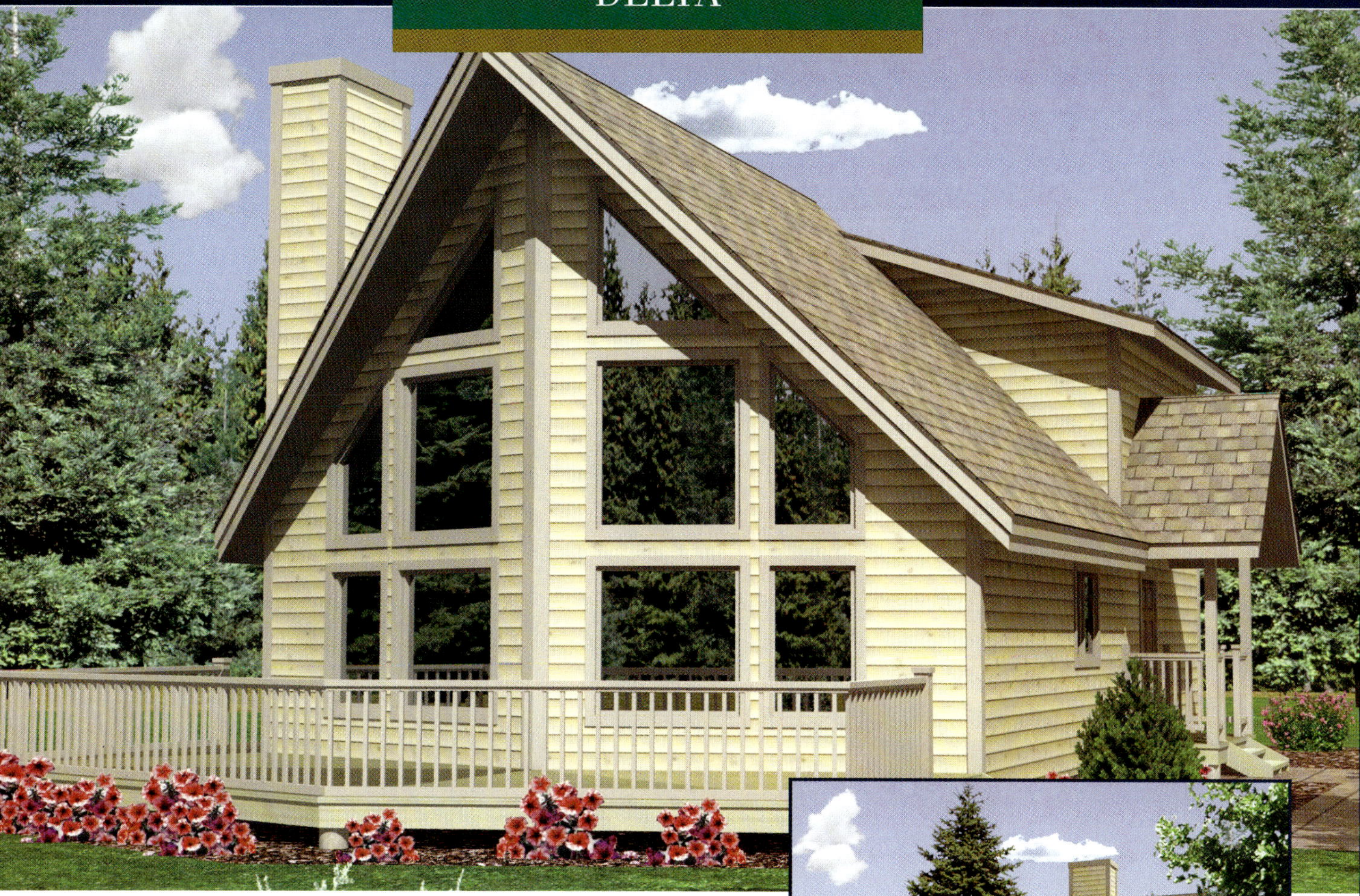

~ DELTA ~

1,816 sq. ft.

- exterior dimensions 28' x 47'
- vaulted master bedroom
- 3 bedrooms, 2 bathrooms
- open great-room, kitchen, and dining room

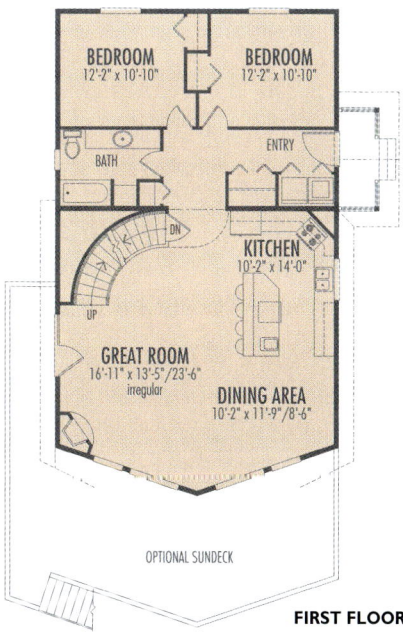

BEDROOM
12'-2" x 10'-10"

BEDROOM
12'-2" x 10'-10"

ENTRY

BATH

DN

UP

KITCHEN
10'-2" x 14'-0"

GREAT ROOM
16'-11" x 13'-5"/23'-6"
irregular

DINING AREA
10'-2" x 11'-9"/8'-6"

OPTIONAL SUNDECK

FIRST FLOOR

MASTER BEDROOM
15'-1" x 17'-1"

ENSUITE

W.I.C.

PLANT
SHELF

DN

OPEN TO BELOW

SECOND FLOOR

PHOTOGRAPHY: JAMES SALOMON

1,112 sq. ft.

- High ceilings and gable windows give the interior of this cozy woodland cottage a light and airy feeling.

- A gracious entry hall separates the two bedrooms from the living room and kitchen.

- The courtyard deck, a screen porch off the living room, and a large rear deck expand the living space outdoors.

- The spacious living room features a fireplace, built-in entertainment center, and a beautiful box-bay window.

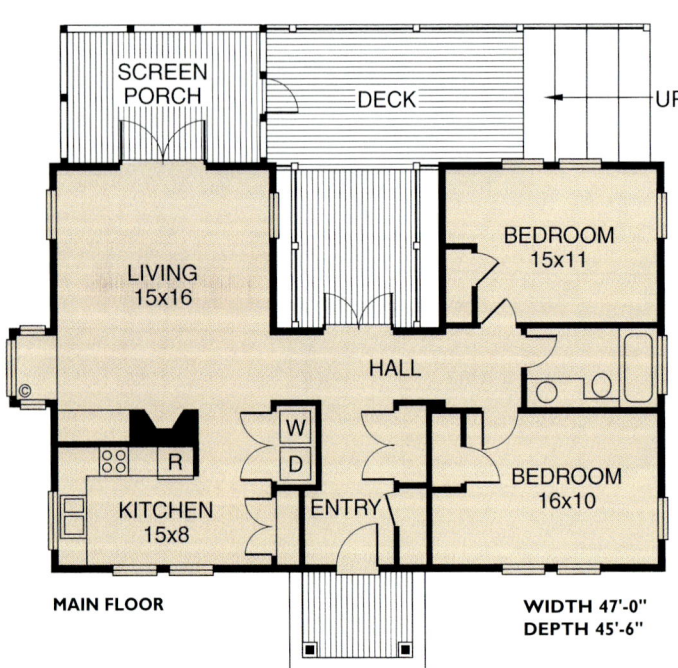

SCREEN PORCH

DECK

UP

LIVING 15x16

BEDROOM 15x11

HALL

W

W D

R

KITCHEN 15x8

ENTRY

BEDROOM 16x10

MAIN FLOOR

WIDTH 47'-0"
DEPTH 45'-6"

2,503 sq. ft.

- exterior dimensions 58' x 38'
- private second-floor master suite
- 4 bedrooms, 2 bathrooms
- vaulted kitchen, living room and dining room

FIRST FLEOOR

58'-0"
17.7 m

COVERED DECK

KITCHEN
14'-0" x 13'-0"
4.3 x 4.0 m

DEN
9'-0" x 11'-10"
2.7 x 3.6 m

BATH

LAUNDRY

FOYER

LINEN

BEDROOM
16'-0" x 11'-10"
4.9 x 3.6 m

DINING ROOM
16'-0" x 13'-0"
4.9 x 4.0 m

DN   UP

LIVING ROOM
26'-0" X 16'-3"
7.9 X 5.0 m

BEDROOM
6'-0" x 11'-10"
4.9 x 3.6 m

OPTIONAL SUNDECK

OPTIONAL SUNDECK

38'-0"
11.6 m

SECOND FLOOR

42'-0"
12.8 m

ENSUITE

LINEN

LOFT

W.I.C.

W.I.C.

MASTER BEDROOM
16'-0" x 14'-9"
4.9 x 4.5 m

DN

OPEN TO BELOW

25'-0"
7.6 m

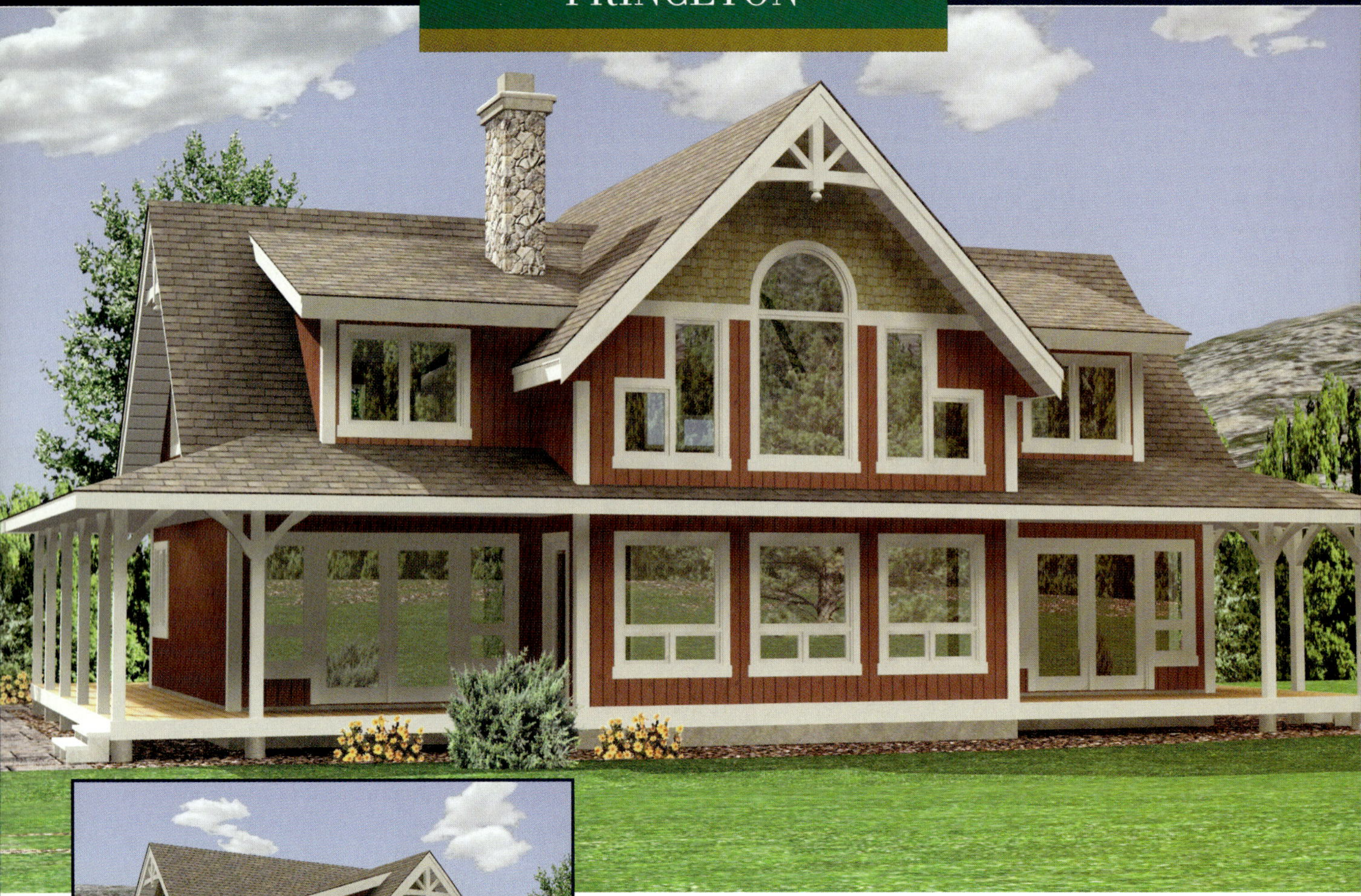

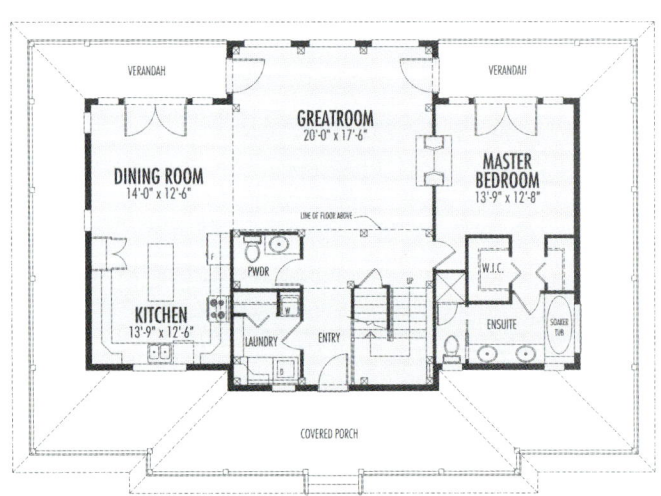

2,264 sq. ft.

- exterior dimensions 50' x 34'
- large vaulted great-room
- 3 bedrooms, 2½ bathrooms
- covered verandah and porch

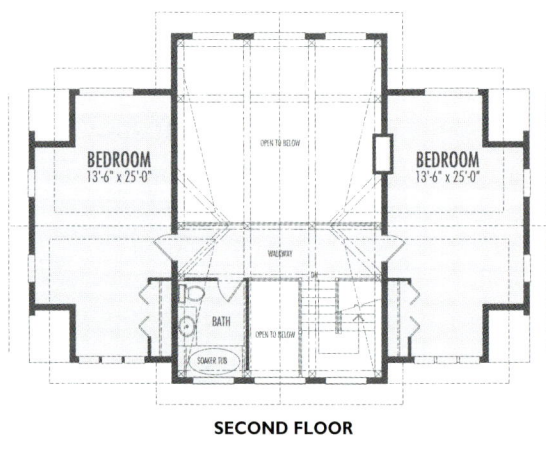

FIRST FLOOR

VERANDAH

VERANDAH

GREATROOM
20'-0" x 17'-6"

DINING ROOM
14'-0" x 12'-6"

MASTER BEDROOM
13'-9" x 12'-8"

LINE OF FLOOR ABOVE

PWDR

W.I.C.

KITCHEN
13'-9" x 12'-6"

LAUNDRY

ENTRY

UP

ENSUITE

SOAKER TUB

COVERED PORCH

SECOND FLOOR

BEDROOM
13'-6" x 25'-0"

OPEN TO BELOW

BEDROOM
13'-6" x 25'-0"

WALKWAY

BATH

OPEN TO BELOW

SOAKER TUB

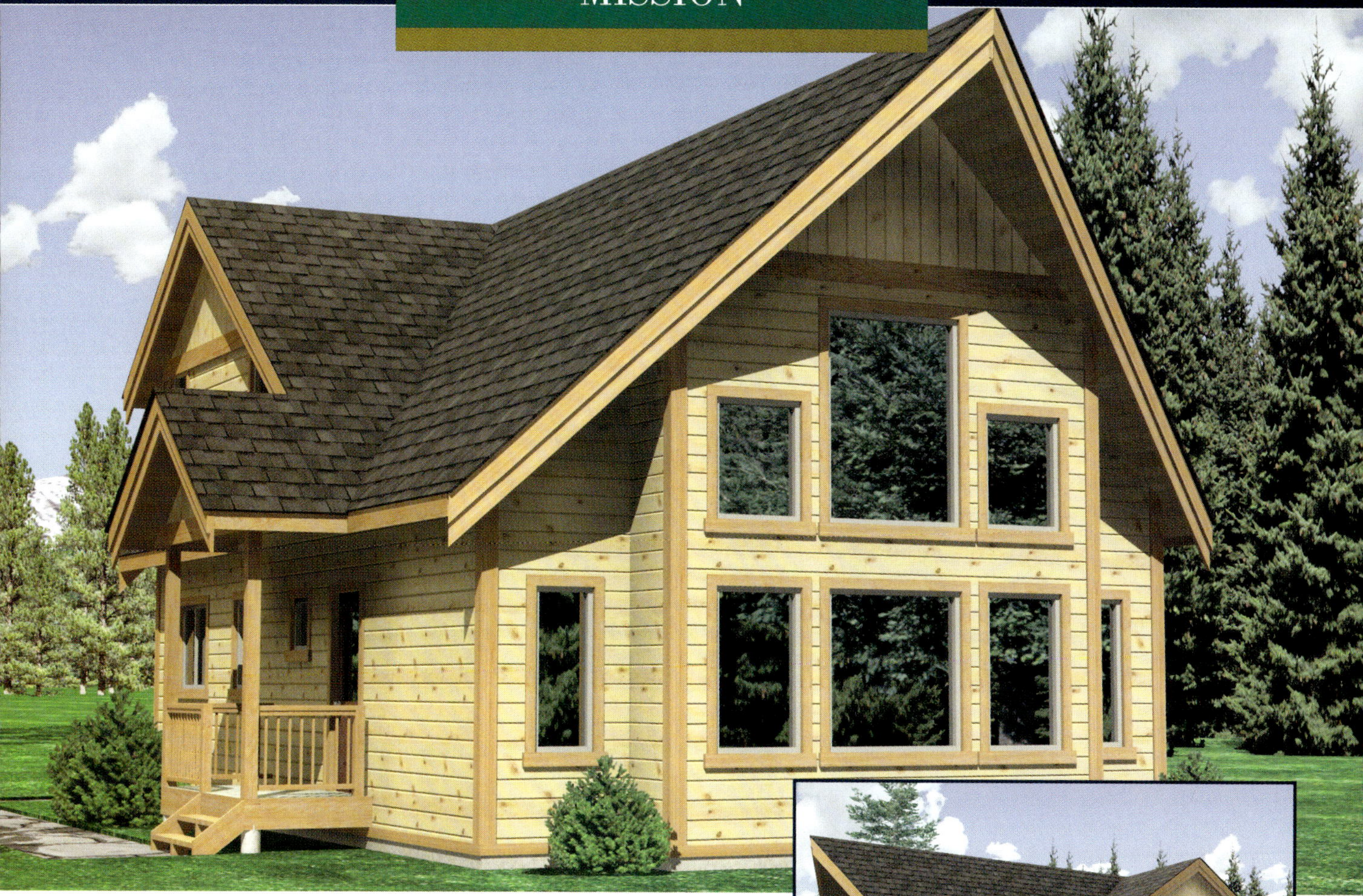

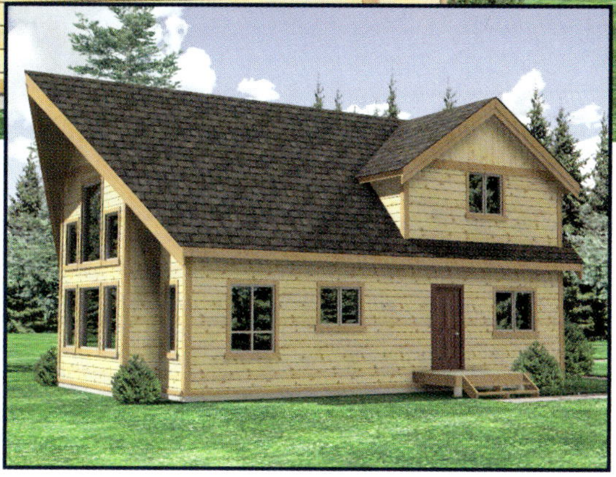

1,558 sq. ft.

- exterior dimensions 26' x 42'
- large vaulted dining, living, and kitchen area
- 3 bedrooms, 2 bathrooms
- vaulted master bedroom with 4-piece ensuite

FIRST FLOOR

SECOND FLOOR

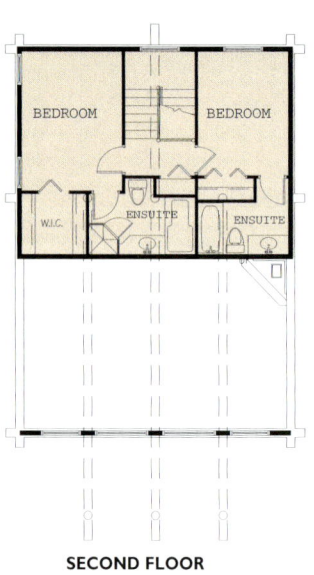

SECOND FLOOR

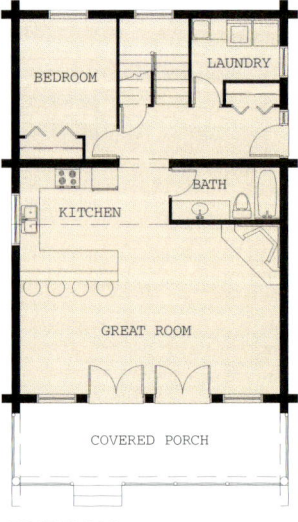

FIRST FLOOR

1,519 sq. ft.

- This log home offers the best in gracious living for the smaller family looking for great style. The great-room with adjacent kitchen is perfect for family gatherings and entertaining.

- Double French doors off of the great-room doors bring the outdoors in, while a corner fireplace keeps the atmosphere warm and cozy.

- Upstairs features two private bedrooms, each with their own luxurious full bathrooms and large closets. This compact design features an abundance of simple pleasures.

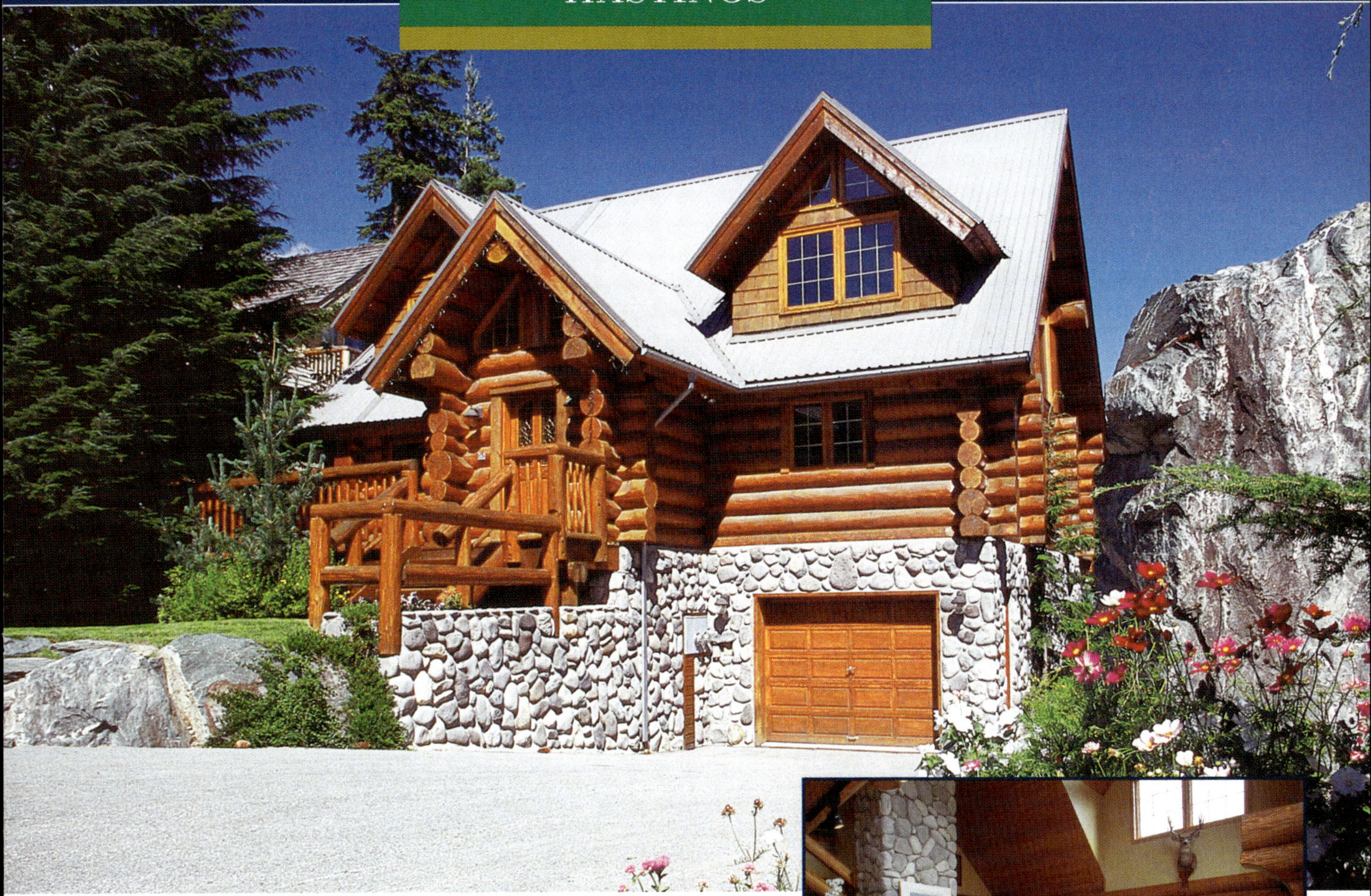

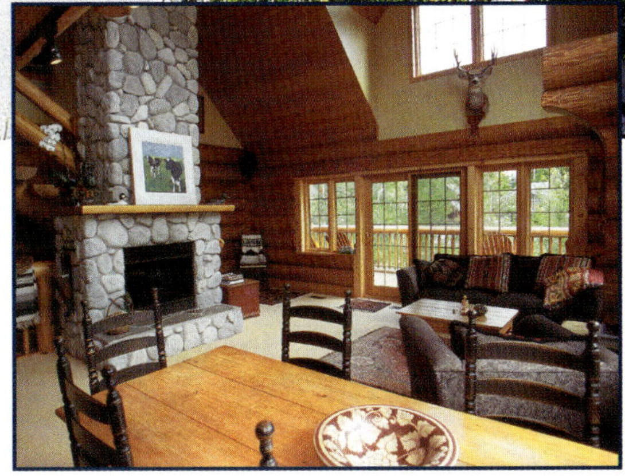

1,885 sq. ft.

- exterior dimensions 40' x 35'9"
- vaulted open-plan living area
- 3 bedrooms, 2 bathrooms
- loft on upper floor

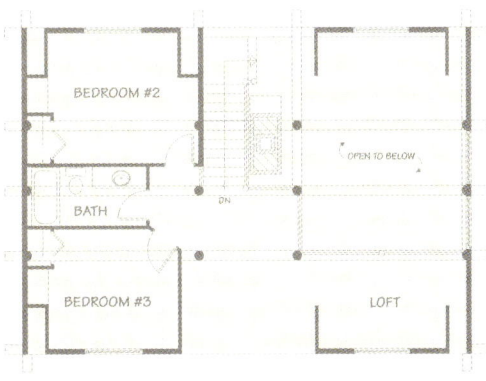

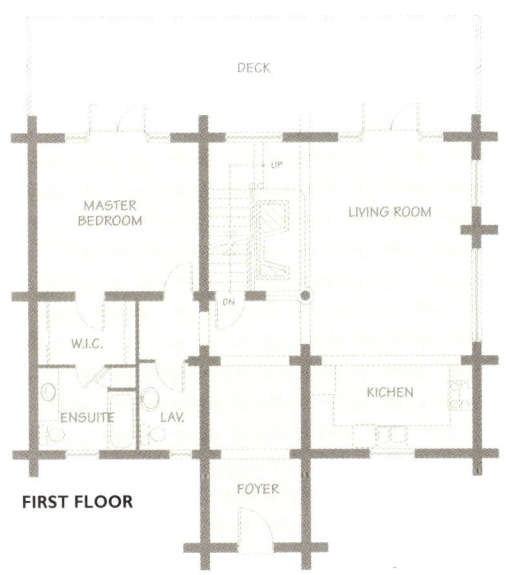

FIRST FLOOR

DECK

UP

MASTER BEDROOM

LIVING ROOM

DN

W.I.C.

ENSUITE · LAV.

KICHEN

FOYER

SECOND FLOOR

BEDROOM #2

OPEN TO BELOW

BATH

DN

BEDROOM #3

LOFT

2,437 sq. ft.

- This truly exceptional three-bedroom (or two bedroom and den) home offers a wonderful range of features and amenities.

- The enormous master bedroom, with adjoining ensuite and spacious walk-in closets, is neatly tucked away, offering the ultimate in privacy.

- The magnificent combination of vaulted living areas with prow front design and wraparound balcony, brings year-round outdoor exposure.

- Enjoy entertaining in your deluxe kitchen with island and adjacent living area.

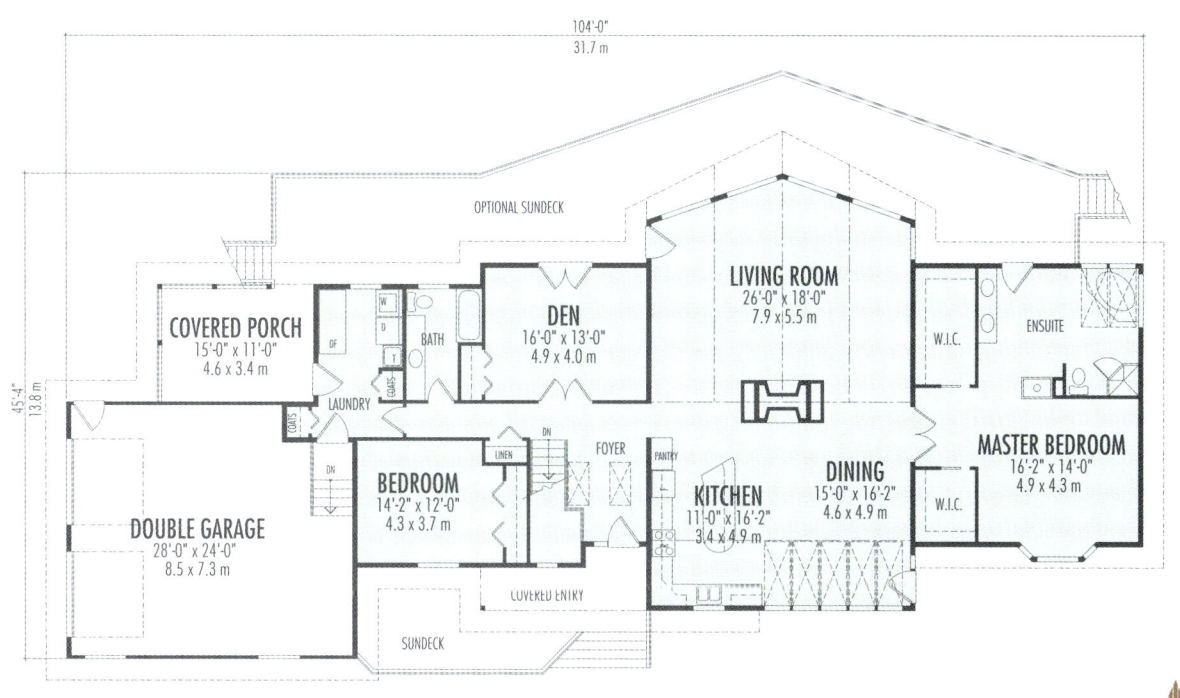

104'-0"
31.7 m

OPTIONAL SUNDECK

45'-4"
13.8 m

COVERED PORCH
15'-0" x 11'-0"
4.6 x 3.4 m

W
D

BATH

DEN
16'-0" x 13'-0"
4.9 x 4.0 m

LIVING ROOM
26'-0" x 18'-0"
7.9 x 5.5 m

W.I.C.

ENSUITE

DF

COATS

LAUNDRY

DN

BEDROOM
14'-2" x 12'-0"
4.3 x 3.7 m

LINEN

DN

FOYER

PANTRY

KITCHEN
11'-0" x 16'-2"
3.4 x 4.9 m

DINING
15'-0" x 16'-2"
4.6 x 4.9 m

W.I.C.

MASTER BEDROOM
16'-2" x 14'-0"
4.9 x 4.3 m

DOUBLE GARAGE
28'-0" x 24'-0"
8.5 x 7.3 m

COVERED ENTRY

SUNDECK

MAIN FLOOR

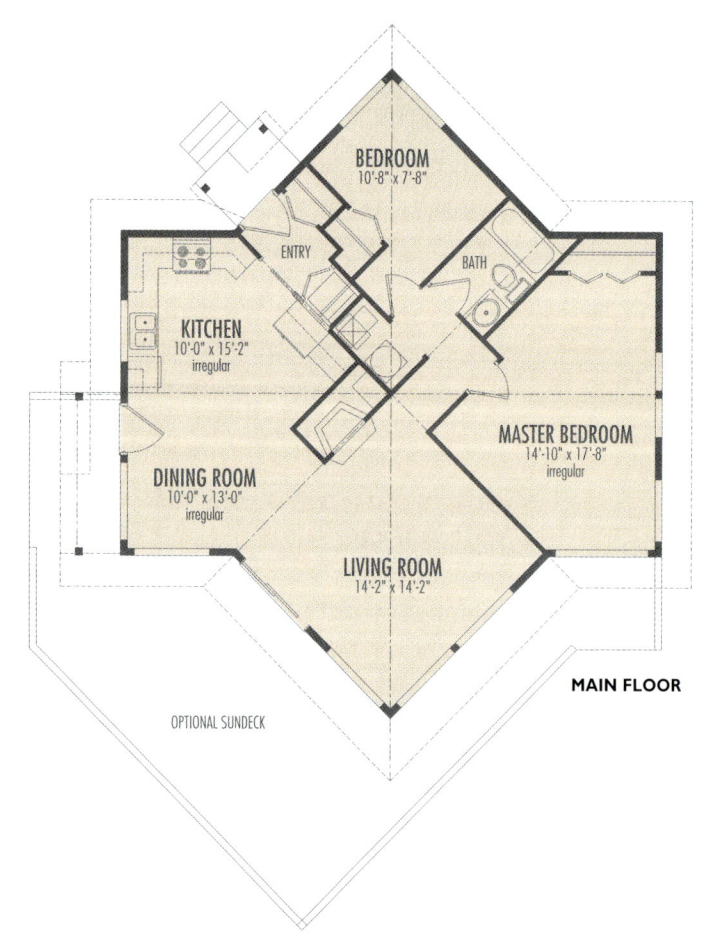

976 sq. ft.

- exterior dimensions 36' x 42'
- unique design with all areas vaulted
- 2 bedrooms, 1 bathroom
- large open-plan kitchen, dining, and living area

BEDROOM
10'-8" x 7'-8"

ENTRY

BATH

KITCHEN
10'-0" x 15'-2"
irregular

MASTER BEDROOM
14'-10" x 17'-8"
irregular

DINING ROOM
10'-0" x 13'-0"
irregular

LIVING ROOM
14'-2" x 14'-2"

MAIN FLOOR

OPTIONAL SUNDECK

~ VANTAGE ~

1,440 sq. ft.

- exterior dimensions 24' x 30'
- large living, dining and kitchen area
- 3 bedrooms, 2 bathrooms
- separate family room on main floor

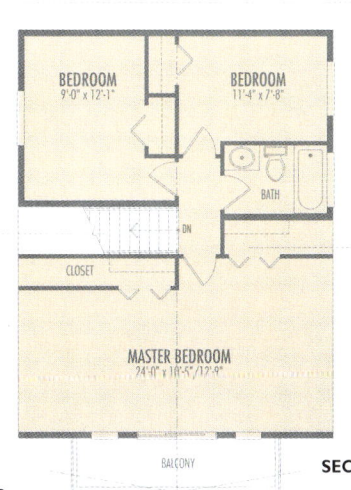

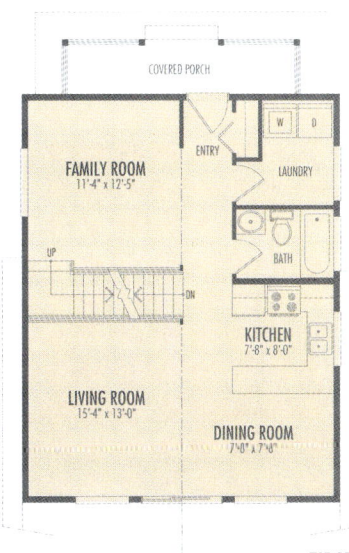

FIRST FLOOR

- COVERED PORCH
- ENTRY
- W D
- LAUNDRY
- BATH
- FAMILY ROOM 11'-4" x 12'-5"
- UP
- DN
- KITCHEN 7'-6" x 8'-0"
- LIVING ROOM 15'-4" x 13'-0"
- DINING ROOM 7'-0" x 7'-6"

SECOND FLOOR

- BEDROOM 9'-0" x 12'-1"
- BEDROOM 11'-4" x 7'-8"
- BATH
- DN
- CLOSET
- MASTER BEDROOM 24'-0" x 10'-5"/12'-9"
- BALCONY

~ LAKEFIELD ~

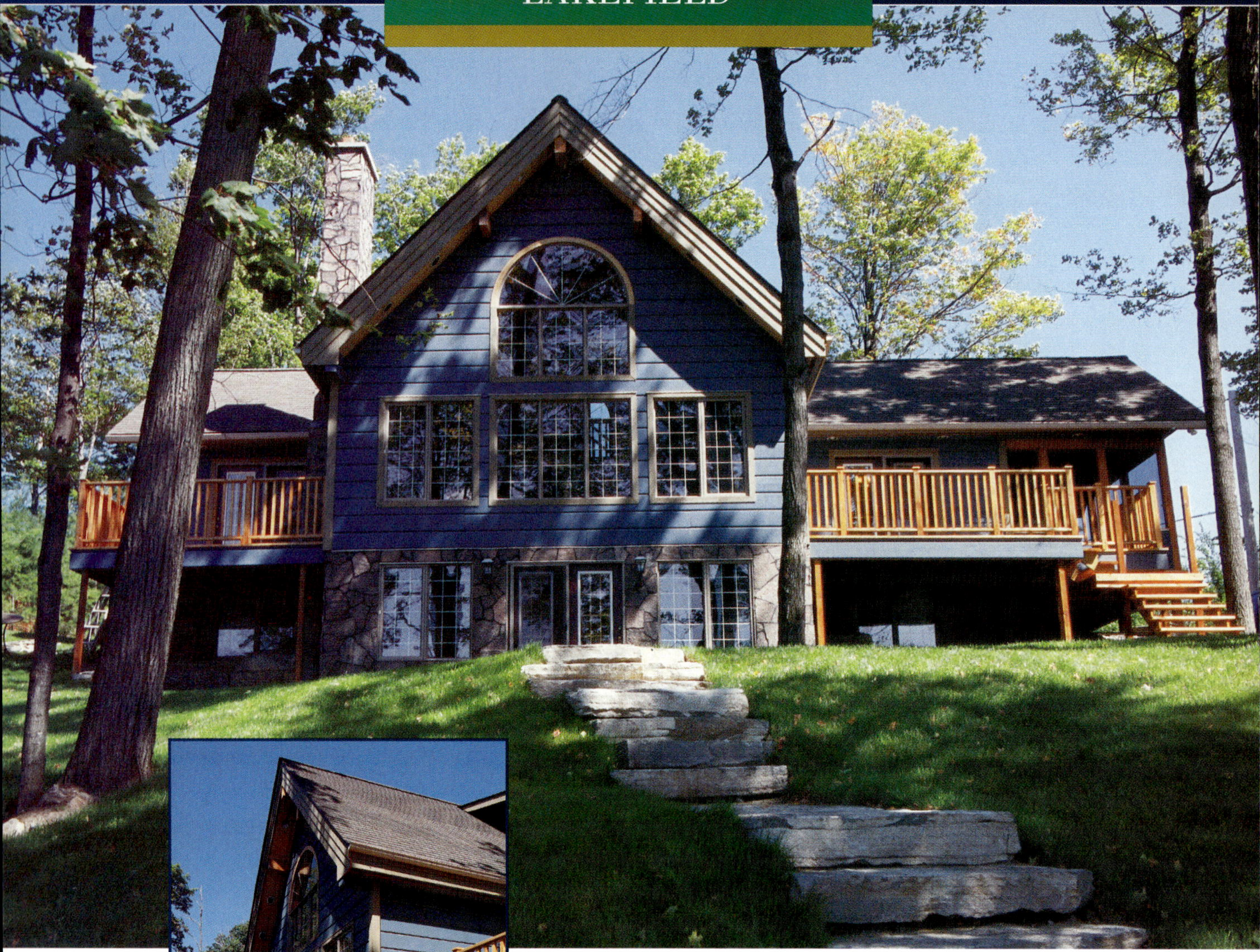

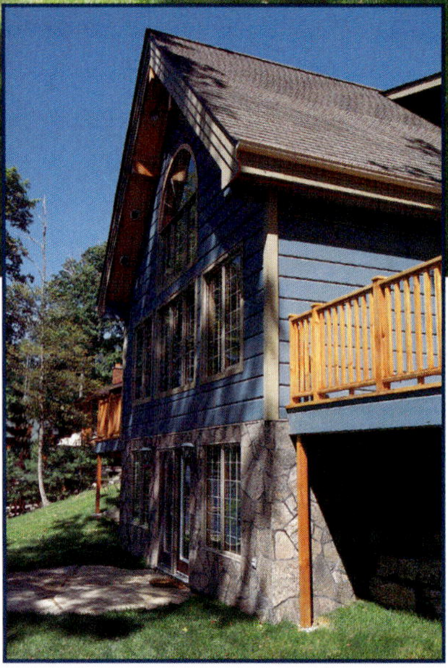

1,873 sq. ft.

- exterior dimensions 53' x 34'6"
- vaulted great-room
- 3 bedrooms, 2½ bathrooms
- covered porch and sundeck

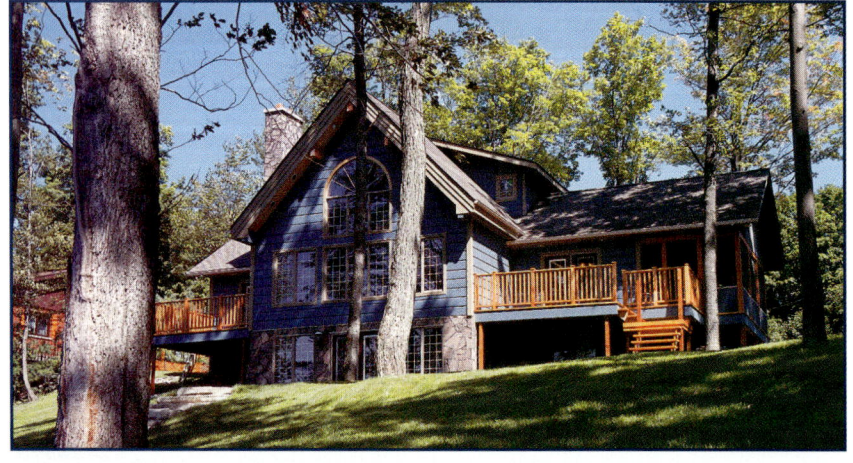

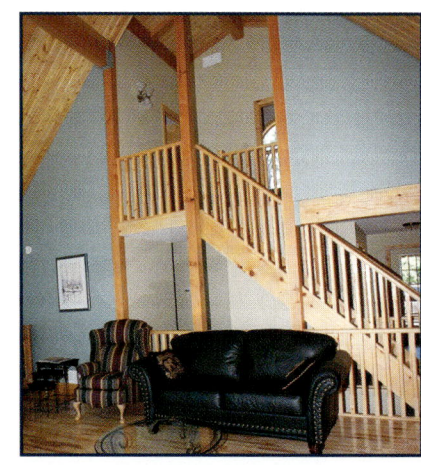

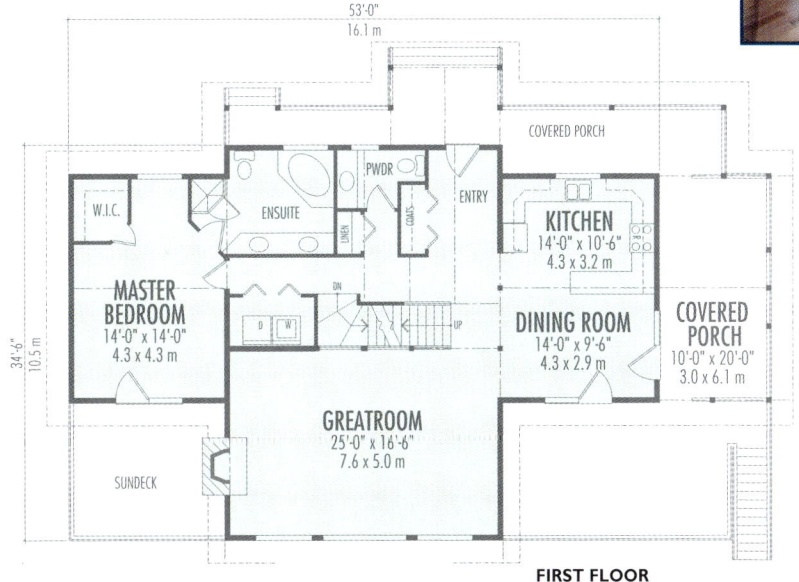

FIRST FLOOR

53'-0"
16.1 m

COVERED PORCH

PWDR

ENTRY

W.I.C.

ENSUITE

LINEN

COATS

KITCHEN
14'-0" x 10'-6"
4.3 x 3.2 m

DN

MASTER
BEDROOM
14'-0" x 14'-0"
4.3 x 4.3 m

D W

UP

DINING ROOM
14'-0" x 9'-6"
4.3 x 2.9 m

COVERED
PORCH
10'-0" x 20'-0"
3.0 x 6.1 m

34'-6"
10.5 m

GREATROOM
25'-0" x 16'-6"
7.6 x 5.0 m

SUNDECK

SECOND FLOOR

25'-0"
7.6 m

BEDROOM
16'-9" x 9'-10"
5.1 x 3.0 m

BEDROOM
8'-3" x 13'-10"
2.5 x 4.2 m

BATH

DN

W.I.C.

18'-0"
5.5 m

OPEN TO BELOW

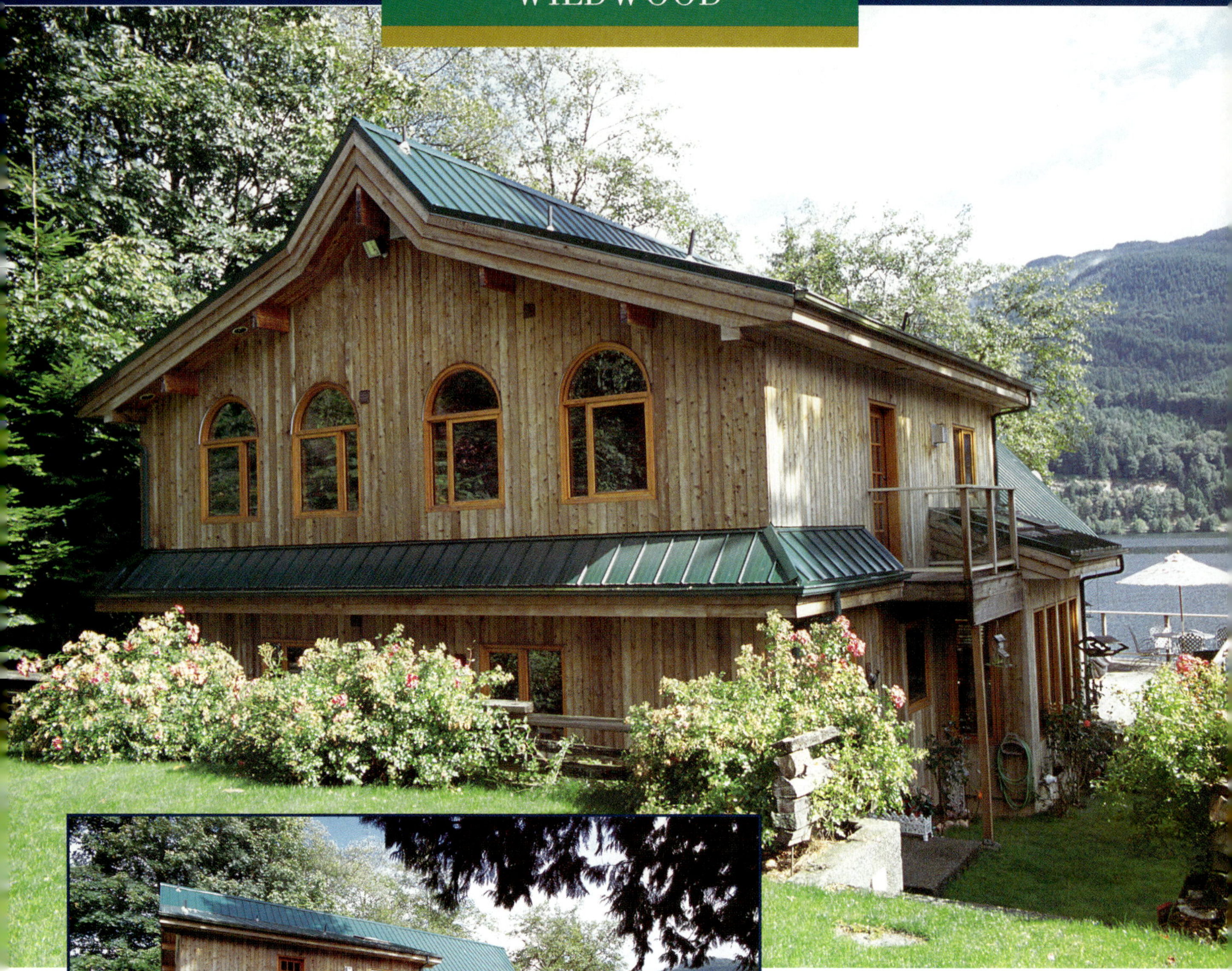

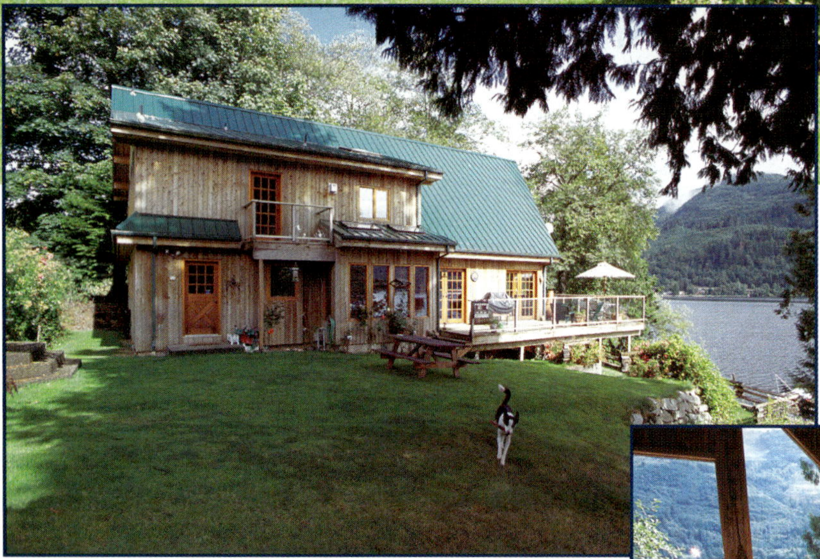

2,640 sq. ft.

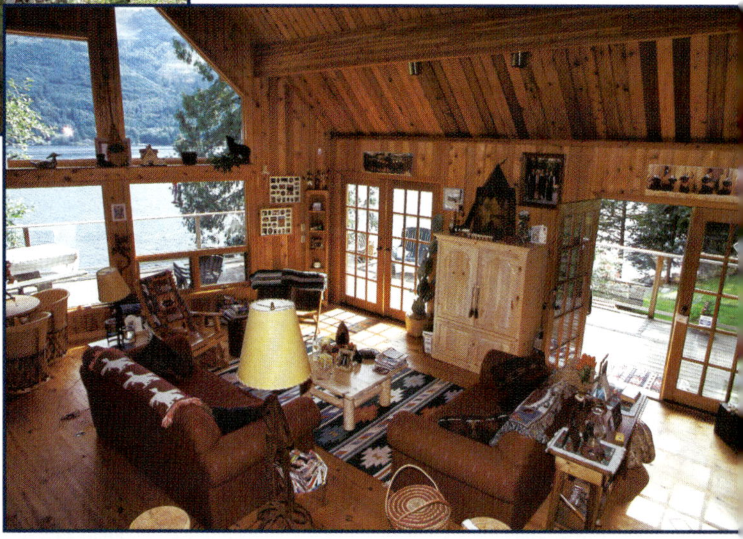

- exterior dimensions 32' x 55'4"
- vaulted living room opens onto sundeck
- 4 bedrooms, 3 bathrooms
- cozy den on main floor, loft on upper floor

SECOND FLOOR

SECOND FLOOR plan labels:
- W.I.C.
- BATH
- BEDROOM 12'-0" x 15'-0" 3.7 x 4.5 m
- MASTER BEDROOM 14'-8" x 14'-0" 4.5 x 4.3 m
- BATH
- BALCONY
- LOFT 16'-0" x 9'-4" 4.9 x 2.8 m
- BEDROOM 12'-0" x 10'-6" 3.7 x 3.2 m
- OPEN TO BELOW
- 32'-0" 9.8 m
- 29'-0" 8.8 m

FIRST FLOOR plan labels:
- 32'-0" 9.8 m
- W
- D
- LAUNDRY
- FOYER
- COATS
- BEDROOM 12'-0" x 12'-1" 3.7 x 3.7 m
- KITCHEN 13'-8" x 8'-0" 4.2 x 2.4 m
- BATH
- LINEN
- DINING ROOM 16'-0" x 12'-0" 4.9 x 3.7 m
- DEN 12'-0" x 9'-3" 3.7 x 2.8 m
- UP
- LIVING ROOM 32'-0" x 24'-4" 9.8 x 7.4 m
- 55'-4" 16.9 m
- OPTIONAL SUNDECK

FIRST FLOOR

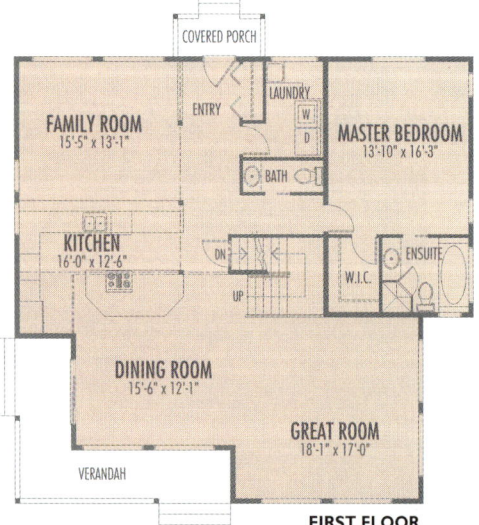

2,235 sq. ft.

- exterior dimensions 45' x 42'
- vaulted great-room and dining room
- island kitchen open to family room
- 4 bedrooms, 2½ bathrooms
- covered verandah and porch

FIRST FLOOR

COVERED PORCH

ENTRY

LAUNDRY
W
D

FAMILY ROOM
15'-5" x 13'-1"

MASTER BEDROOM
13'-10" x 16'-3"

BATH

KITCHEN
16'-0" x 12'-6"

DN

ENSUITE

UP

W.I.C.

DINING ROOM
15'-6" x 12'-1"

GREAT ROOM
18'-1" x 17'-0"

VERANDAH

SECOND FLOOR

BEDROOM
13'-1" x 9'-7"

BEDROOM
11'-5" x 10'-11"

BEDROOM
13'-1" x 9'-7"

BATH

DN

OPEN TO BELOW

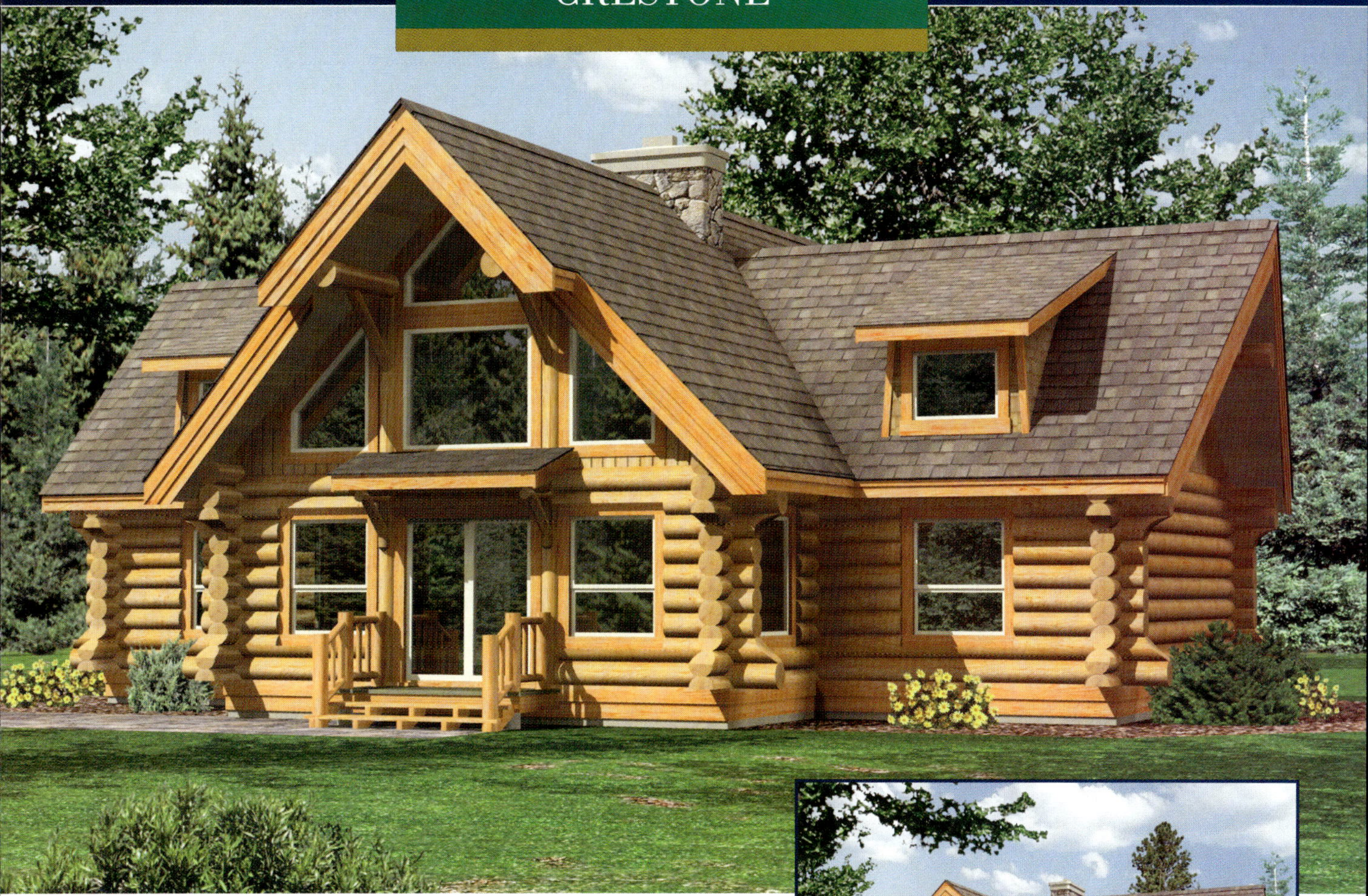

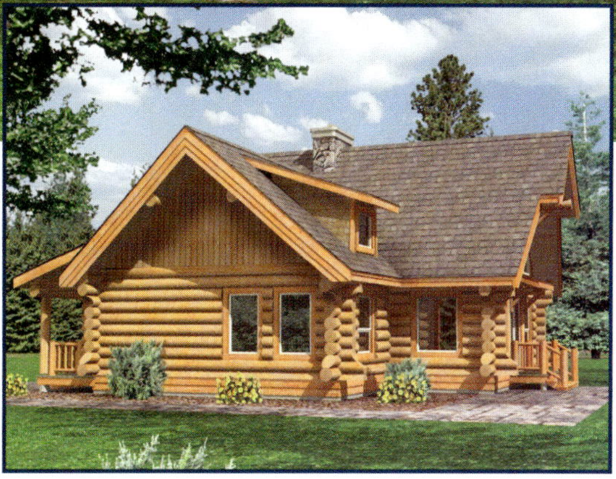

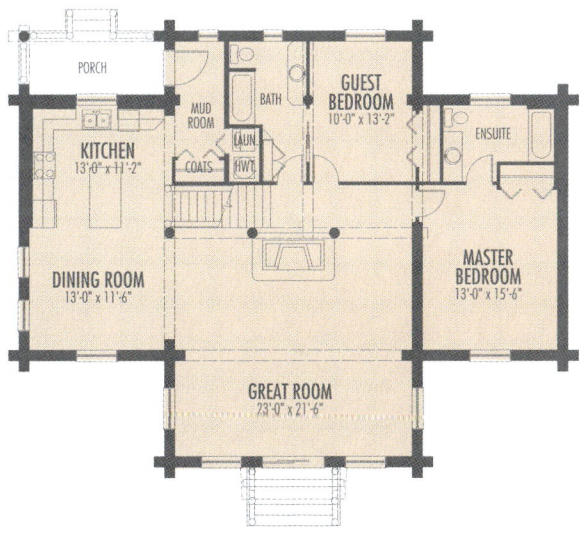

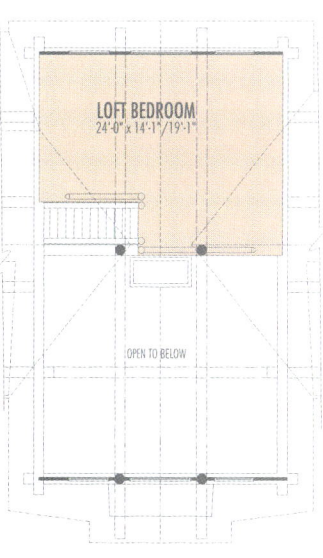

2,042 sq. ft.

- exterior dimensions 52' x 40'
- large great-room with cathedral ceiling
- open vaulted kitchen and dining area
- 3 bedrooms, including a generous vaulted loft bedroom, 2 bathrooms

PORCH

KITCHEN
13'-0" x 11'-2"

MUD ROOM

BATH

GUEST BEDROOM
10'-0" x 13'-2"

LAUN.

COATS

HW

ENSUITE

DINING ROOM
13'-0" x 11'-6"

MASTER BEDROOM
13'-0" x 15'-6"

GREAT ROOM
23'-0" x 21'-6"

FIRST FLOOR

LOFT BEDROOM
24'-0" x 14'-1"/19'-1"

OPEN TO BELOW

SECOND FLOOR

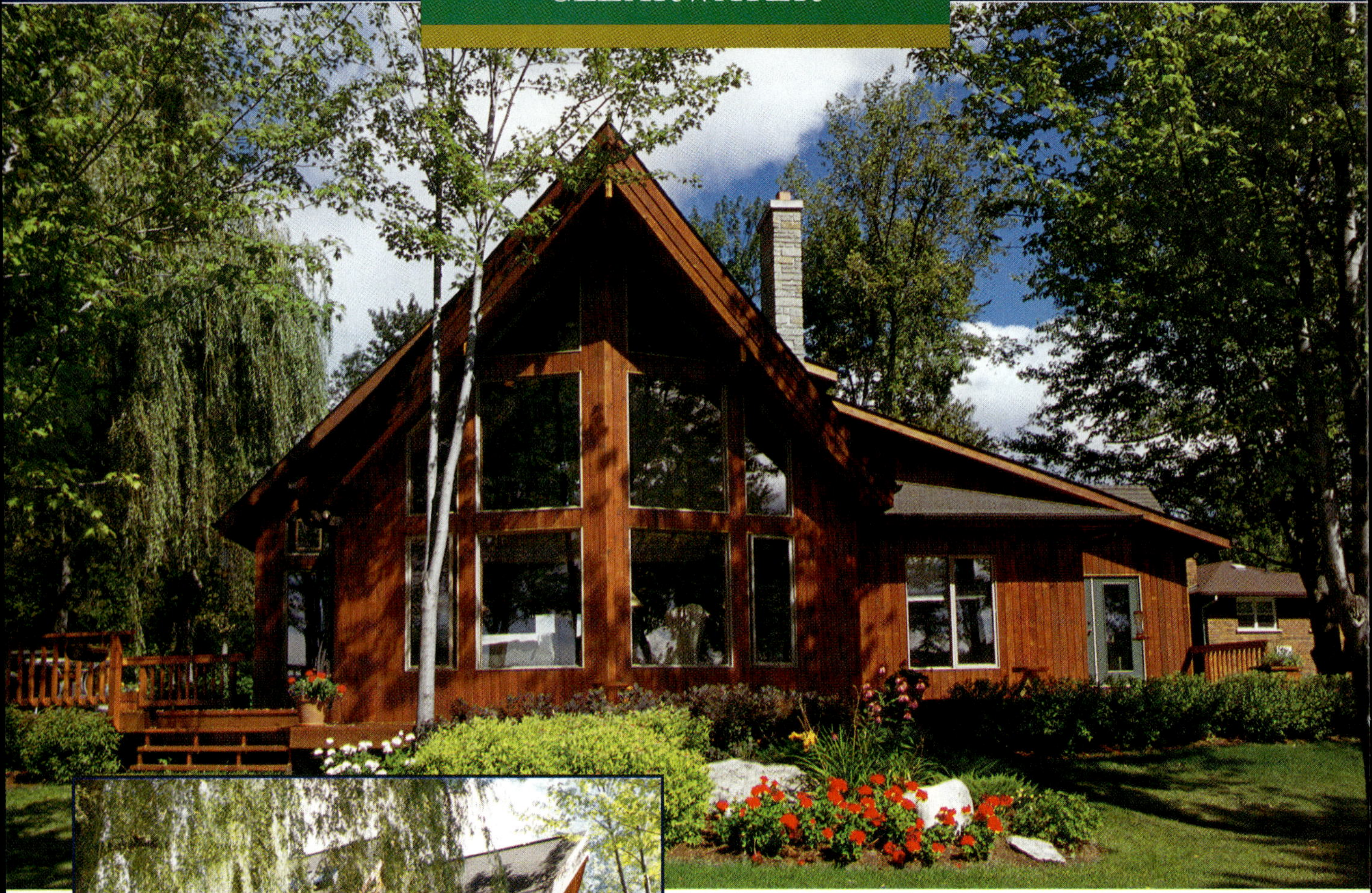

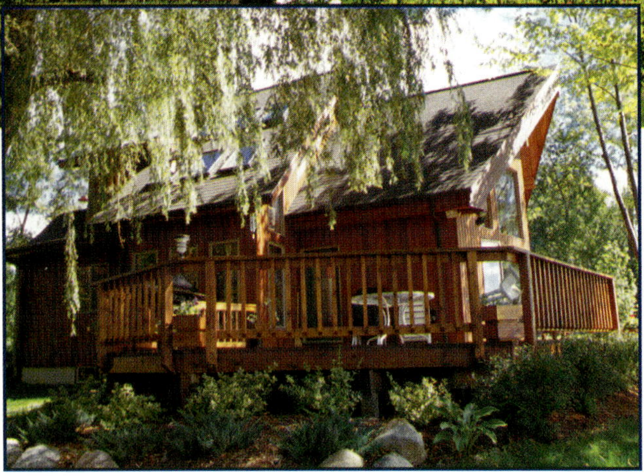

2,507 sq. ft.

- exterior dimensions 56' x 62'
- vaulted living room, master bedroom, and loft
- 3 bedrooms, 2 bathrooms
- multiple skylights

FIRST FLOOR

GARAGE
28'-0" x 24'-0"
8.5 x 7.3 m

KITCHEN
12'-0" x 14'-0"
3.7 x 4.3 m

FOYER

BATH

PANTRY

BEDROOM
12'-0" x 14'-4"
3.7 x 4.4 m

DINING ROOM
20'-2" x 12'-0"
6.1 x 3.7 m

BEDROOM
11'-4" x 11'-0"
3.5 x 3.4 m

LIVING ROOM
24'-0" x 16'-0"
7.3 x 4.9 m

62'-0"
18.9 m

56'-0"
17.1 m

SECOND FLOOR

LOFT
14'-0" x 24'-0"
4.8 x 7.3 m

MASTER BEDROOM
15'-6" x 22'-0"
4.7 x 6.7 m

W.I.C.

ENS.

OPEN TO BELOW

38'-0"
11.6 m

46'-0"
14.0 m

~ TYNDALE ~

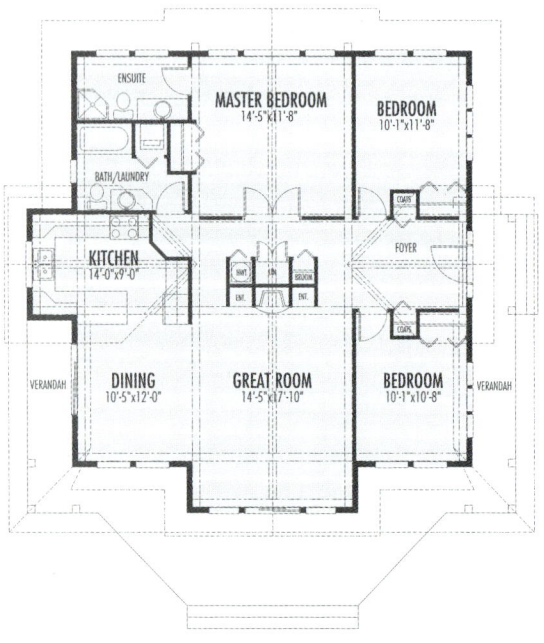

MAIN FLOOR

1,396 sq. ft.

- exterior dimensions 44' x 40'
- all living areas vaulted
- 3 bedrooms, 2 bathrooms
- covered verandahs

130 TIMBER CRAFTED HOMES

~ WESTMERE ~

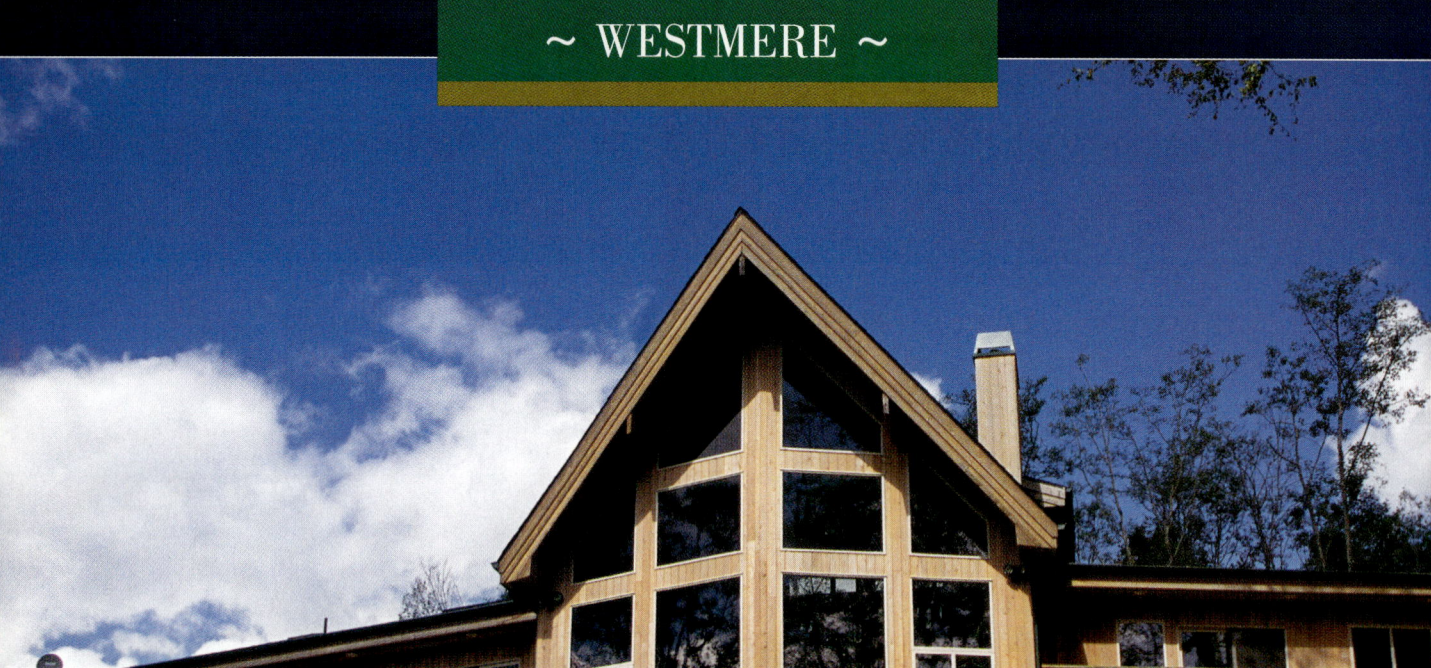

2,415 sq. ft.

- exterior dimensions 84'9" x 47'11"
- vaulted living room, with many skylights in dining room and kitchen
- 2 bedrooms and loft, 2½ bathrooms
- separate mudroom, laundry room, and walk-in pantry

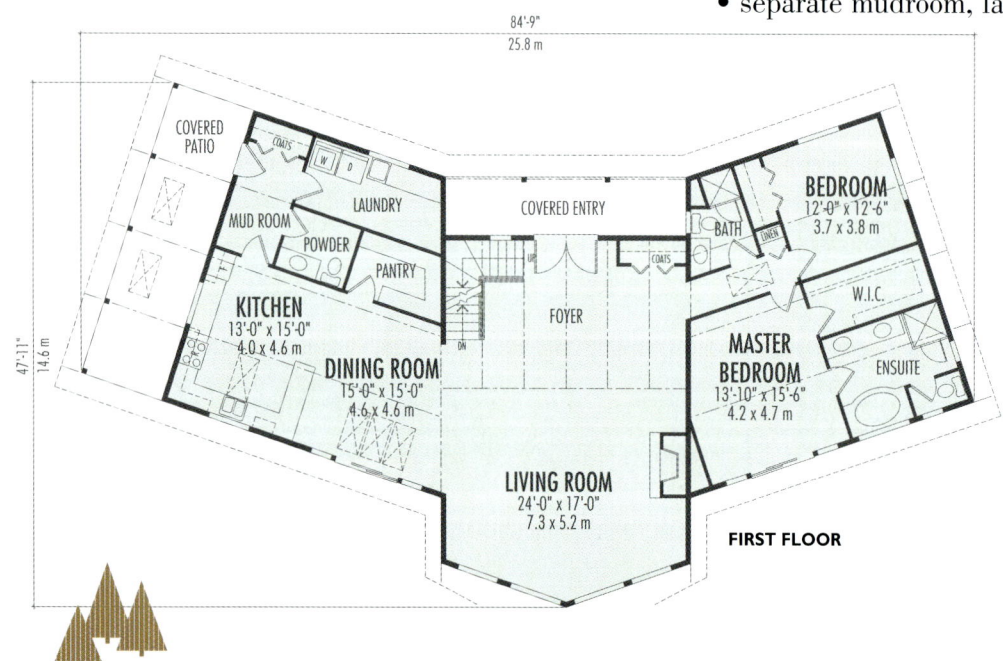

FIRST FLOOR

84'-9"
25.8 m

47'-11"
14.6 m

COVERED PATIO

COATS
W D
LAUNDRY
MUD ROOM
POWDER
PANTRY
KITCHEN
13'-0" x 15'-0"
4.0 x 4.6 m
DINING ROOM
15'-0" x 15'-0"
4.6 x 4.6 m
COVERED ENTRY
FOYER
DN
UP
COATS
BATH
LINEN
BEDROOM
12'-0" x 12'-6"
3.7 x 3.8 m
W.I.C.
MASTER BEDROOM
13'-10" x 15'-6"
4.2 x 4.7 m
ENSUITE
LIVING ROOM
24'-0" x 17'-0"
7.3 x 5.2 m

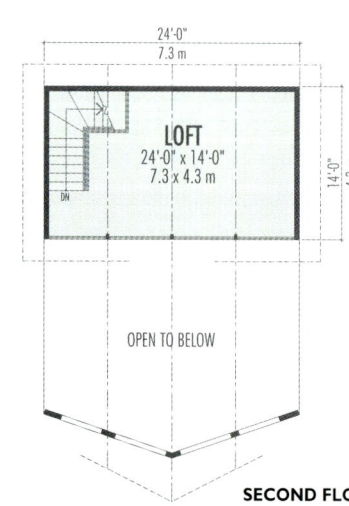

SECOND FLOOR

24'-0"
7.3 m

14'-0"
4.3 m

LOFT
24'-0" x 14'-0"
7.3 x 4.3 m
DN

OPEN TO BELOW

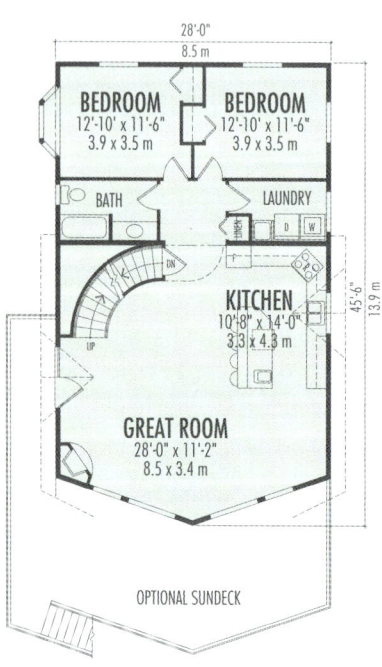

FIRST FLOOR

28'-0"
8.5 m

BEDROOM
12'-10' x 11'-6"
3.9 x 3.5 m

BEDROOM
12'-10' x 11'-6"
3.9 x 3.5 m

BATH

LAUNDRY

DN

KITCHEN
10'-8" x 14'-0"
3.3 x 4.3 m

UP

GREAT ROOM
28'-0" x 11'-2"
8.5 x 3.4 m

45'-6"
13.9 m

OPTIONAL SUNDECK

SECOND FLOOR

28'-0"
8.5 m

BALCONY

MASTER
BEDROOM
15'-9" x 18'-0"
4.8 x 5.5 m

ENSUITE

W.I.C.

18'-0"
5.5 m

PLANT
SHELF

DN

OPEN TO BELOW

1,741 sq. ft.

- exterior dimensions 28' x 45'6''
- lovely open-plan kitchen and great-room
- 3 bedrooms, 2 bathrooms
- feature staircase

Making a House a Home

Welcome to the world of interior design and finishing, where you can create distinctive living spaces as unique as you are. Given ever-changing hectic lifestyles, with work, travel, and the constant juggling of schedules, our homes have once again become a gathering place.

A home is more than walls, floors, doors, windows, and a roof. A home is a haven—a place that provides its owners with a warm welcome, sanctuary, and a sense of pride. Turning a house into a home requires thoughtful planning to ensure all your needs are met.

When choosing and designing your home, there are some fundamental questions to ask yourself:

- *How do you move through your surroundings during the day?*
- *What would be a logical flow from room to room for your daily routines?*
- *Do you spend a lot of time in a formal living room or dining room, or would these traditional spaces be better utilized as part of an open-plan kitchen and great room?*
- *Do you need a media room, home office, or hobby space?*
- *Do you like to entertain casually or formally, big groups or small?*
- *Where do you like to eat? Read? Listen to music? Watch TV?*
- *Have you made room for private space?*

Once you have determined your lifestyle needs, then you can begin the wonderful process of creating your exclusive home. There are many design features that turn an ordinary plan into an original masterpiece. Signature windows showcase not only the exterior of your home, but they also highlight your views from the interior. Well-placed windows maximize the natural light, bringing a spacious, soft glow to every room. Great rooms, with cathedral ceilings and distinctive windows, become the heart of your home.

Windows, skylights, and solariums are usually the first architectural details to attract attention in creating a stunning exterior look. They're also the first things we notice when we walk into a room. Windows and skylights infuse our homes with natural light, and an open and airy feeling of spaciousness and comfort. Sunrooms and solariums bring the beautiful outdoors into our homes, while protecting us from inclement weather.

Dream Homes specializes in designing timber crafted homes which maximize the use of light. Post and beam construction allows high vaulted ceilings and walls of windows to let in as much natural light as possible. It also allows many options in combining the warmth of natural wood in ceilings with a bold use of colors. The result is a feeling of spaciousness and tranquility.

Lighter colored hardwood floors work well in this setting by way of contrast. The effect is to make vaulted ceilings feel more intimate without losing the feel of spaciousness. Area rugs as accent pieces on the flooring can be particularly effective in making a major design statement. The floorings you choose have a big impact on the overall impression of each room, and will add feelings of coziness, elegance, or drama.

Many people use a formal living room or dining room only on rare occasions, so there is more call for open floor plans, combining kitchen, dining, and entertaining areas into one magnificent, multiuse space. Porches, decks, and patios extend your living quarters during good weather, and add a visual welcome all year round.

Luxury in private spaces like bedrooms, ensuites, and studies are a way to create "a room of your own" for when you need time to relax and reflect. Keep in mind your art and collections, the things that you love, so that you can design special wall areas to showcase them.

When it comes time to decorate your new home, there are many tricks that professional designers use to make distinguishing statements. If you like color, don't be afraid to use it! Choose colors you are drawn to, colors you like wearing, colors that inspire you to smile. Homes have a personality, humor, and style that reflect their owners. Use dimmer switches with your lighting so you can adjust the light with the time of the day, the weather outside, and your own mood.

Alcoves and built-in benches, cabinets, and bookshelves are timeless additions that can be customized to create one-of-a-kind rooms. Fireplaces add a warm ambience in any room, including master bedrooms and kitchens.

Above all, remember that this house is your home. It's a wood and glass reality born out of your desire to create the perfect place to hang your hat.

From concept to completion, we can help bring your dream home to life. Our complete interior design service includes color schemes, space planning, designer boards, virtual tours, and budget planning. After an initial consultation, we will gain insight into how you want your home to look and feel. We then make it simple for you by being your one reliable source for all the interior products you'll need.

Visit our website at **www.mapleinteriors.com**

How to Proceed

We hope you have enjoyed this outstanding selection of designer homes and are inspired by the ideas you have seen. Further exploring your dream home couldn't be more simple. There is no obligation and no cost when you contact us.

Choose a Design

This is one of the most comprehensive collections of high quality homes ever published and available for sale. These are not line drawings but real homes crafted with great attention to detail and built with pride. Initially, all you have to do is select the name of the design(s) in which you are interested. This design can be fully customized at a later stage to suit your own specific needs should you so desire.

Contact Us at Garlinghouse

the
Garlinghouse
company

Helping to build dreams since 1907

Call Garlinghouse toll free at 1-800-235-5700 or fax to 1-800-659-5692.
All foreign residents call 1-860-659-5667.
Monday to Friday 8:00 am to 8:00 pm
Eastern Standard Time.

The operator will take your name and contact information, including the design in which you are interested, where you live, and where you intend to build.

Alternatively, you can simply fill in the attached information sheet and send it to:

The Live Your Dream Collection
Garlinghouse Company
174 Oakwood Drive
Glastonbury, CT 06033

NAME: _____

STREET: _____

CITY: _____

STATE/PROVINCE: _____ ZIP/POSTAL CODE: _____

DAYTIME PHONE NUMBER: _____

E-MAIL: _____

NAME OF DESIGN: _____

_____

LOCATION OF BUILDING LOT: _____

ESTIMATED CONSTRUCTION DATE: _____

Receive Expert Assistance

Within 48 hours of receiving your call or written information sheet, you will be contacted by your nearest Dream Homes consultant. The representative will provide you with full details of the standard features contained in the home package you have selected, as well as the package cost. If required, the consultant will also help you fully customize the house to suit your needs, and assist you in determining any of these design changes.

Additionally, your consultant will assist you in calculating the cost of all the other components of your new home, as well as offer tips and advice on how to deal with contractors and obtain building permits. If you do not have your own contractor, we can help you to find a reliable and competent team to build your dream home.

Select Your Package Design

With Dream Homes, you are purchasing a complete home package. This package includes the following:

- Construction blueprints
- Framing lumber and plywood to build walls and floors
- Siding in a wide variety of materials, styles, colors, and finishes
- Customized windows and skylights
- An extensive selection of exterior doors
- Roofing materials
- House wrap
- Rust-proof nails

Many options are also available including:

- Sunrooms and solariums
- Decking and railing
- Interior doors in many styles
- Wall and roof panelization
- Drywall and insulation

Your home package will have all the components you need to complete your home to "lock-up stage." This means that you can then complete your interior finish, electrical, and plumbing in a fully weatherproof environment—and at your own pace. Individual considerations, needs, and styles vary considerably for interior finishing. Consult your Dream Home sales and design consultant for more details.

Order Your Home Package

Only when you have finalized your design and are satisfied with the corresponding package price will you be asked to sign a purchase order. At this stage, you will need to make a down payment to commence the production process. You will then receive construction blueprints meeting the building and code standards for your intended location. The building materials will be shipped when and where you want them with a detailed construction manual. You may also contact the factory at any time for further assistance.

Building a custom-designed home has never been this easy!

Important Information to Remember:

- You are purchasing a home package based on the architectural design you have selected.

- This design can be fully customized to meet your exact requirements.

- The home package contains the materials required to construct and finish the exterior of your home with the exception of the concrete foundation and stonework.

- The construction blueprints will conform to local building department guidelines.

- Shipping can be arranged to anywhere in the world.

- A Dream Homes representative will work with you all the way through the design and construction process.

- Your home package will only contain high quality building materials, and is supported by a full manufacturer warranty.

- These designs are copyrighted and may not be reproduced in whole or in part without express written permission.

- Photographs and plans may differ slightly due to individual customer preferences. Check with your sales representative to confirm construction details.

~ INDEX OF HOMES ~

Dream Homes of America and Garlinghouse gratefully acknowledge the willingness
of the proud owners of these outstanding homes to share their vision.